I0819264

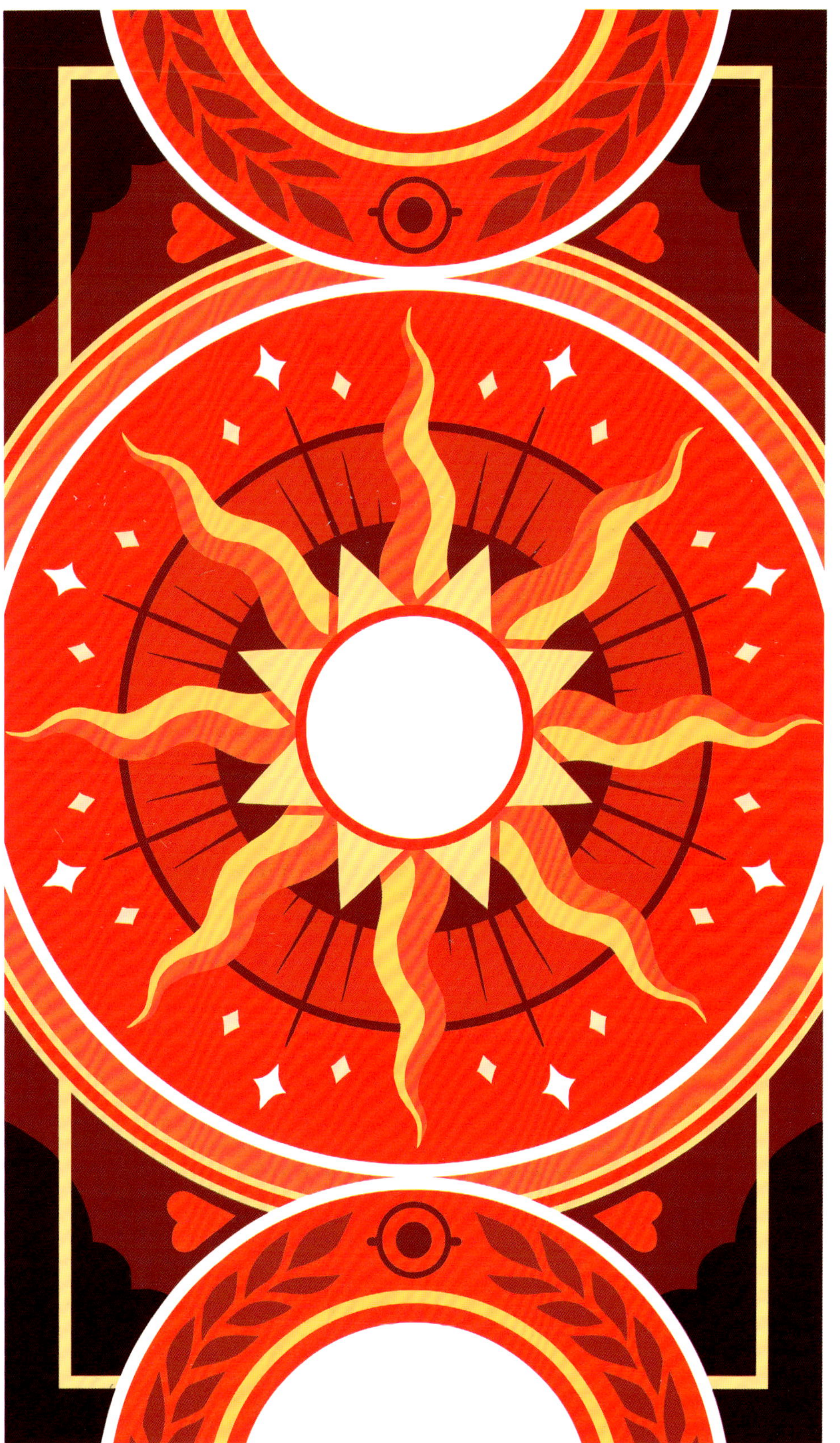

Around the Sun

STORIES *and* SYMBOLS *from* ACROSS *the* WORLD

Yoshi Yoshitani

TEN SPEED PRESS
California | New York

Contents

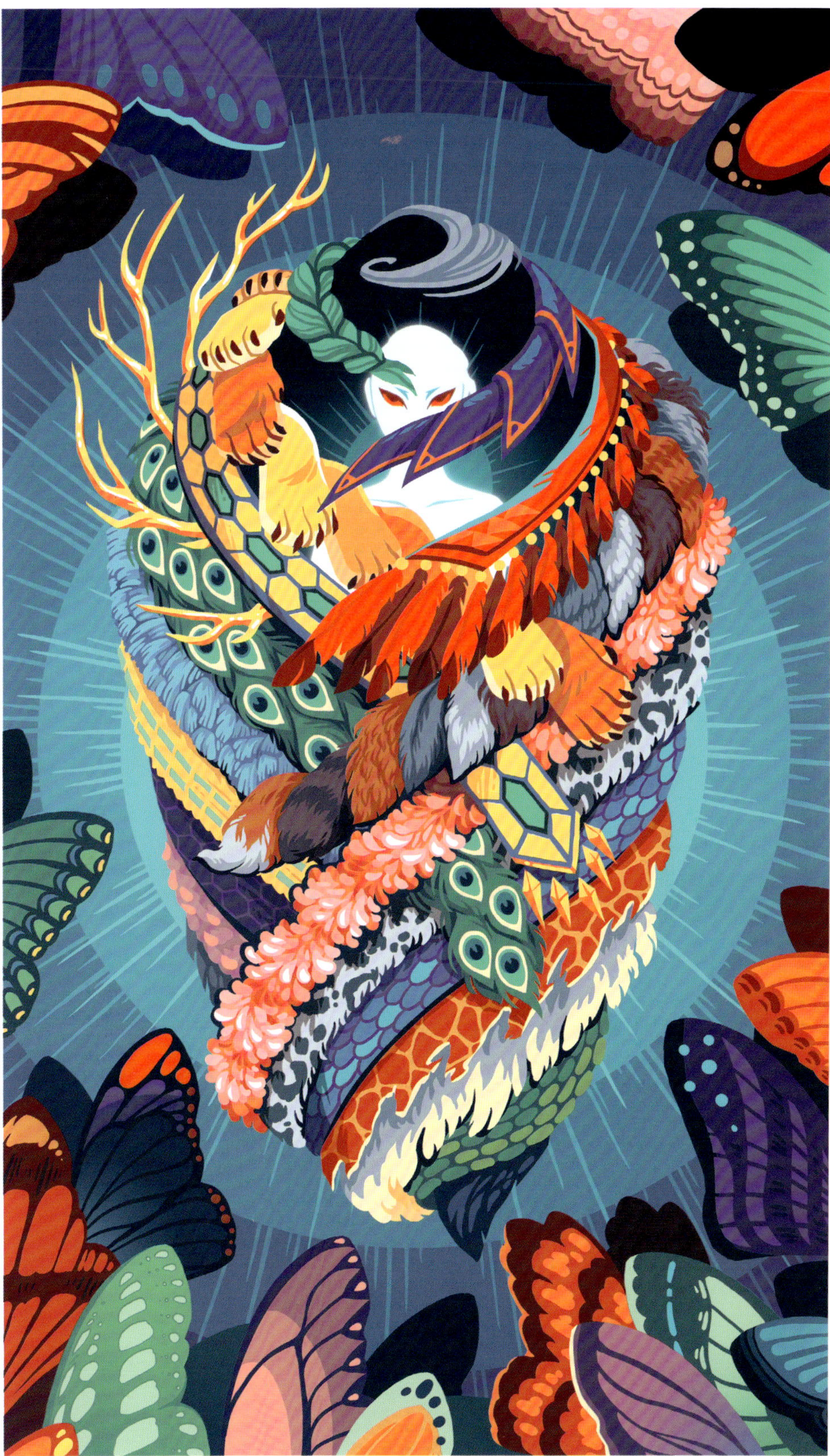

Introduction

Growing up in a multicultural household, I was surrounded by myths and fairy tales from different traditions, each shaped by its own culture, beliefs, and environment. Yet as a child, I noticed that even though these stories came from such disparate backgrounds, they shared the same human experiences of high adventure, forbidden doors, fated romance, and tragic loss. These tales showed me that we can find connections in the stories we share and celebrate the differences in the ways we choose to tell them.

As I grew older, I found that my childhood convictions remained true—stories both bind and individualize us. I began collecting as many stories from as many different places as I could. Used bookstores, museums, libraries, research journals, personal blogs, and social media all helped feed my fixation. But where I began to experience true joy was when I started sharing those stories back out.

A decade ago, I started on what I thought would be a small project, matching a few fairy tales with tarot cards. That grew into the card deck and guidebook *Tarot of the Divine* and the storybook *Beneath the Moon*. In the years since, I have met countless people who have told me how this collection of stories impacted

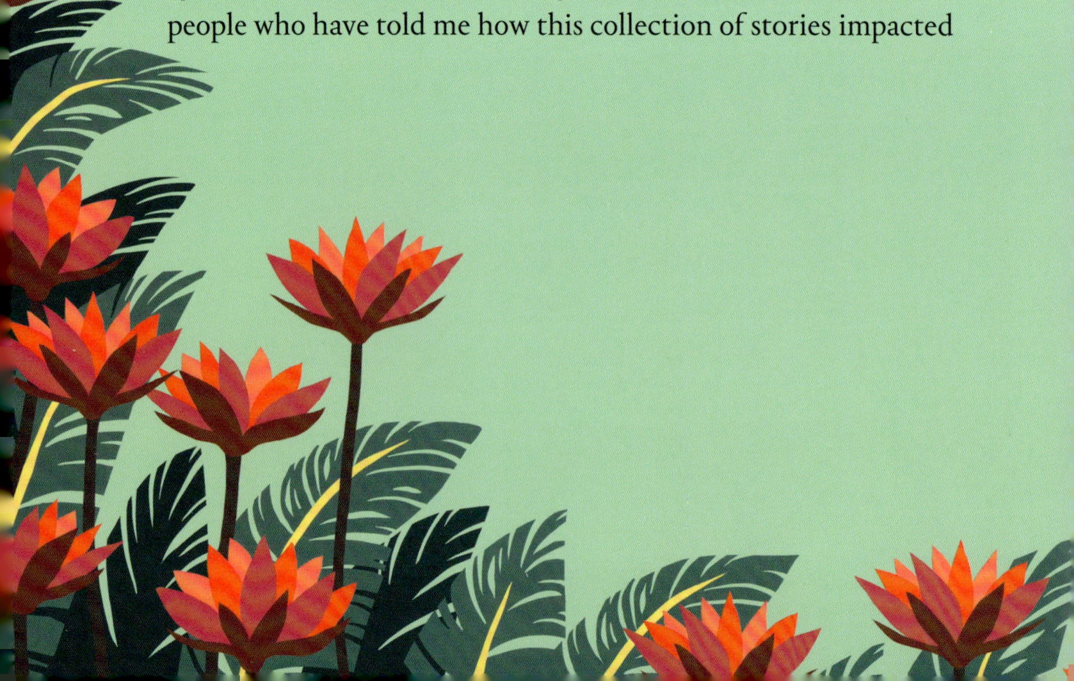

them. Some were thrilled to finally see on paper stories they had been taught as children, some felt connected to an unseen history, some were excited to learn about the world in new ways, and some resonated deeply with ancient stories they had never heard before. Over and over, I am awed at the power of stories and the connections they bring.

Now I want to share even more stories. Where *Beneath the Moon* lightly summarized nearly eighty myths, legends, and fairy tales from across the world, in *Around the Sun* and the accompanying card deck and guidebook *Oracle of the Divine*, I choose to dive deeper into twelve stories and give readers more of a chance to fall in love with the characters and unique cultures they came from. But I also want to emphasize global similarities, so for that I choose twelve motifs that appear repeatedly in multiple unrelated cultures from around the globe.

I hope you enjoy this collection and leave wanting to learn even more about one another, all of us spinning around the same sun.

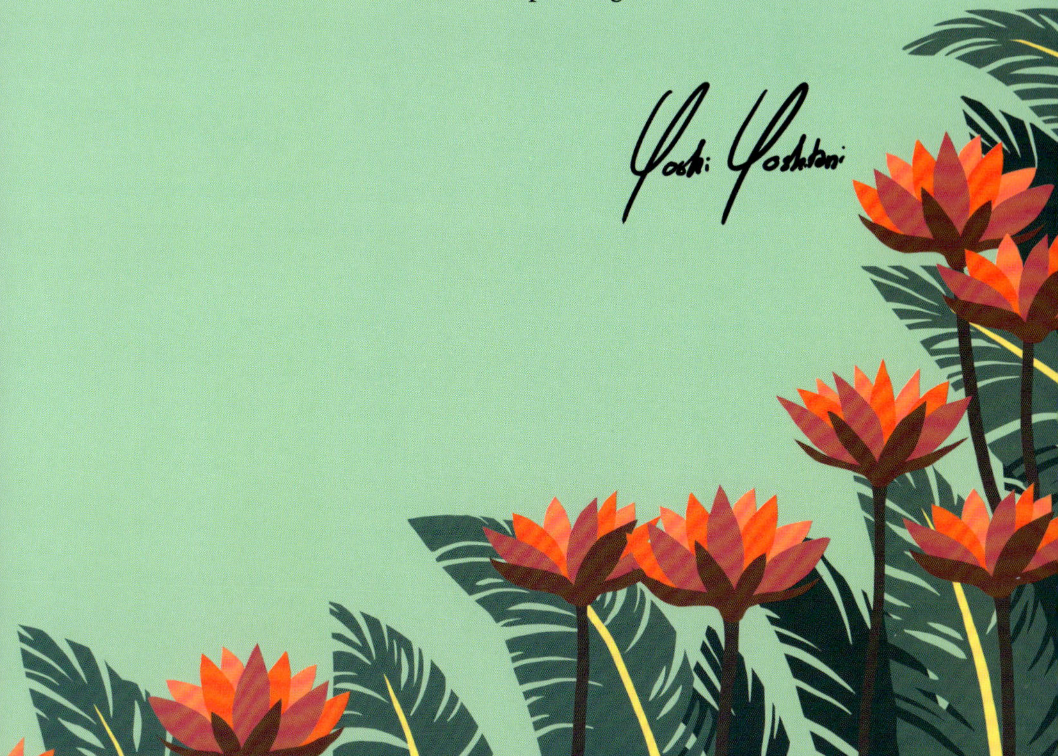

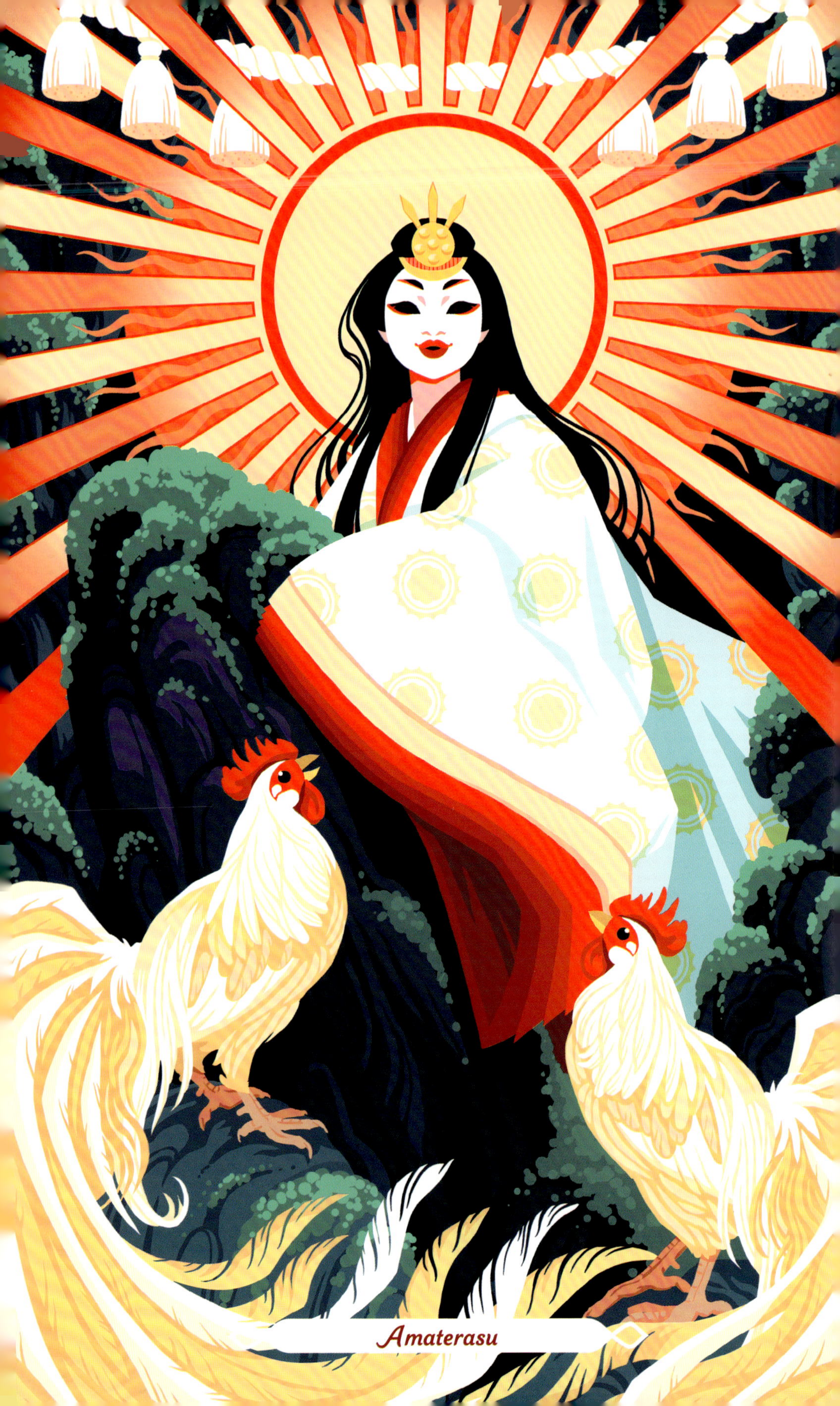
Amaterasu

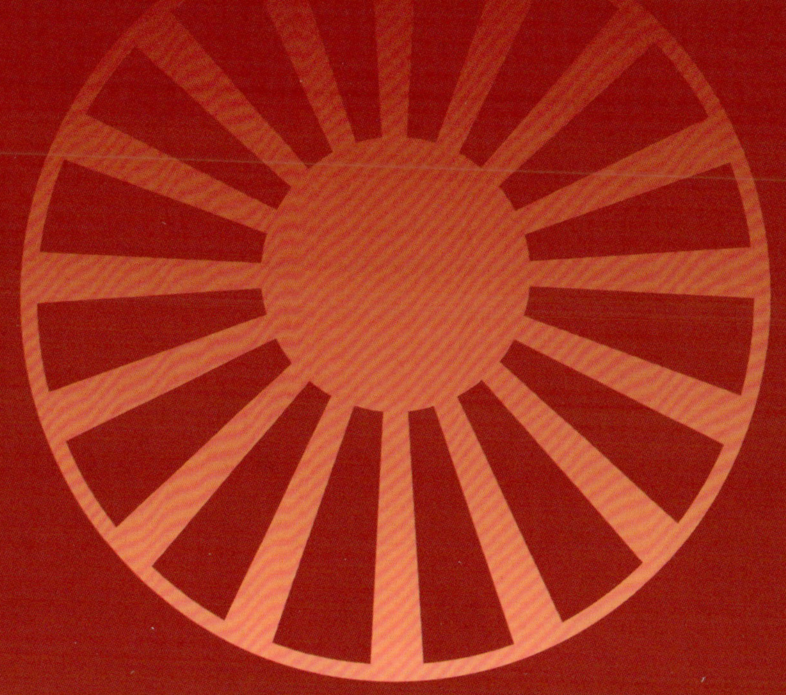

AMATERASU
and the Heavenly Rock Cave

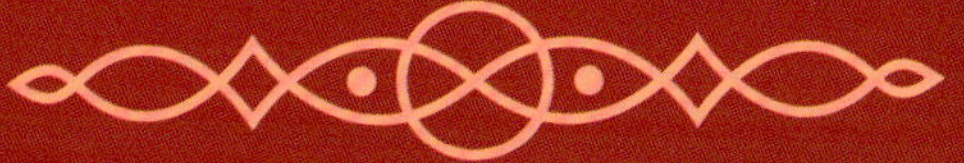

JAPANESE MYTHOLOGY | JAPAN

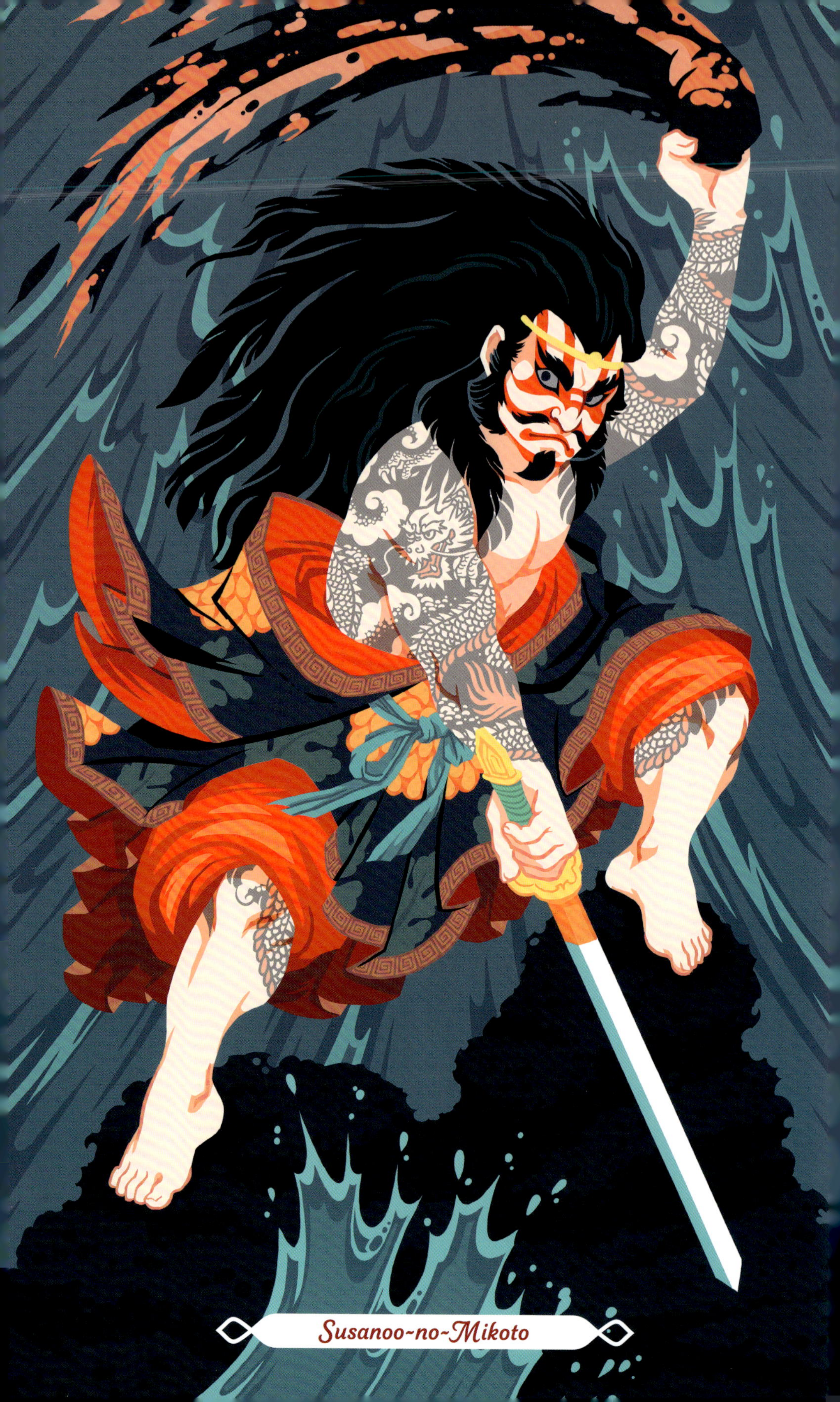
Susanoo-no-Mikoto

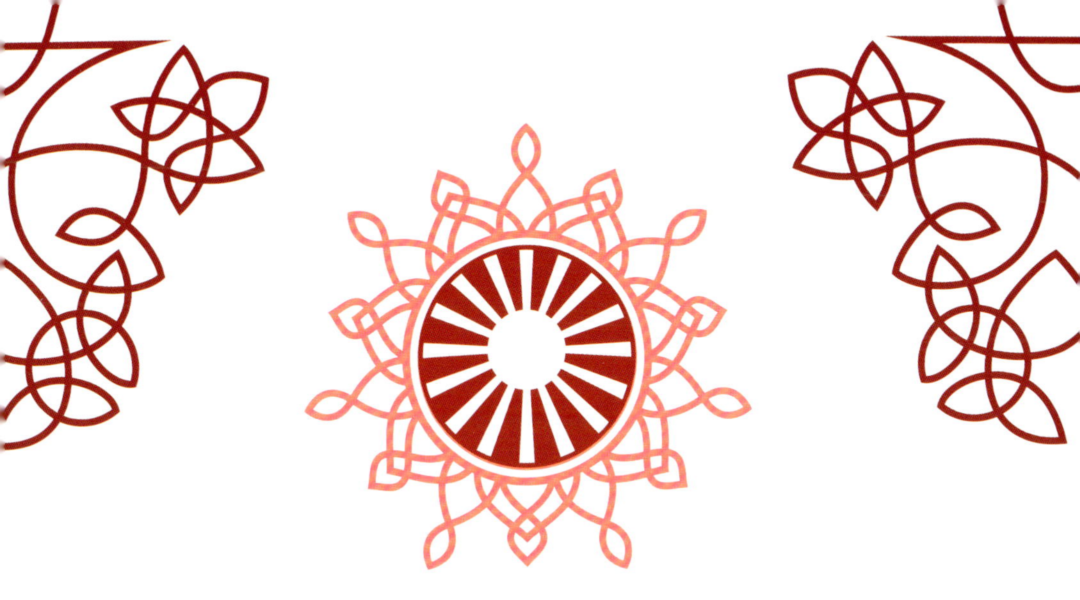

Long ago, when the islands of Japan had only just been formed by the god Izanagi and the goddess Izanami, there lived the Sun Goddess, Amaterasu Omikami, the most radiant of the deities and ruler of the heavens.

Amaterasu had many siblings, but none was more troublesome than her younger brother, Susanoo-no-Mikoto, the God of Storms and Pestilence. Wild and destructive, he was fond of loud wailing and wicked wrath, leaving a trail of chaos wherever he went. He was so disruptive that eventually he even wore out the patience of his father, Izanagi. The founding god finally banned Susanoo from Takamagahara, the high plain of heaven, for his unruly conduct.

Before leaving, Susanoo sought to bid farewell to his sister Amaterasu. Suspicious of his intentions, Amaterasu met him in her full warrior attire and demanded proof that his visit was one of peace. Susanoo suggested that they engage in a divine contest, and if he won, it would count as validation of his sincerity. Amaterasu agreed. She took Susanoo's sword, broke it into three pieces, chewed each piece, and spat three times. From each chewed piece rose a deity, until three new goddesses stood

before them. Then Susanoo took Amaterasu's necklace, pulled off five magatama beads, chewed each bead, and spat five times. From each chewed bead rose a deity, until five new gods stood before them.

Susanoo crowed his victory, as he had made more gods than the number of goddesses Amaterasu was able to produce. But Amaterasu argued that she had won, as the gods had been created from her necklace, which proved to be better source material.

Either furious that Amaterasu refused to acknowledge his superiority or flushed with triumph, Susanoo proceeded to rage unchecked across Amaterasu's home. In his wrath, he tore up her rice fields, defecated in her palace, and flayed the heavenly piebald horse from tail to head. But worst of all, he completely sundered the peace and tranquility of his sister's home by hurling the remainder of the horse at Amaterasu's loom, causing the shuttle to kill her beloved handmaiden Ame-no-Hatorime, Goddess of Weaving and Order.

Devastated, heartbroken, and livid, Amaterasu fled to Ama-no-Iwato, the Heavenly Rock Cave, sealing herself inside with a massive boulder. With the light of the sun locked away, heaven and earth were plunged into complete darkness. Crops withered, animals died, and evil demons roamed unchecked. Divine order was in shambles, and the world was engulfed in chaos.

The eight hundred myriad *kami*, gods both lesser and greater, quickly gathered outside the cave and begged Amaterasu to return to the world. But the goddess was so engulfed in her pain and grief that she would not heed them. The kami didn't know what to do until Ame-no-Uzume, Goddess of Mirth and Revelry, suggested they hold a loud celebration outside the cave to pique Amaterasu's curiosity and lure her out.

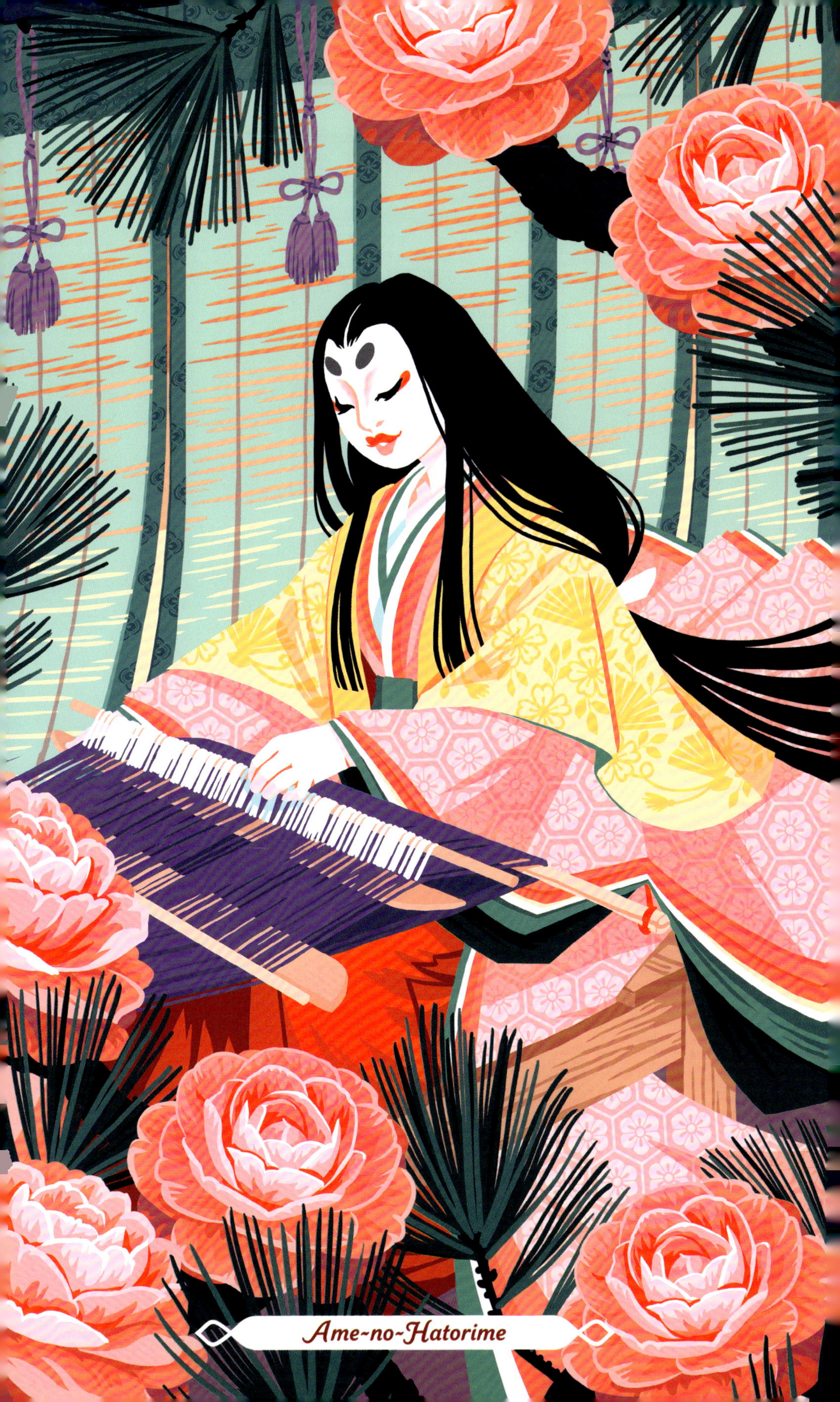
Ame-no-Hatorime

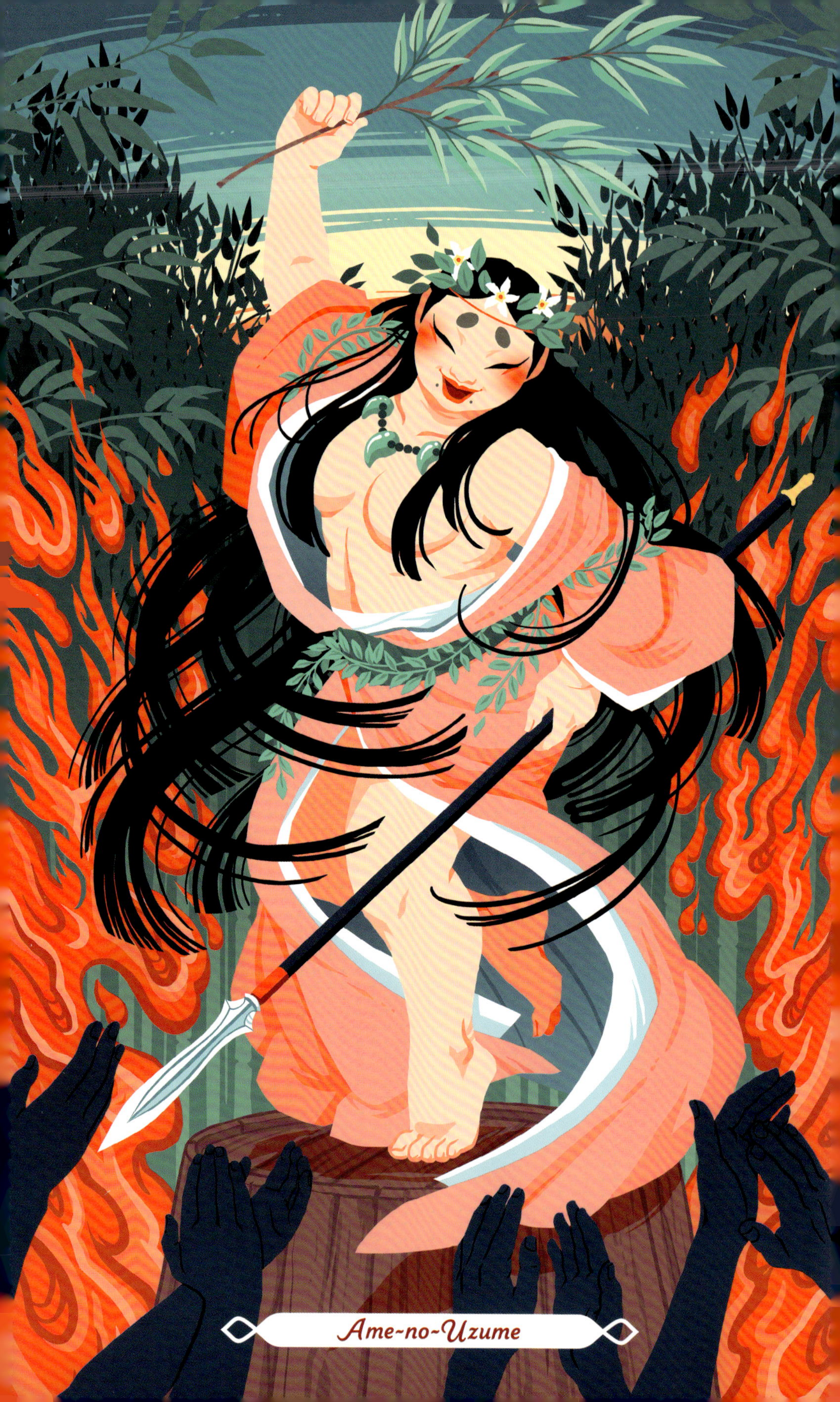
Ame-no-Uzume

The kami all agreed, setting up decorations of ribbons and jewels. Then Ame-no-Uzume bound up her sleeves with a cord of hikage vine, tied a headband of masaki vine, grabbed bundles of sasa leaves, then turned over a wooden tub and began to stomp her feet atop it. The dance she performed was so wild, so hilarious, and so lewd that all of the eight hundred gathered kami erupted into rambunctious laughter—the first heard since the world had gone dark.

Their joy was so raucous and infectious that even Amaterasu, deep in her cave and even deeper in her misery, heard them. She was puzzled, confused at how there could be happiness in a world shrouded in darkness and despair. Slowly, she crept to the door of her cave and slid back the rock to peer outside. Quickly, the kami by the entrance held up a mirror, known as Yata-no-Kagami, which reflected Amaterasu's own radiant light back at her. Stunned by her own power, resplendence, and beauty, she stepped forward and fully emerged. As soon as Amaterasu was out, more kami pushed the boulder back and sealed the entrance with a shimenawa rope so she could never again retreat to the cave.

Amaterasu laughed with the other kami at Ame-no-Uzume's antics, and agreed to resume her place in heaven. The myriad eight hundred kami then caught and punished Susanoo for his many transgressions. He was fined a thousand tables of restitutive gifts, the nails of his hands and feet were cut off, and he was divinely expelled from heaven, forced to wander the earth until redeemed.

Dawn broke, light returned to the world, and harmony was restored. From then on, Amaterasu's brilliance continued to shine upon the heavens and earth, symbolizing the triumph of light over darkness, order over chaos, and the enduring hope that even in the darkest moments, joy can lead us back to the light.

THE OLDEST KNOWN WRITTEN accounts of Japanese Shinto mythology are the *Kojiki*, written around A.D. 710, and the *Nihon Shoki*, written in A.D. 720, but the oral tradition they capture dates back to the start of the Yayoi period in 300 B.C. As such, even though both works appear to have been written at around the same time and commissioned by the Japanese imperial family, they contradict each other. The *Nihon Shoki* even contradicts itself—as it tells the mythical creation of Japan, footnotes appear with alternative versions of the myth that often run counter to the main narrative. Nor can the political motives of the writers themselves be overlooked, particularly in the *Kojiki*, which takes pains to trace the lineage of every noble family of the eighth century to a deity serving the Sun Goddess Amaterasu. But even as the *Kojiki* and the *Nihon Shoki* were written, most people in Japan remained illiterate, and the recitation of stories through dance, plays, and storytellers meant that Japanese myth and folklore continued to grow and change through the centuries. Just as nearly every physical crossroad had a small shrine to a kami, or Shinto god, nearly every village had a different variant of the same stories. Amaterasu is a perfect example of these divergences. While many maintain she is an unmarried virgin goddess, some say she was married to the Moon God Tsukuyomi before they parted. Others believe she was in a romantic relationship with her handmaiden before she died. Still others say her handmaiden was her daughter with an unnamed father. Despite the myriad of divergent stories, one thing all Amaterasu's worshippers agree on is that she is the goddess of the sun. While most other female celestial goddesses are associated with the moon, she is one of the very few female sun deities in the world.

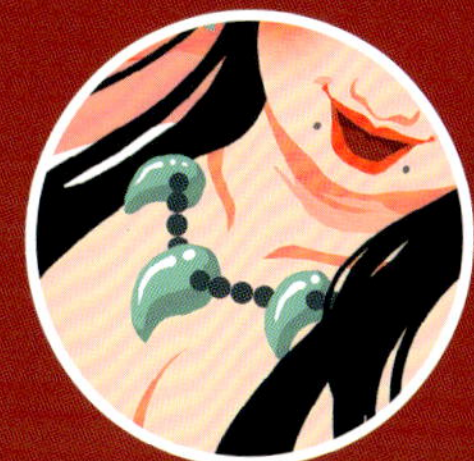

Magatama beads are made of jade, glass, agate, or other stones and are magical protective charms. They ward off evil spirits and bring good fortune.

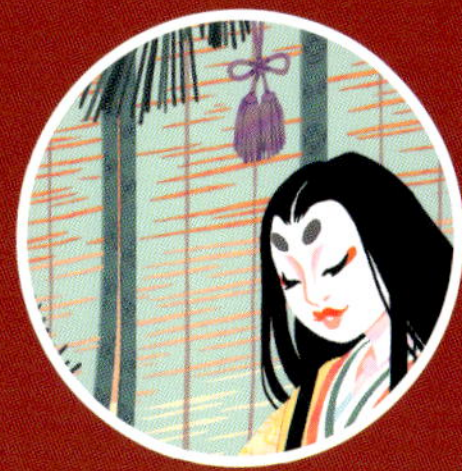

During the Heian period, *misu*, or curtains made of finely woven green bamboo, were used to conceal women from the male gaze. Slightly transparent, they allowed women to see without being seen and evoke mystery.

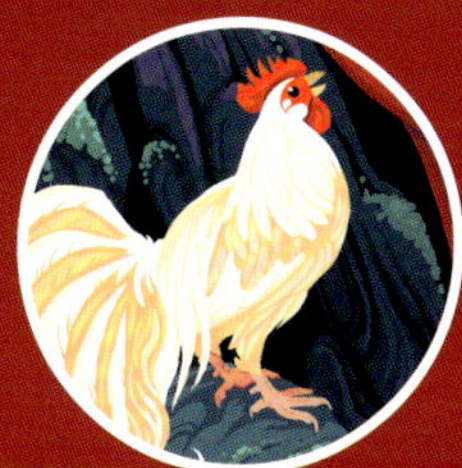

Often associated with Amaterasu, roosters embody vigilance, awakening, good fortune, and hope. Their crow is symbolic of the sun's return and the dispelling of darkness.

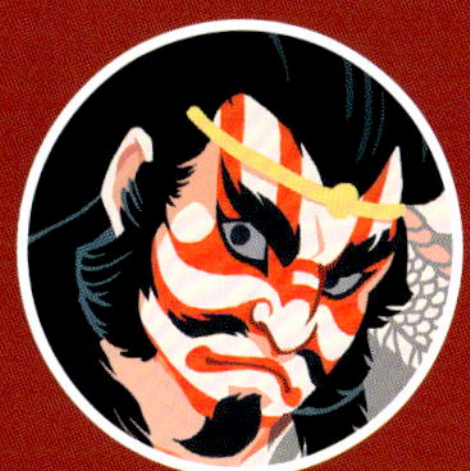

In Japanese Kabuki theater, *kumadori* makeup uses bold lines and colors to convey to the audience a character's disposition. The red *sujiguma* pattern represents roles with superhuman strength and filled with intense anger.

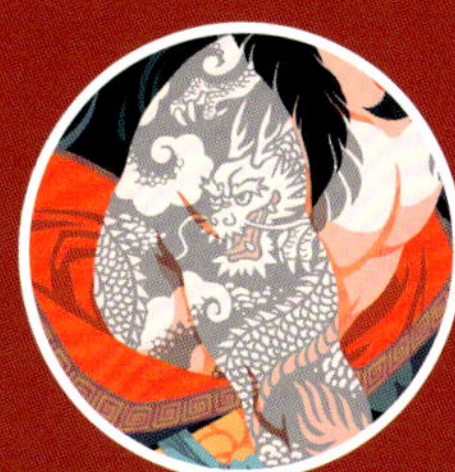

After being expelled from heaven, Susanoo slays the eight-headed dragon Yamata-no-Orochi with his ten-span sword Totsuka-no-Tsurugi.

THE MIRROR

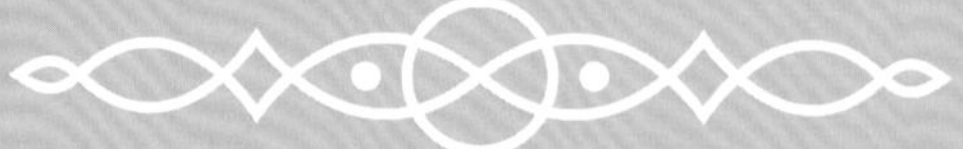

The Mirror is an object that reflects not only appearance but also the soul. In mythology and folklore, mirrors—often represented by still water, polished metal, or enchanted glass—reveal inner truths, subconscious desires, and spiritual realities. Mirrors in these stories do not change the world; they only reflect what is hidden and the truths the viewer is not ready to confront.

Mirrors are often symbols of divine insight. In Japanese mythology, the Yata-no-Kagami is a heavenly mirror that represents wisdom and truth. It is used to lure the Sun Goddess Amaterasu from hiding by showing her own radiant reflection—reminding her of the joy she had forgotten. In Aztec mythology, the god Tezcatlipoca, whose name means "Smoking Mirror," wields a polished obsidian mirror that reveals all things—truth, lies, and fate itself. His mirror is both a tool of prophecy and a weapon of chaos, exposing hidden sins and unraveling illusions.

Other stories warn of the evils of one's reflection. In Greek myth, Narcissus falls in love with his own image reflected in a pool of water. Unable to look away, he withers and dies, a lesson of how self-absorption and illusion can consume a person. In the German fairy tale *Snow White*, the evil queen's Magic Mirror confirms her worst insecurities. Its unwavering honesty drives her to jealousy and attempted murder. The Mirror does not deceive—but its truth becomes a catalyst for cruelty. Similarly, in the Greek legend of Medusa, her own reflection in Perseus's mirrored shield turns her to stone—a warning that facing one's true self can be fatal.

The Mirror is a tool of revelation and reflects what already lies within. Whether it leads to wisdom, ruin, or transformation depends on the soul that dares to look.

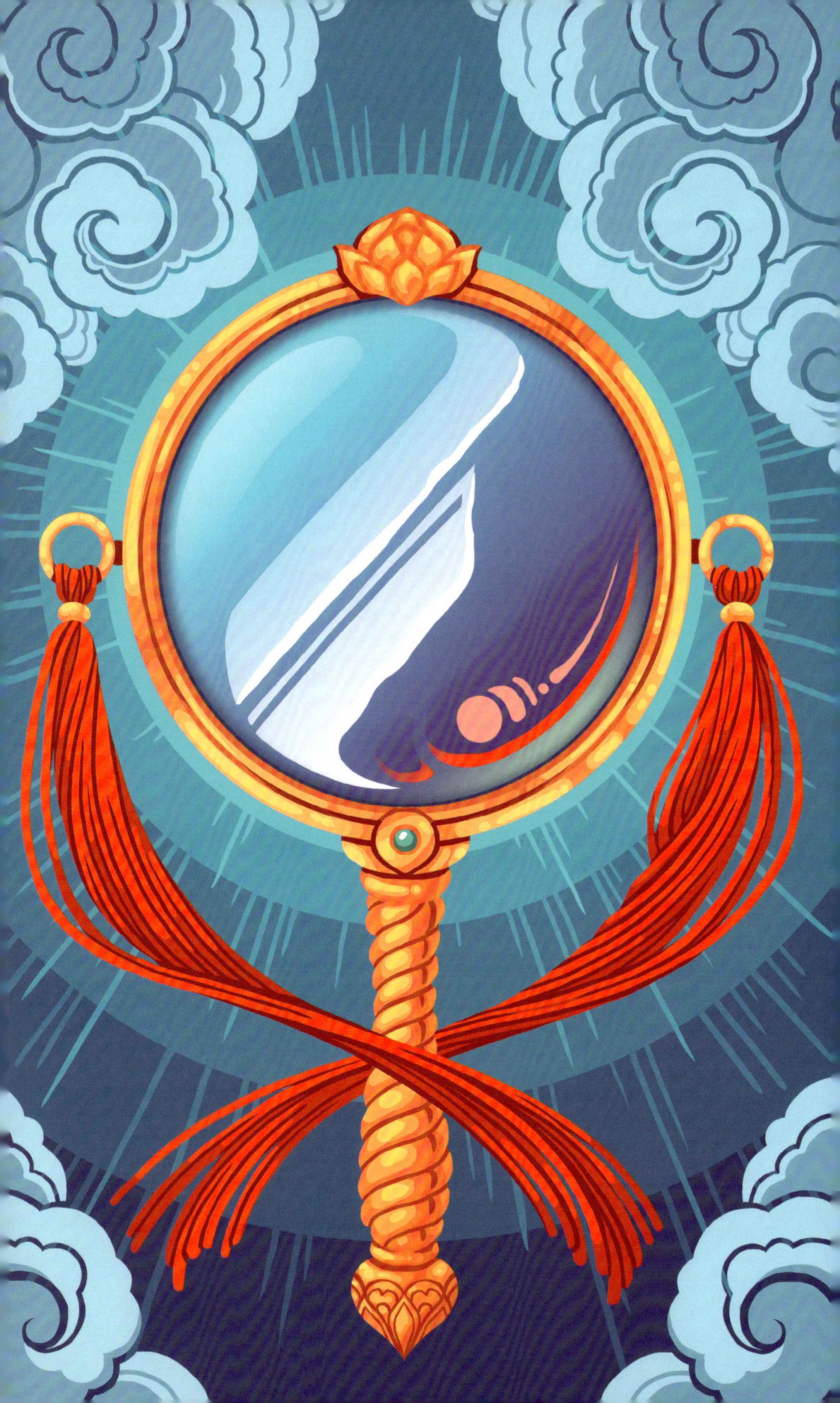

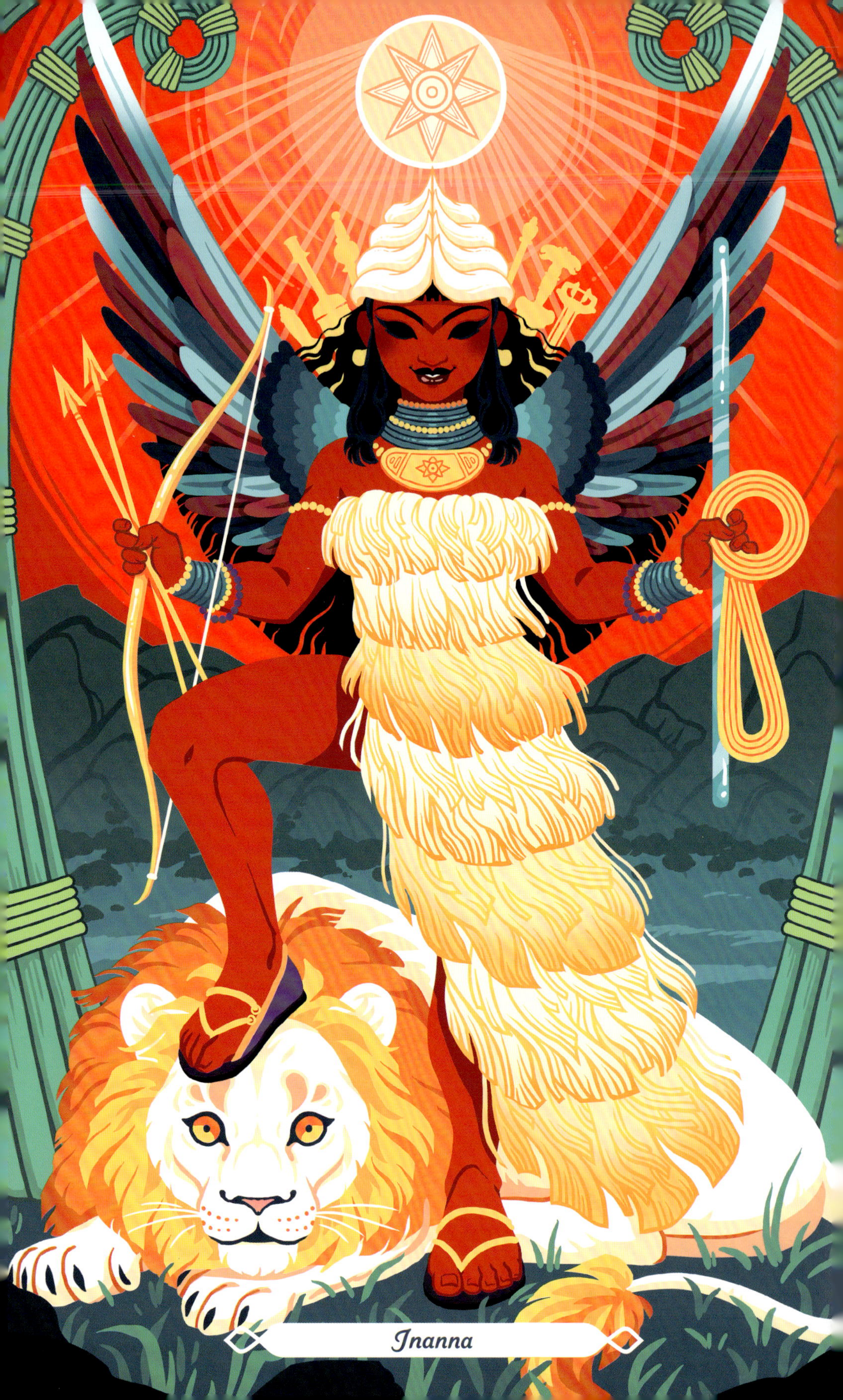
Inanna

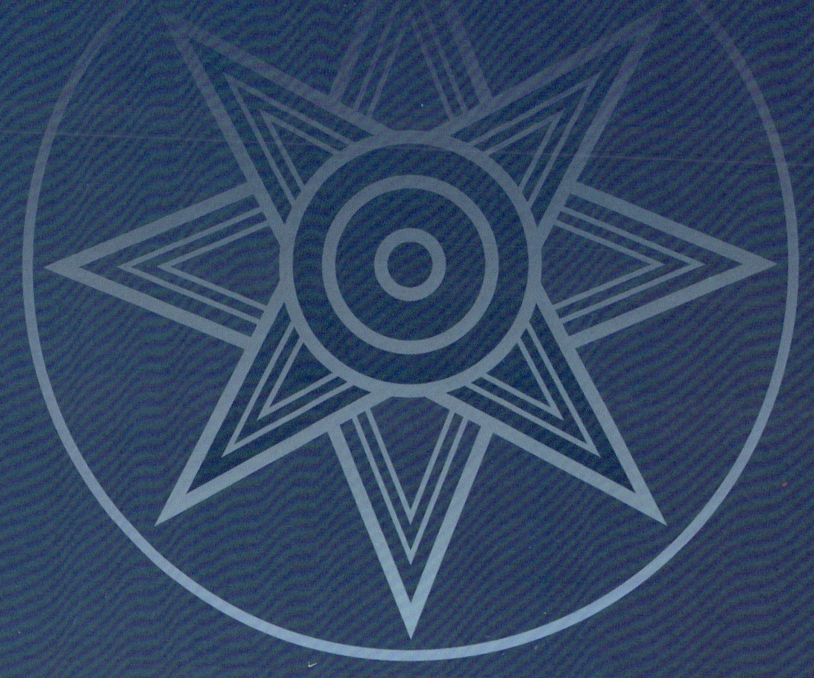

INANNA'S *Descent into the Underworld*

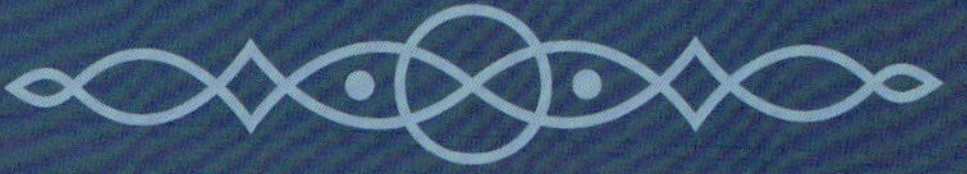

SUMERIAN MYTHOLOGY | IRAQ

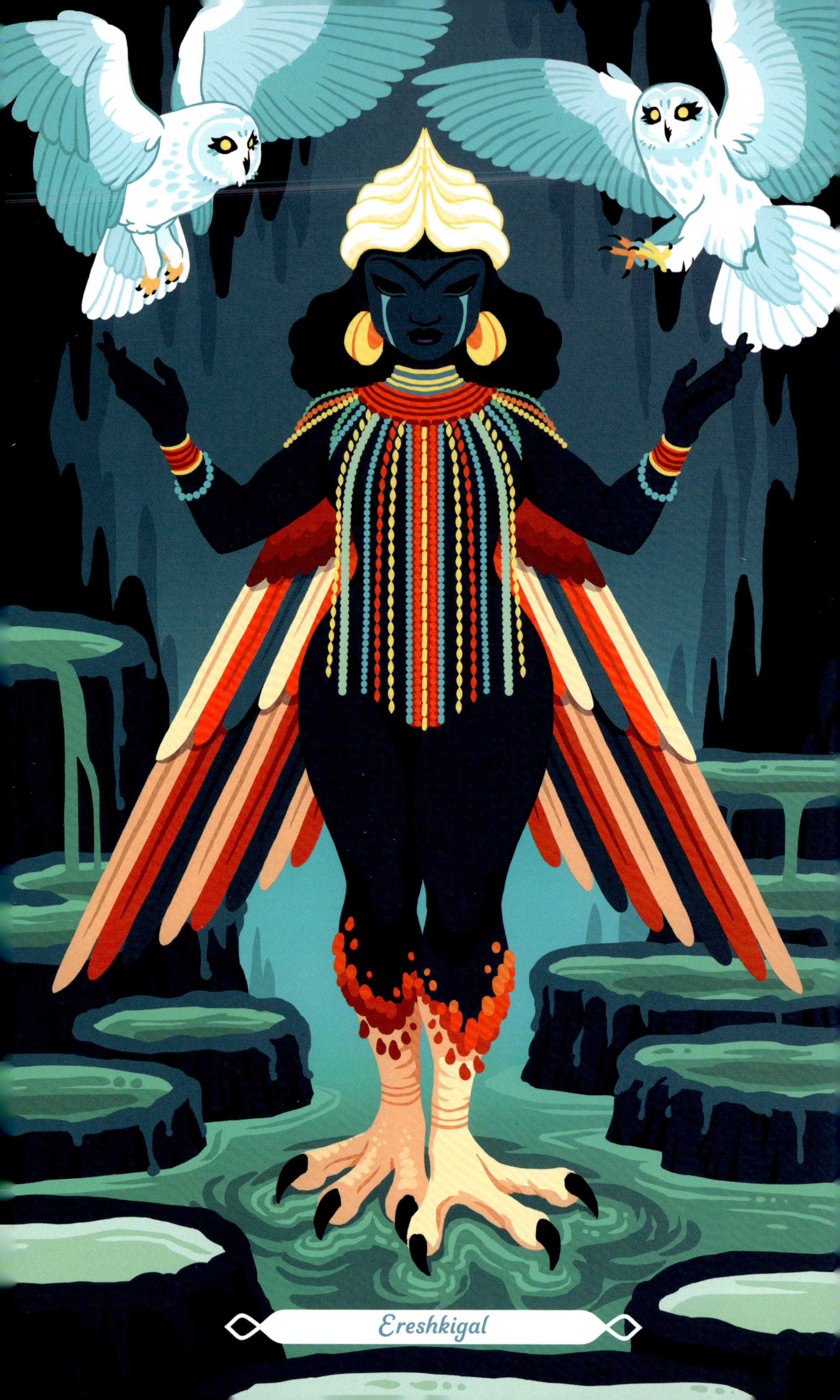
Ereshkigal

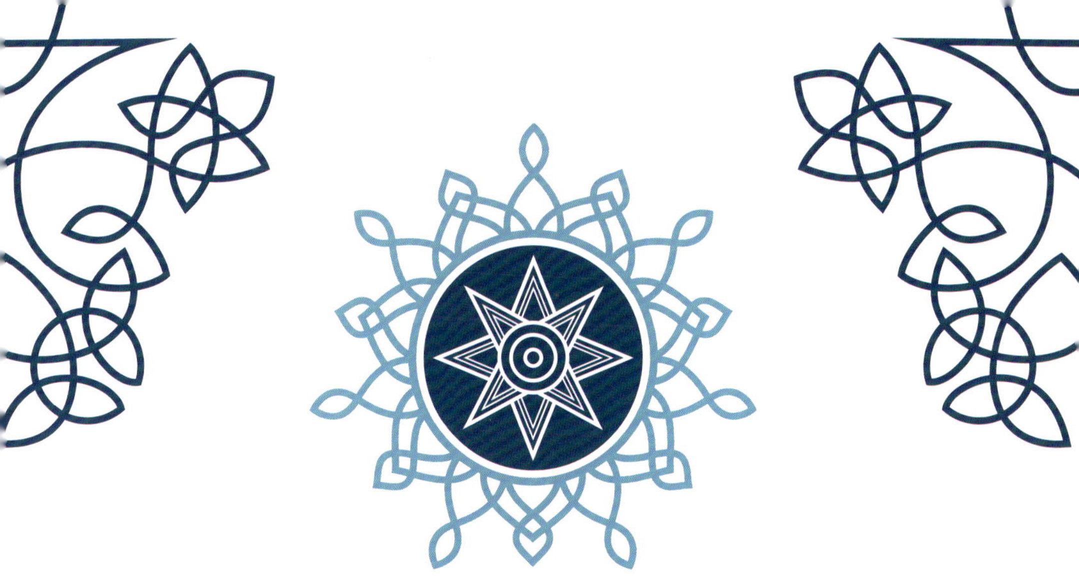

There was once a time when Inanna (later called Ishtar), Queen of Heaven and Earth, Goddess of Power and Ambition, wished to expand her domain to include the Underworld, which was ruled by her older sister, the goddess Ereshkigal.

This was not the first time the goddess Inanna had coveted what another deity had. When she was still a young, weak goddess with only a few *Me*, or divine objects of power, to her name, she saw that Enki, the God of Wisdom, had many. Desiring his power, clever Inanna went to Enki's home in his city of Eridu and challenged him to a drinking contest. Charmed by the beautiful goddess, Enki agreed and was soon so drunk that he willingly bestowed upon her his most powerful *Me:* the shugurra crown, the lapis lazuli measuring rod, the divine sword, and many more. Inanna quickly departed Eridu with her winnings, but Enki sobered up as she fled and realized what he had done. He tried to send monsters after Inanna, but her personal advisor and divine attendant, the goddess Ninshubur, fought them all off. So Inanna returned to her city of Uruk victorious and stronger than before, becoming the goddess who ruled over beauty, love, conquest, justice, luck, kingship, and war.

Inanna went on to capture the temples of other gods, crush mountains, and assert her own authority across the world. As she gained more power and divine objects on these conquests, Inanna naturally set her sights on one of the strongest *Me* of all, the Throne of the Underworld.

To prepare for her journey down into the shadowy realm, Inanna did three things. First, she put on seven of her most powerful *Me*: the shugurra crown, the small lapis bead necklace, the double strand necklace, the pectoral necklace, the kaunakes dress, the gold bracelet, and the lapis lazuli measuring rod. Second, she told the faithful Ninshubur what to do if she did not return. Third, she came up with an excuse to visit her sister Ereshkigal.

Before Inanna schemed for the Underworld, she had desired for the great hero Gilgameš (later called Gilgamesh) to become her consort. Gilgameš refused her, saying she was too insatiable, and instead chose to continue adventuring with his companion Enkidu. Inanna was furious with his rejection and sent the Bull of Heaven to destroy him. After a great battle, Gilgameš and Enkidu were able to kill the Bull of Heaven, who was then revealed to be Gugalanna, husband of Ereshkigal, Queen of the Underworld.

As the Goddess of Conquest, Inanna felt neither remorse nor sorrow for her actions, but she pretended to be upset as a pretense to visit the funeral of Gugalanna. And so, wearing all her fine *Me*, applying divine eyeliner, and fixing her hair beautifully, the Goddess of Changing Fortunes descended to the cave of the Underworld. Ereshkigal saw her sister approaching and was not deceived. Although Inanna might claim she had arrived for the funeral, she was dressed too brilliantly, disrespecting the dead. The Queen of the Underworld ordered all seven gates barred tight against Inanna, and each one would open only if Inanna

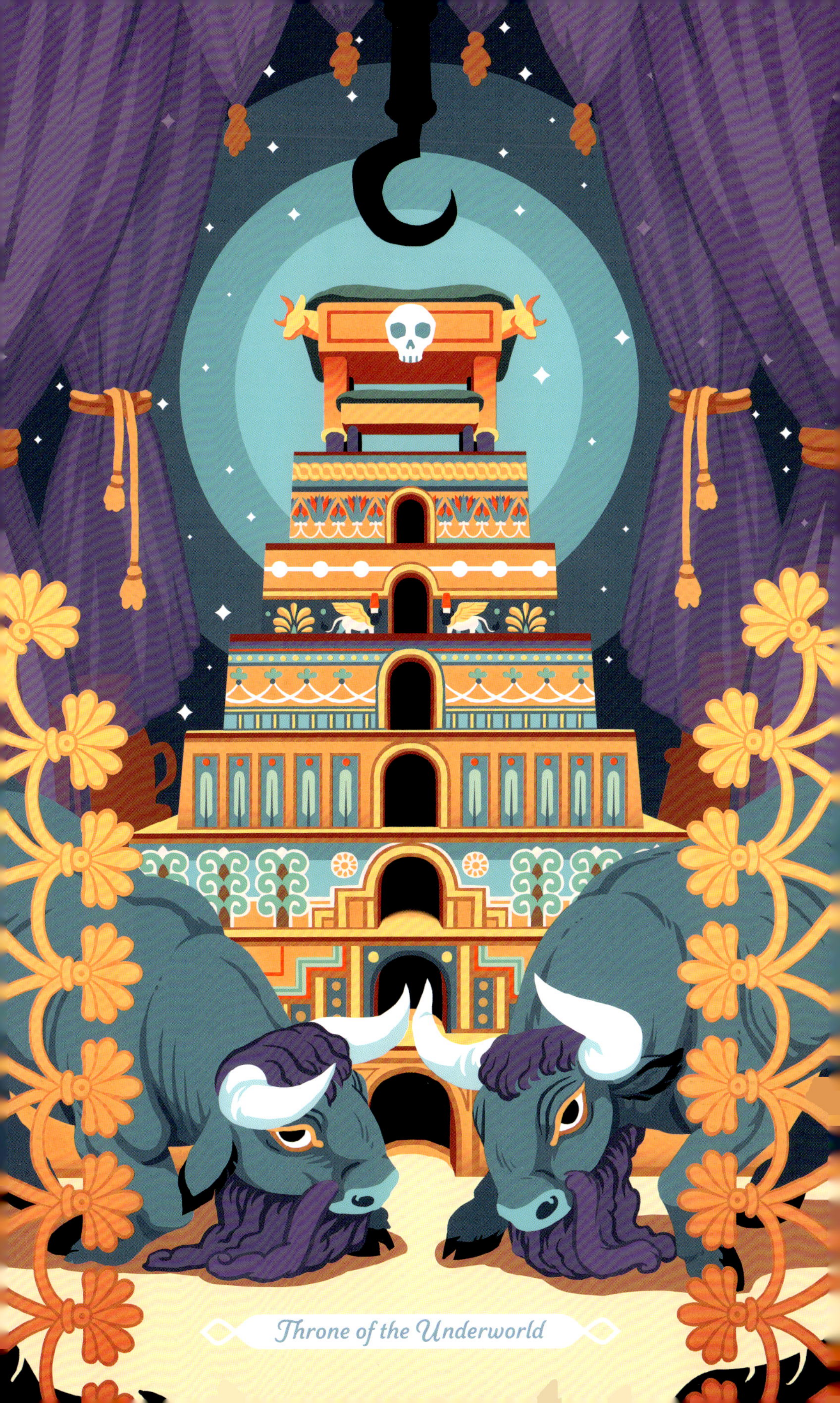
Throne of the Underworld

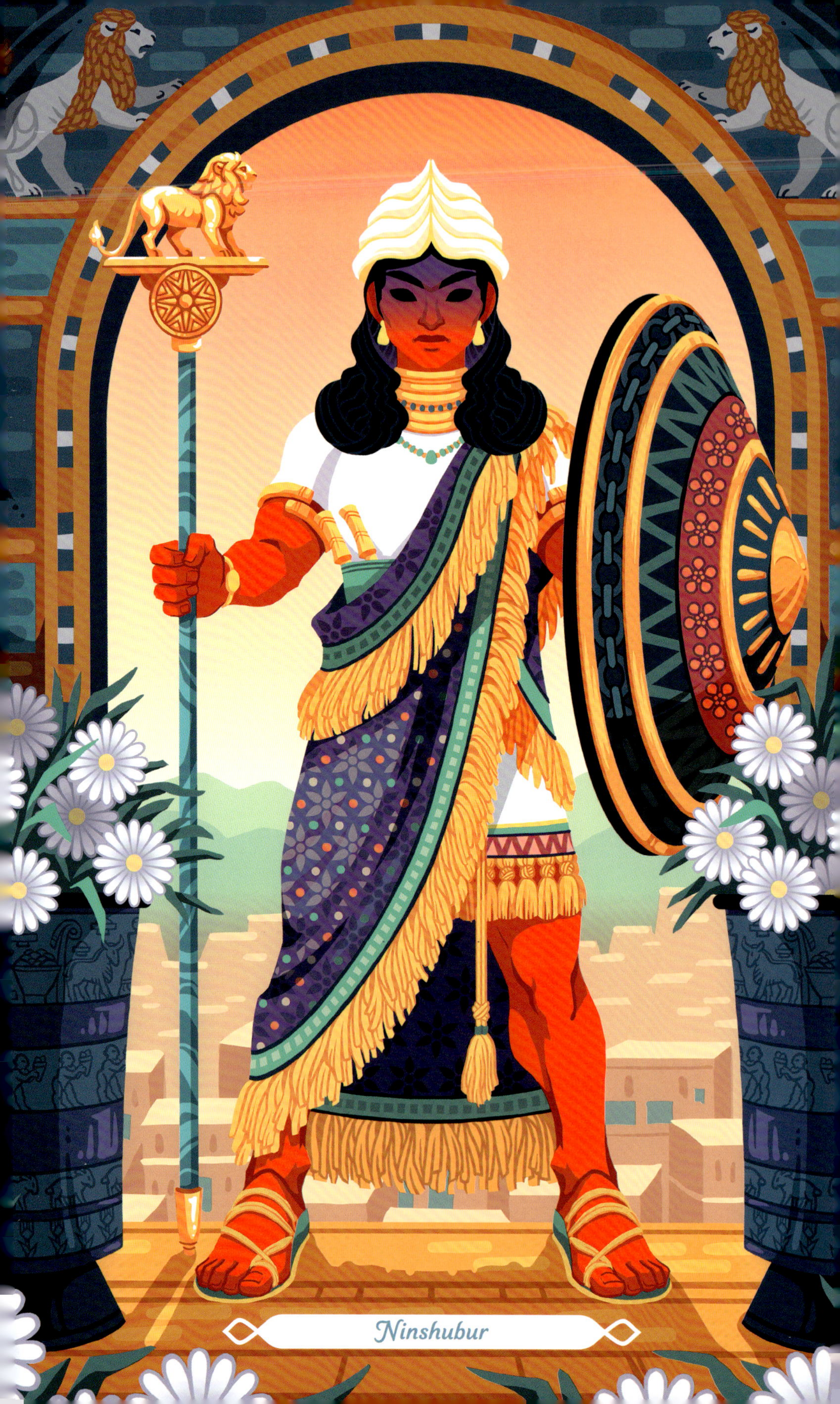
Ninshubur

relinquished one of her seven divine objects. Inanna, blinded by desire for a new queendom, did not hesitate.

Thus, Inanna arrived naked before Ereshkigal. Unashamed and without hesitation, she ascended the dais and sat down on the throne and prepared to rule. But Inanna, in her haste and greed, forgot that she had willingly stripped herself of power. Ereshkigal's wrath struck her dead, and the Queen of the Underworld hung the Goddess of Beauty's rotting corpse on a hook.

Three days later, Inanna had not returned home. So Ninshubur did as Inanna had instructed and began to loudly mourn the death of the goddess. The attendant tore at her wailing eyes in sorrow, dressed in simple rags, and beseeched the gods to free Inanna. Ereshkigal, moved by Ninshubur's devotion, reluctantly agreed to resurrect the goddess, but only if someone would take Inanna's place in the Underworld.

Inanna rose, accompanied by seven demonic guardians of the Underworld, and scoured the earth for someone to send in her stead. But all she found were her loyal and devoted followers, all crying and dressed in rags mourning her. She would not have any of the faithful replace her, and she did not know whom to choose. That is, until she walked into her palace and found her husband, Dumuzid, dry-eyed, dressed in his fine *Me,* and sitting upon her very own throne.

Enraged at his disrespect, Inanna slew her husband and handed him to the seven demonic guardians. They dragged him down into the Underworld while the Goddess of Justice roamed free once more. Queen of Heaven and Earth, but never the dead.

THE SUMERIAN GODDESS INANNA was likely first worshipped as a small goddess with a scattering of odd, uncorrelated powers and attributes in the real-life city of Uruk, now known as Warka, in Iraq. But over time, as the mortal Uruk grew and gradually conquered and gained dominion over nearby city-states, so too did the divine Inanna's power. Many of Inanna's myths revolve around her defeating or tricking other gods in her pantheon and taking their powers and earthly temples, as with the tale of Enki. These divine losses may have been used as explanations for human battles and conquests, and why some cities ceased the worship of their own local god and began to venerate Inanna. With each defeated god, Inanna's catalogue of gifts grew, until she was a goddess who reigned over fertility, wheat, passion, vengeance, thunderstorms, rain, fortune, and more. Eventually she subsumed a god named Ishtar and took his name as her own and became the highest deity in the Assyrian pantheon, which adopted much of Sumerian mythology. While today in the Western world, she is often summarized as a goddess of love and war, she is better understood as a goddess of power, as all of her myths can be interpreted as either solidifying or seeking to gain more authority and rule. She uses all the tools at her disposal to expand her dominance, not just over the domains of lust and battle, but also trade, music, deceit, beauty, politics, justice, and games. Interestingly, although she is a goddess of love, sexuality, and fertility, the one power she is never associated with is motherhood and children. She is a ruler and a taker, not a supporter or giver.

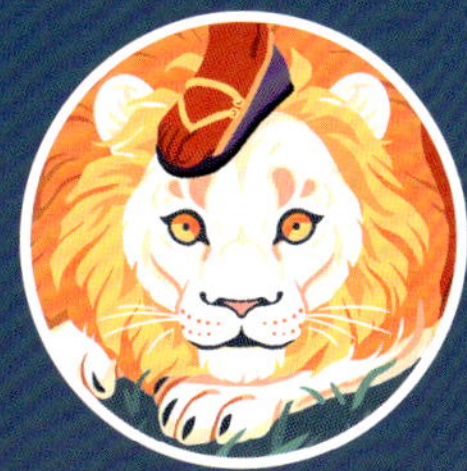

Classically, Ishtar, or Inanna, is depicted standing on top of lions. She never stands beside them, but always shows her dominance over them.

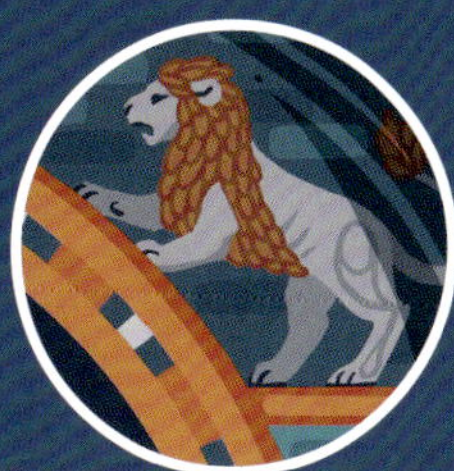

The Gate of Ishtar was the eighth gate to the inner city of Babylon. Glazed to look like precious lapis lazuli and gold, it was an impressive monument to the most favored goddess of the Akkadian pantheon.

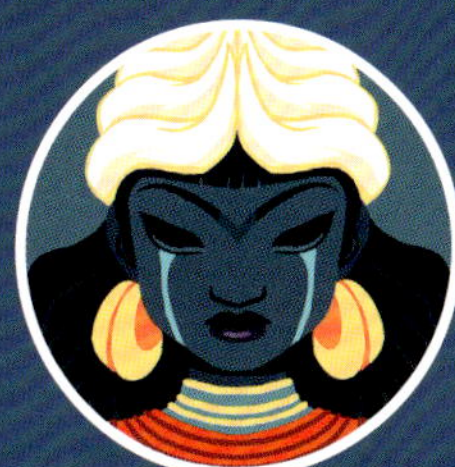

Very few images remain of the goddess Ereshkigal, and historians disagree about which of those images, if any, depict her. Some suspect that the people in ancient Mesopotamia considered it bad luck to preserve any imagery of her.

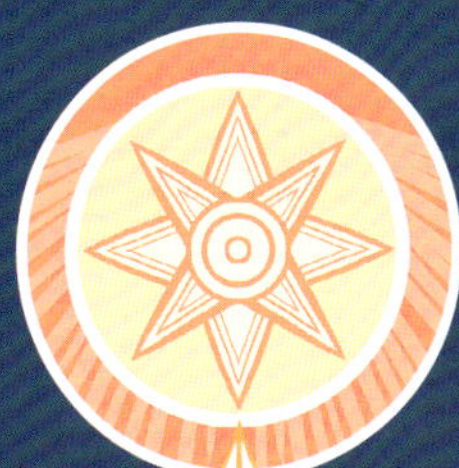

The goddess Inanna is associated with the planet Venus, which is the third brightest object in the sky after the sun and moon. In Sumerian art, it is depicted as an eight-pointed star.

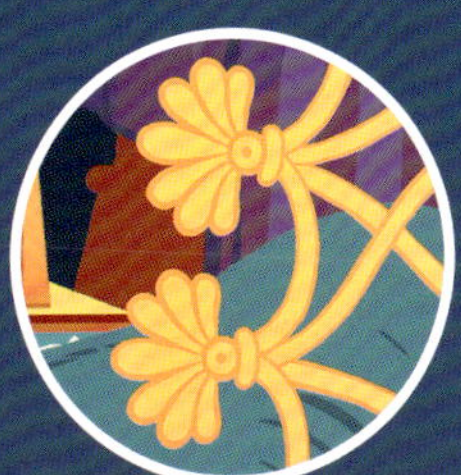

Called the "Tree of Life" by modern scholars, this stylized plant in Assyrian art symbolized cosmic divine order, the authority of royalty, and regeneration.

THE REAPED GOD

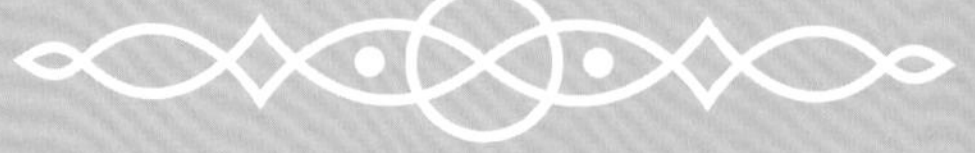

Reaped Gods are nature deities whose life and death correlate to the growth and harvesting of plants, most typically a culture's staple crop.

While stories of Reaped Gods are similar to myths with the theme of Yearly Rebirth, the two are ultimately different. In a Yearly Rebirth story, the deity dies or travels to the underworld for half the year, until the next planting cycle, when they rise again or are reborn. This trope is ultimately used to symbolize the passage of seasons, as in the Greek story of Persephone and the Sumerian story of Dumuzid. By contrast, Reaped Gods are figures who die permanently near the beginning of creation, after which their physical bodies become vegetation. They symbolize sacrifice, fertilization, and new beginnings. While both types of myths are about resurrection, Yearly Rebirth is about the *cyclical* nature of life and death whereas the Reaped God is about new life after the *severing* nature of death.

Reaped Gods are most often murdered by other gods. The Norse giant Ymir is slain by the god Odin who fears him, and his bones become the mountains, his blood the oceans, and his hair the trees and plants of the world. The Japanese goddess Ukemochi is killed by her disgusted guest when he realizes the delicious food she is serving him has been pulled from her nose and vomited. Various pieces of her become the seeds for rice, soybeans, wheat, and more. In the Indonesian myth of Hainuwele, the girl is buried alive by her male suitors when they discover the beautiful golden gifts she gave them are made from her defecations. The pieces of her decomposing body become the first tubers.

However, not all are slain: The Cherokee goddess Selu sacrifices herself for her people. She willingly lies down in a field and becomes maize. The Hawaiian boy Hāloa-naka was stillborn, and when his parents bury him, he becomes the first taro plant.

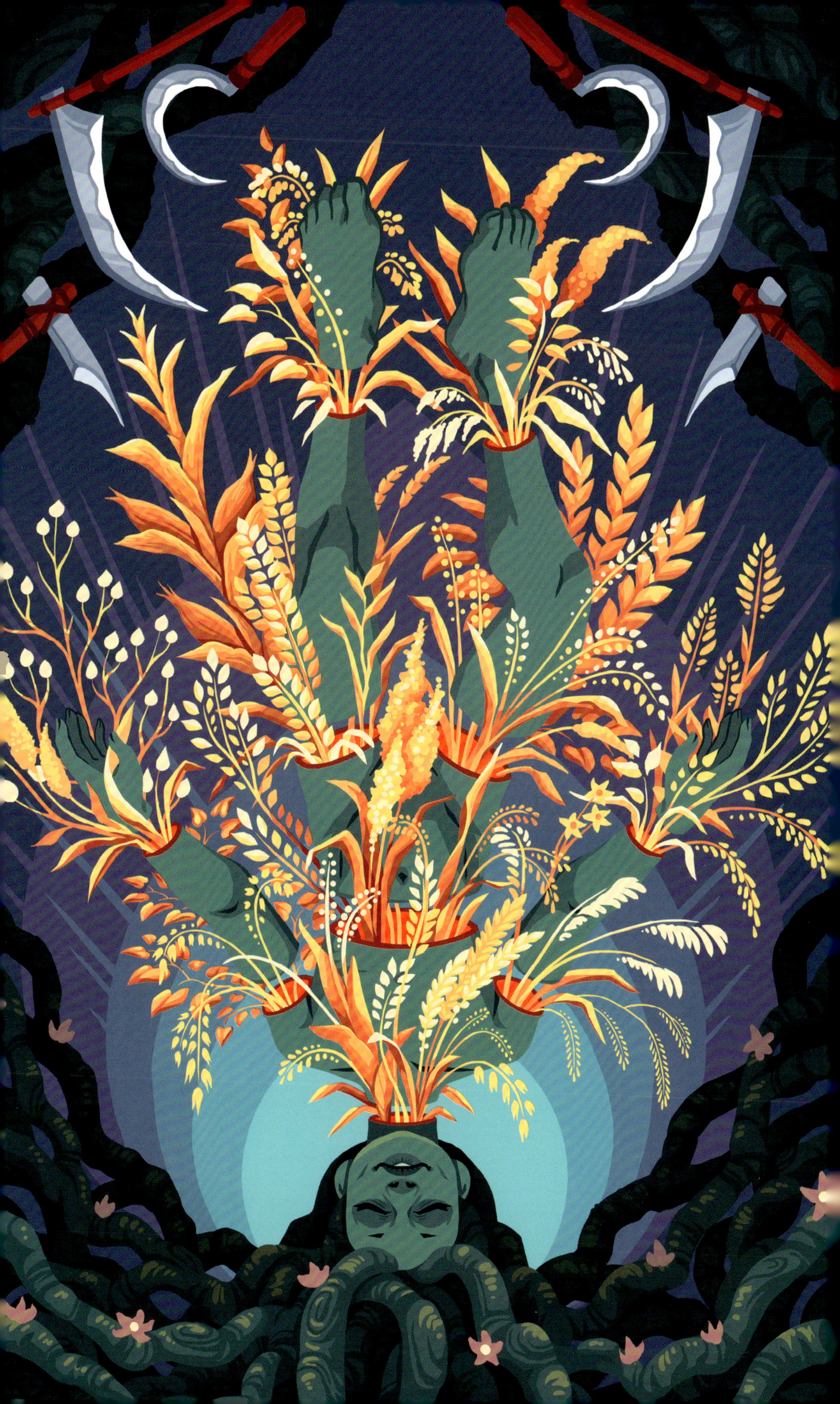

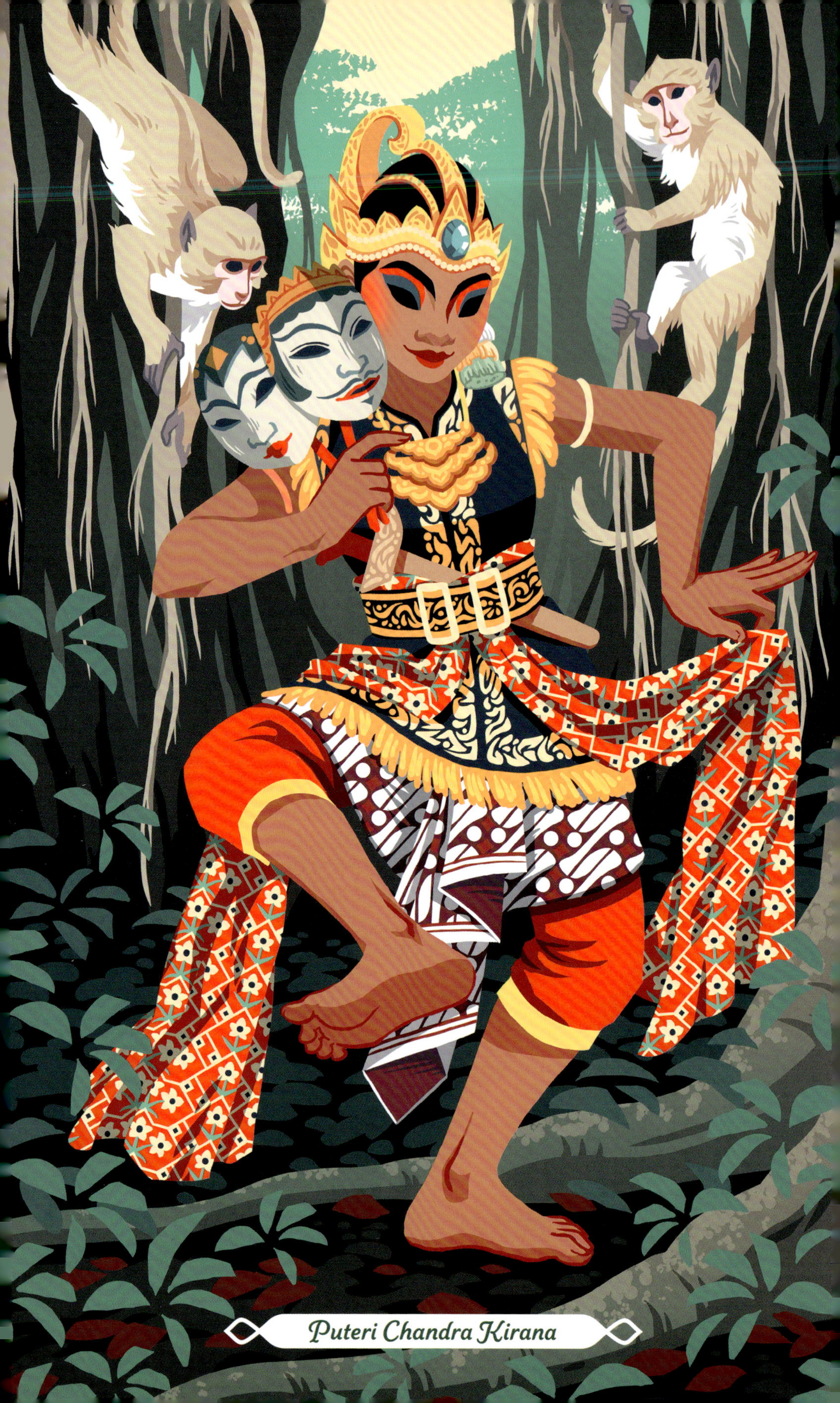
Puteri Chandra Kirana

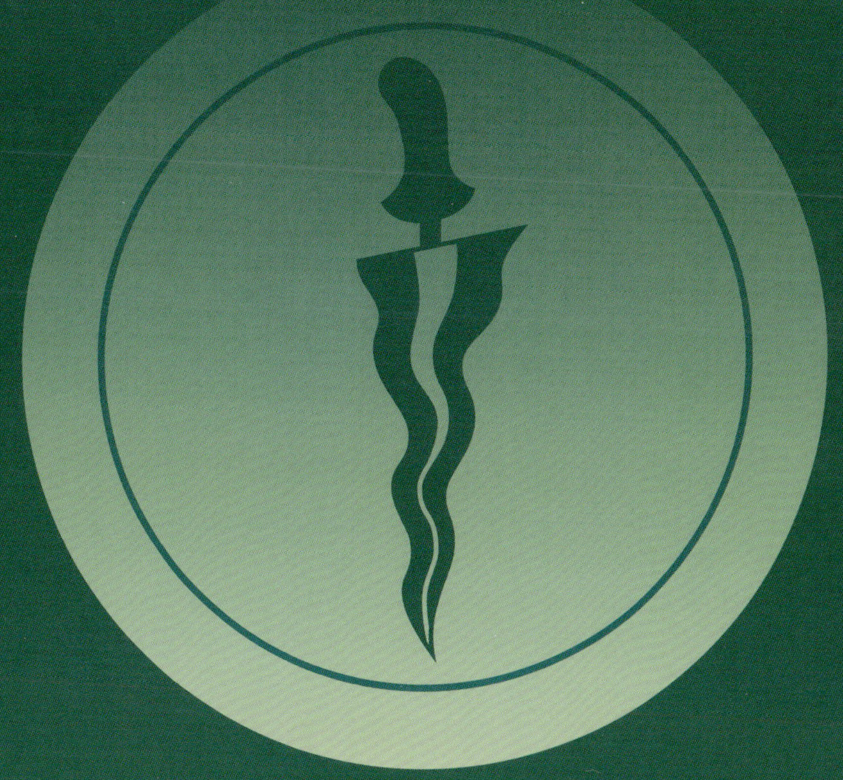

Hikayat PANJI SEMIRANG

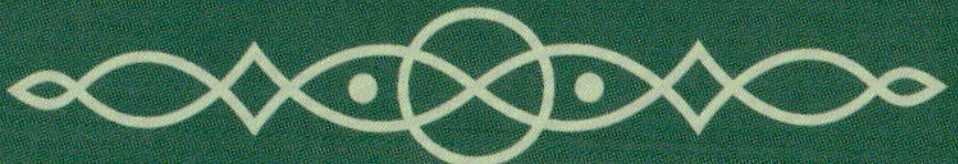

MALAY VERSION OF JAVANESE MYTHOLOGY | INDONESIAN ARCHIPELAGO

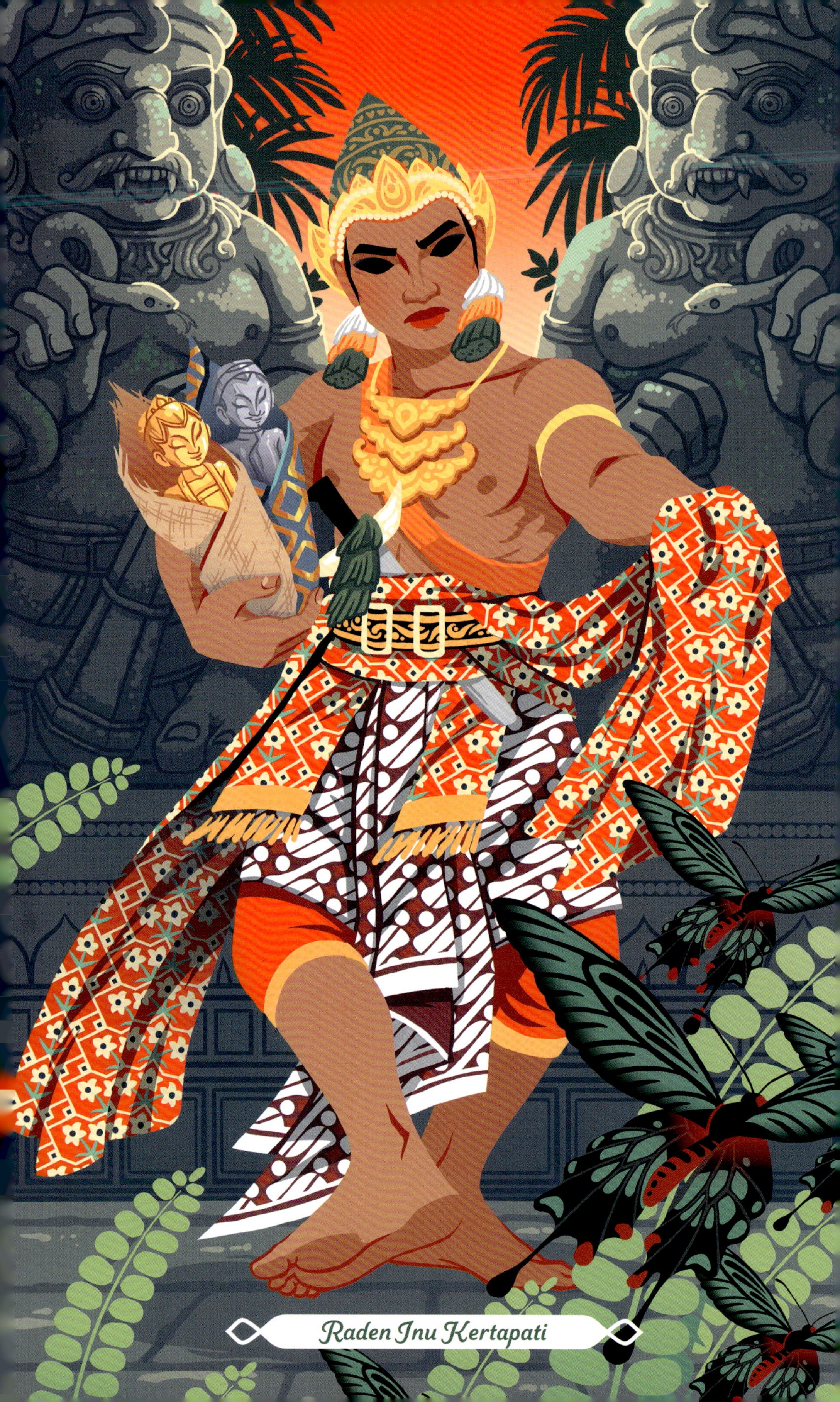
Raden Inu Kertapati

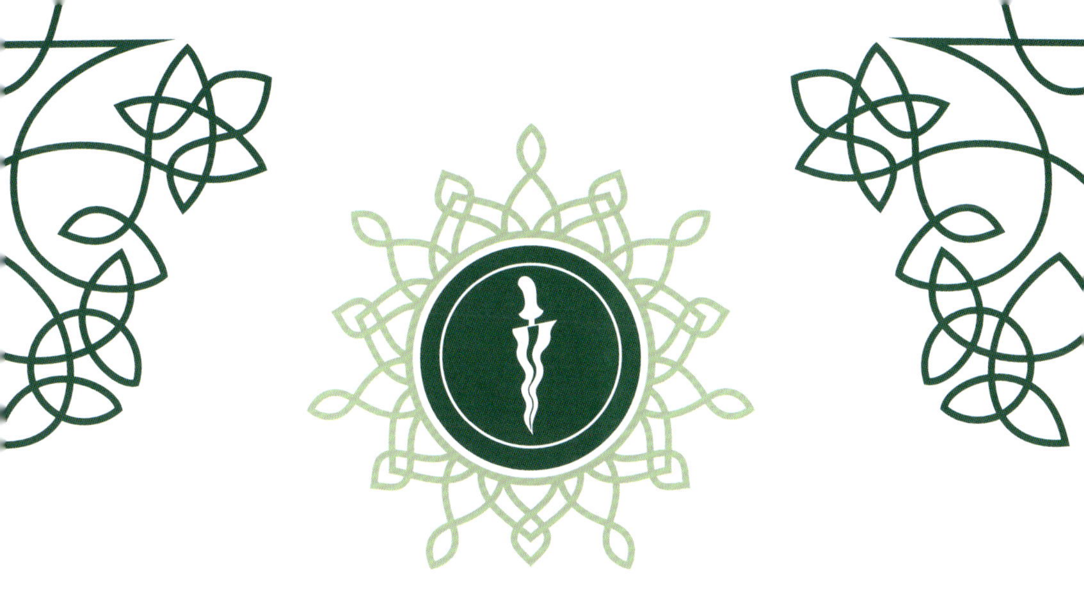

A long, long time ago, four divine siblings descended to earth. The three brothers formed three mighty kingdoms: Daha, Kuripan, and Gagelang. Meanwhile, their only sister, Biku Gandasari, climbed to the top of a high mountain to meditate and observe the world.

The brother who became the Raja, or King, of Daha married two women. One was Tuan Puteri, or queen, Ratu Ningrat, who gave birth to the beautiful Puteri, or Princess, Chandra Kirana. The other was his consort, Paduka Liku, who gave birth to the lovely Puteri Galuh Ajeng. Although the king loved both his wives, Paduka Liku was jealous of Tuan Puteri Ratu Ningrat's higher position, so she secretly poisoned her. Although many in the kingdom suspected Paduka Liku was responsible for the queen's death, the king's love for Paduka Liku made him blind to her wickedness. Without a mother to defend her, Puteri Chandra Kirana grew up neglected. With only her malicious mother to raise her, Puteri Galuh Ajeng grew up spiteful.

Meanwhile, the divine brother who became the Raja of Kuripan married and had a son named Raden, or Prince Inu Kertapati. Raden Inu grew up to be a skillful warrior, a

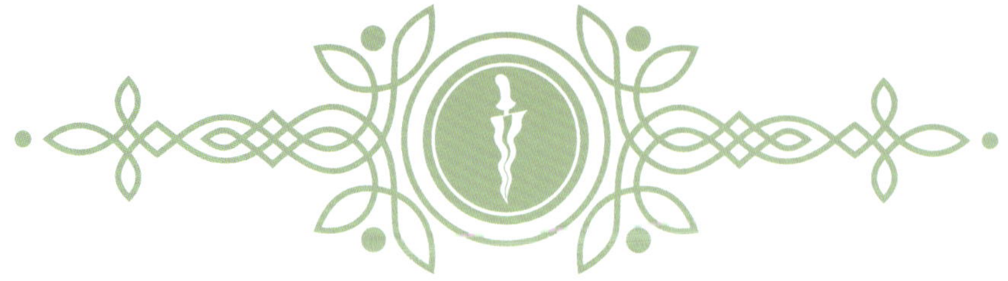

charismatic diplomat, and a handsome young man. When he came of age, his father suggested he marry one of the two princesses of Daha.

To help him decide which princess to marry, the clever prince devised a test to see which princess was purer of heart. He sent two gifts to the two princesses of Daha, one wrapped in fine silk and the other in coarse fabric. When Puteri Galuh Ajeng saw the gifts, she quickly snatched the silk-wrapped gift and opened it to reveal a beautiful doll made of silver. Puteri Chandra Kirana happily unwrapped the humble gift and revealed a sumptuous doll made of gold and covered in gemstones. Paduka Liku, recognizing the golden doll as the true proposal gift, raged with jealousy so viciously that Puteri Chandra Kirana began to fear for her own life. So that night, Puteri Chandra Kirana and her handmaidens secretly fled with the golden doll to the forest outside the kingdom. There, they all disguised themselves as men and lived as bandit warriors with Puteri Chandra Kirana as their leader. She became known as Bandit Prince Panji Semirang, the fiercest fighter of his warrior band.

Unaware of what had happened, Raden Inu set off to Daha with the intention of marrying the princess who had chosen the golden doll. Unfortunately, his caravan full of lavish wedding gifts was attacked en route by none other than Bandit Prince Panji Semirang and his band of warriors. Raden Inu and Panji Semirang fought, and though they were closely matched, Panji Semirang was the ultimate victor. As he stood over the defeated Raden Inu, Panji Semirang realized who the prince was and invited him back to his growing bandit city in the forest.

Raden Inu spent many wonderful days in the company of Panji Semirang. Although Panji Semirang never revealed who he was, Raden Inu came to love his time with the charming and intelligent bandit. It was only with great reluctance that the prince

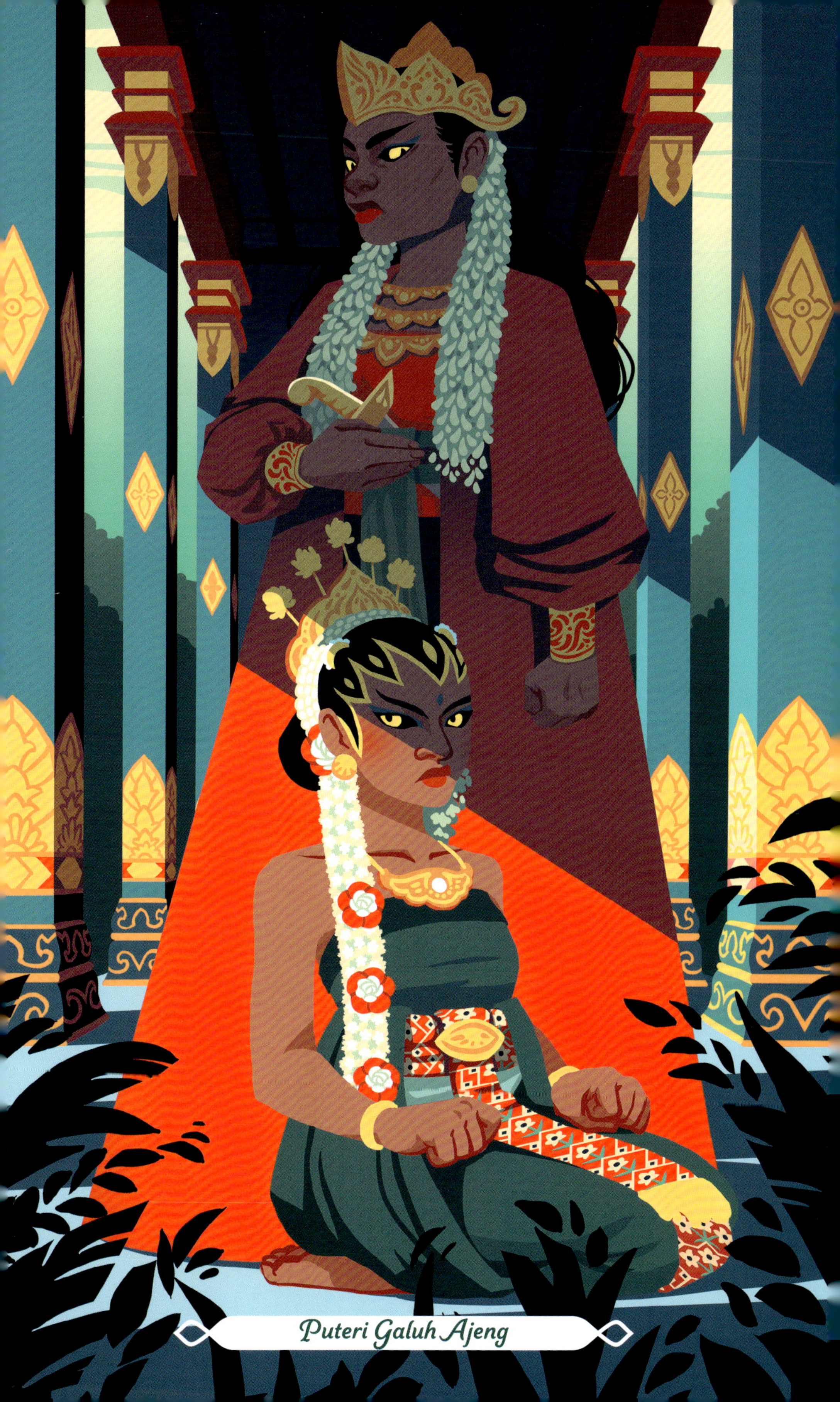
Puteri Galuh Ajeng

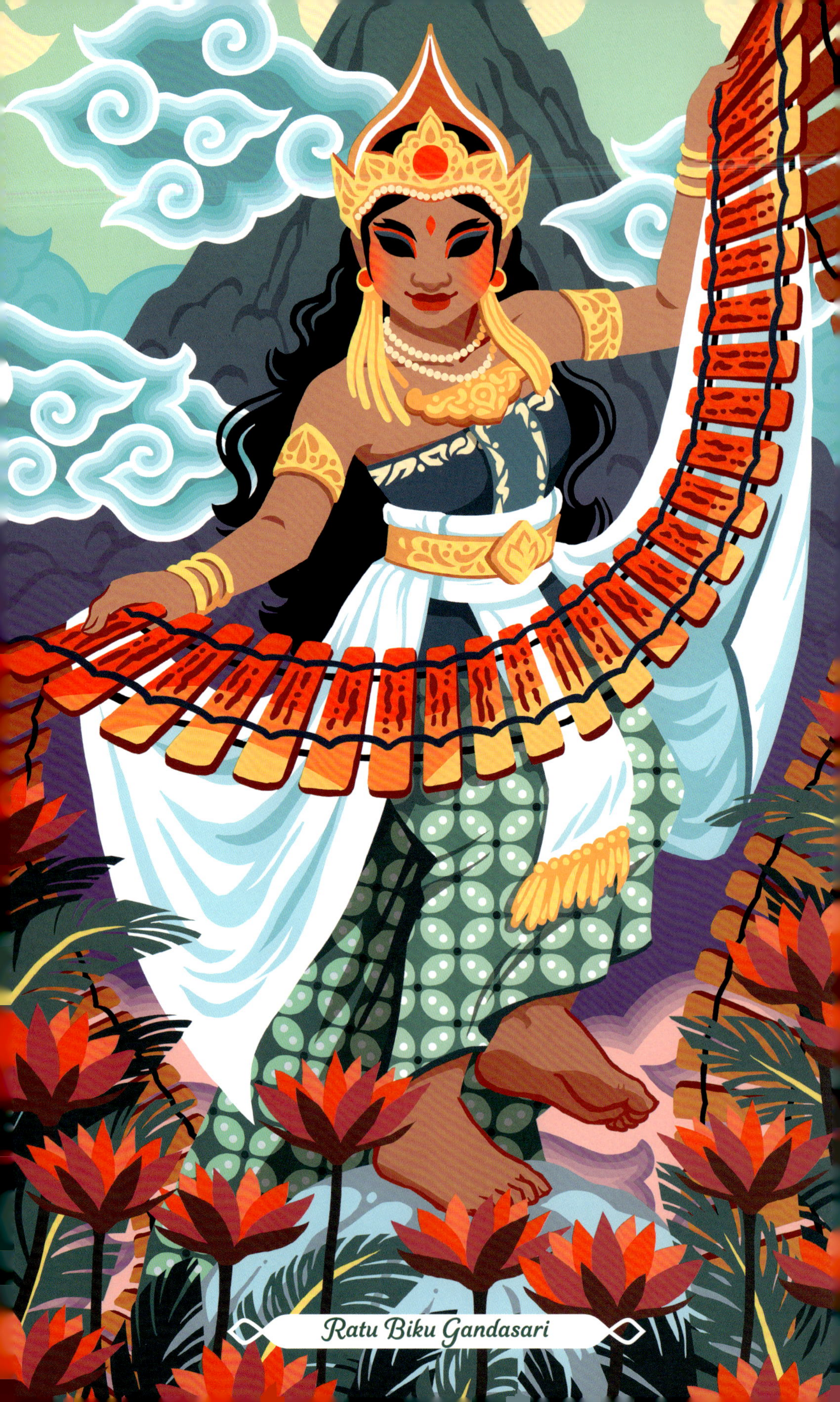
Ratu Biku Gandasari

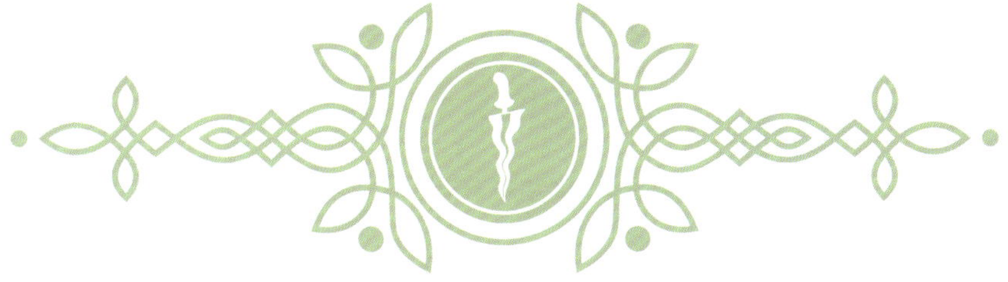

remembered his duty to the two princesses. He said farewell to Panji Semirang and continued to the kingdom of Daha.

After the prince left, Panji Semirang realized he had fallen in love with the prince. Unsure what to do, he climbed the mountains to ask advice from his aunt, the great sage Biku Gandasari. From her high perch, the all-seeing Biku Gandasari had observed Panji Semirang's plight. She told him he must disguise himself as the male dancer Warga Asmara and bring along his warrior bandits disguised as a group of traveling minstrels. Then they must all travel to the kingdom of Gagelang and perform before the king.

Meanwhile, Raden Inu arrived at the kingdom of Daha and asked after the two princesses and the golden doll. He was greeted by Puteri Galuh Ajeng, who told him that a jealous Puteri Chandra Kirana had stolen the golden doll and run away in shame. Puteri Galuh Ajeng insisted that he should marry her and not Puteri Chandra Kirana. But even though she was beautiful, Raden Inu could not forget the feelings he had begun to feel for Panji Semirang. Unable to tolerate marrying another, Raden Inu broke off his engagement to the kingdom of Daha and returned to the forest only to find Panji Semirang and all his retinue gone. A heartbroken Raden Inu turned for home.

Stopping in his uncle's kingdom of Gagelang on his way back, Raden Inu arrived in the court to see a play being performed by the talented Warga Asmara and his troupe. Before the king, Warga Asmara waved his sword in the way Panji Semirang had, and displayed the golden doll given to the Princess of Daha. It was then that the prince recognized the dancer Warga Asmara, first as Bandit Prince Panji Semirang, and then ultimately as Puteri Chandra Kirana—and he loved her in all her guises. He asked for her hand in marriage, and she happily agreed. The two traveled to Kuripan, where they loved and lived in joy.

PANJI SEMIRANG'S STORY BEGAN as an oral tradition in East Java sometime before the fourteenth century. Its popularity resulted in widespread translation throughout Indonesia and farther to Malaysia, Thailand, Myanmar, Cambodia, Laos, and Vietnam. As it migrated, it transformed and became the basis for epic poems, operas, artwork, dance dramas, puppet plays, movies, and novels. With so many variants, a consistent core story is hard to find. While almost all feature a handsome prince and the beautiful Puteri Chandra Kirana, who exactly Panji Semirang is and how he fits into the story changes. Sometimes he is the prince engaged to Puteri Chandra Kirana, with her disappearing on the eve before their wedding and replaced by a demoness. Sometimes Raden Panji Semirang is engaged to Puteri Chandra Kirana but falls in love with a common girl who dies tragically. Sometimes Panji Semirang is the name Puteri Chandra Kirana takes when she disguises herself as a man and goes on many adventures. Supporting characters morph or disappear completely, names and locations alter, and who the villain of the story is shifts. Gender changes, queer romances, disguises, battles, and the intervention of the divine or demonic are all elements that vary wildly among narrators and the interests of their audiences. Panji tales live on today in dances rooted in the tradition of the Javanese court and also in modern comic book and animated adaptations. Therefore, the variant contained above must be described as only a singular thread in a rich and growing tapestry.

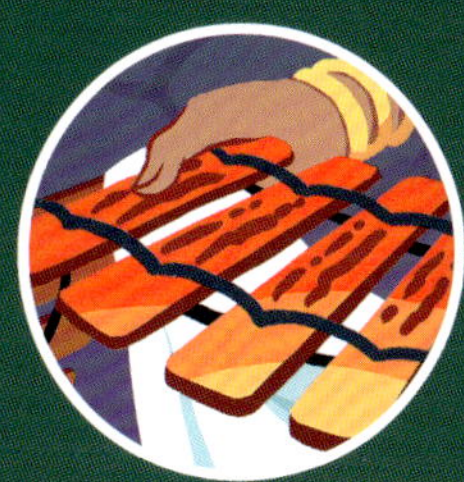

In Indonesia, books were traditionally written on *lontar*, cut and cured palm leaves strung together with string. Words were then carved into the lontar and darkened with black ink.

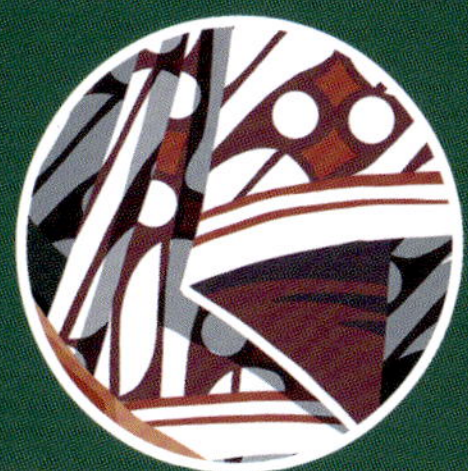

Batik is the traditional Indonesian method of dyeing cloth, using wax to resist the dye to create elaborate patterns with symbolic meaning. This red-and-white pattern is called Parang batik and symbolizes strength and perseverance.

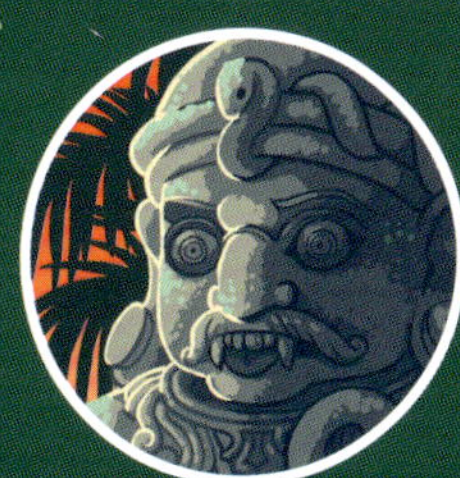

Dwarapala are fierce gate guardians that fend off evil and help maintain balance in the world between the active and the passive, the sacred and the profane.

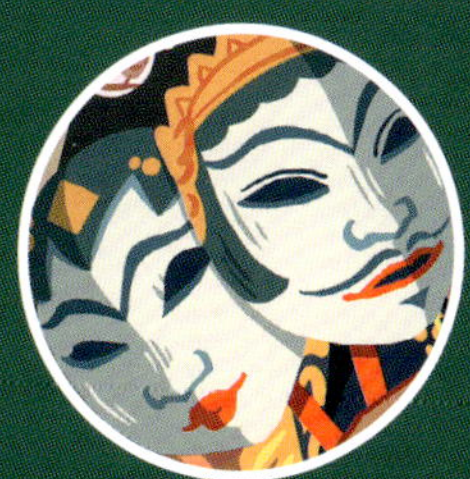

Indonesian *topeng* dance dramas tell mythological, historical, or moral stories like Panji Semirang, and use carved and painted wooden masks to embody key characters, like a king, a princess, a villain, or a clown.

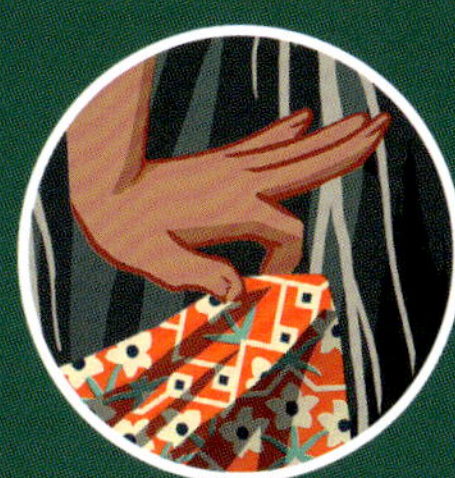

Traditional Indonesian dance features a rich vocabulary of poses that use highly stylized hand, feet, and hip gestures to indicate to the audience femininity, masculinity, assertiveness, or serenity.

THE INSTRUMENT

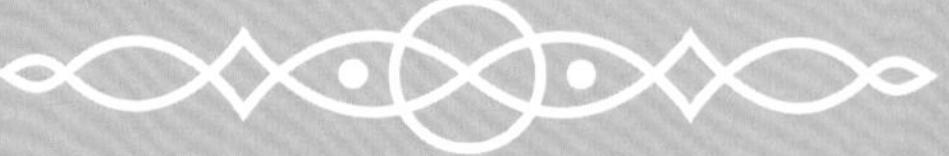

Music and musical instruments often appear in myth and legend as embodiments of creativity, transformation, and pleasure. Instruments are often associated with Tricksters, as they both represent human spontaneity, expressions of the heart, and fluidity that defies description.

Tricksters disrupt the ordinary, and music alters reality. A sudden song can calm a monster, seduce a lover, summon a god, or stir a revolution. A Trickster can make a mortal a god, create feasts from crumbs, and rewrite the rules of the universe. Both can change the atmosphere in subtle or dramatic ways. Tricksters live between categories: god and human, animal and man, sacred and profane. Music, too, is liminal—it flows between the physical and spiritual, between communication and emotion. It can serve as language without words, prayer without religion, or power without violence.

In the American Southwest, Kokopelli, the humpbacked flute player, ushers in spring, seduces lovers, ends conflict, and stirs madness. In Greek mythology, Pan's pipes awaken desire and panic, unraveling order with wild ecstasy. In Hindu mythology, Krishna's flute enchants nature, liberates the soul, and evokes divine love.

Equally, music is used as temptation. The Devil's fiddle from Christian folklore appears as an instrument that drives players mad or entices them into dark bargains. The Akan god Anansi uses his drums to lure others into his traps, where he steals his victims' secrets. And the Hindu Apsaras use their singing to beguile mortals away from the ascetic practices that would give them power.

Whether used to charm, seduce, confuse, teach, or transcend, music represents the raw, emotional force of creation. It disturbs, heals, transforms, and liberates. It is at once divine structure and dangerous freedom.

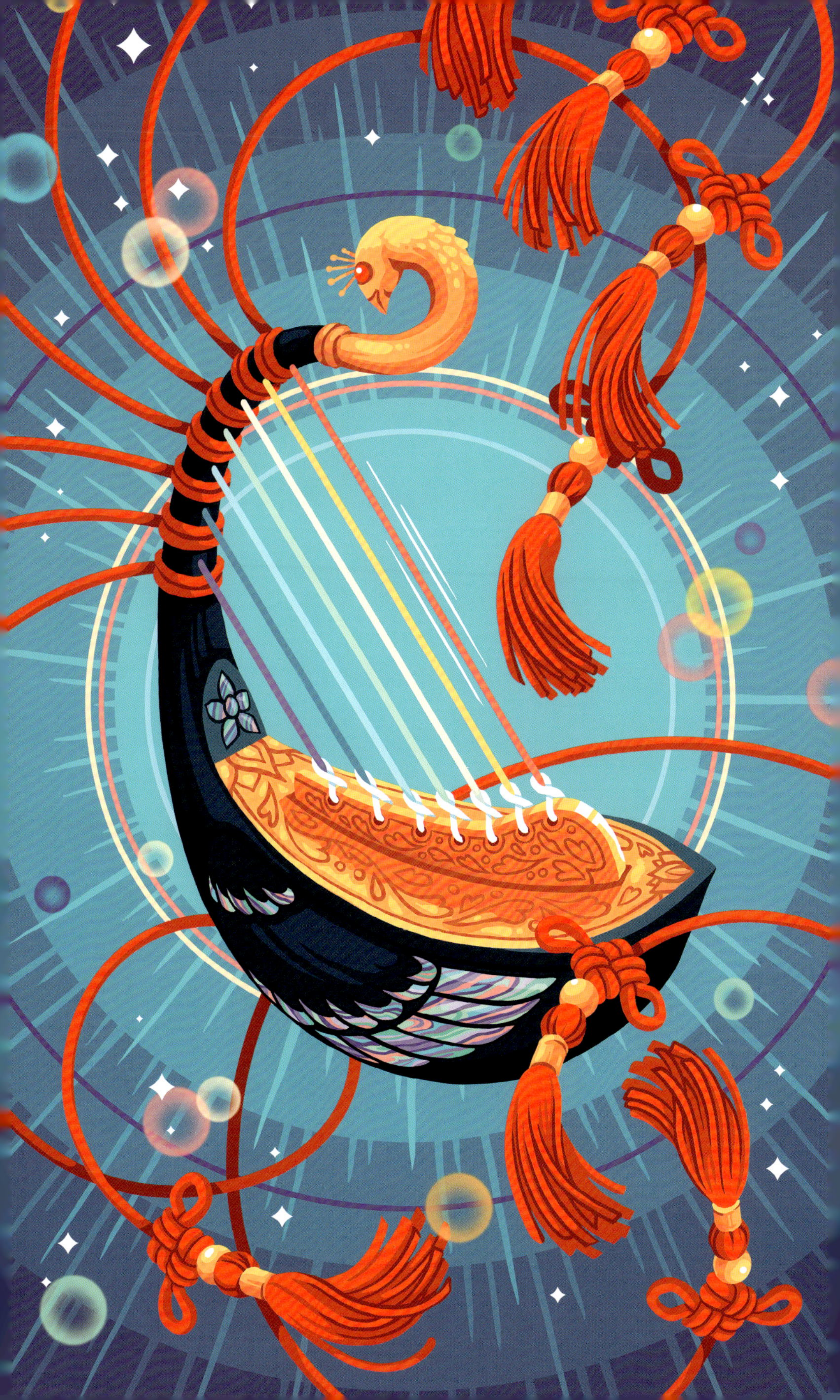

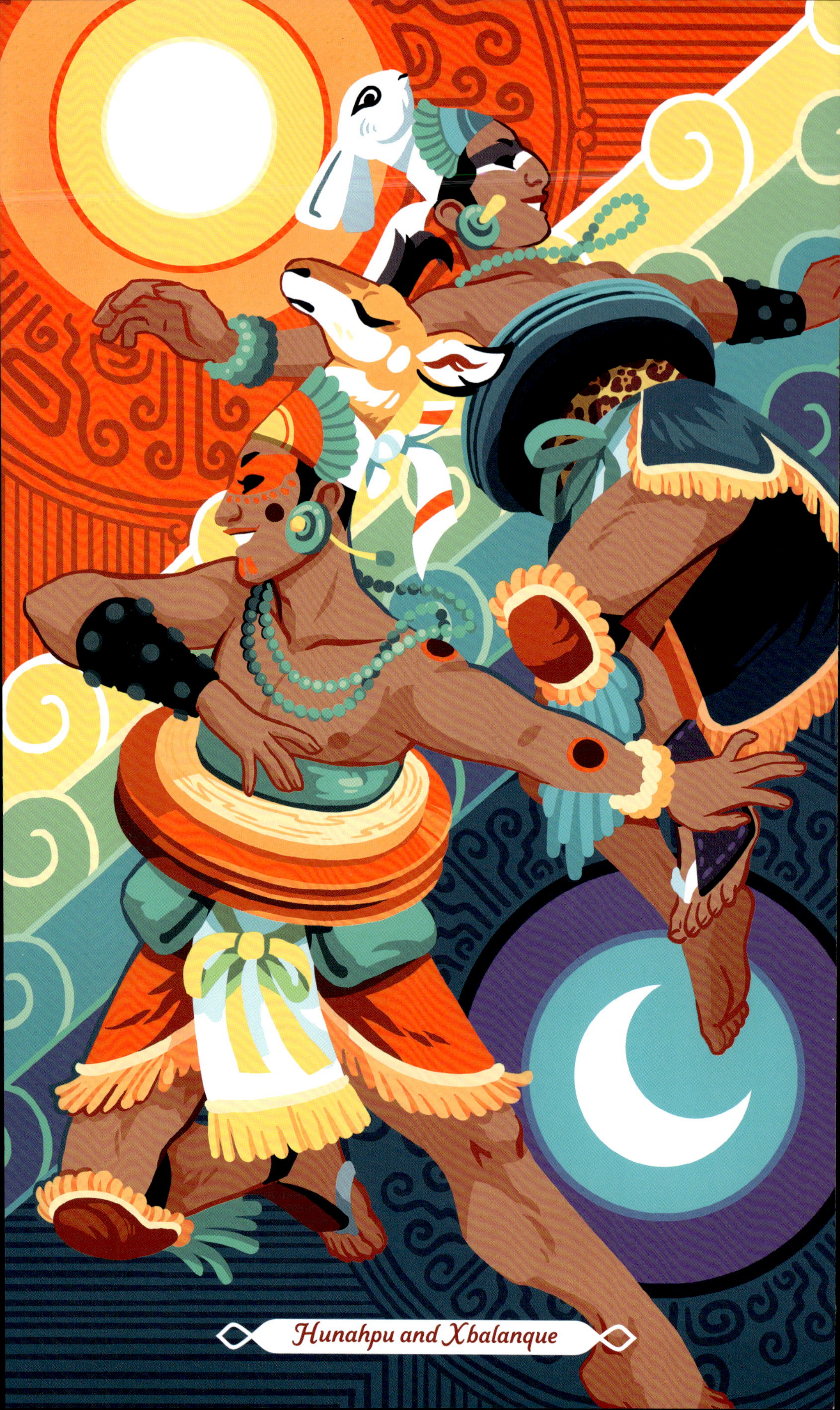
Hunahpu and Xbalanque

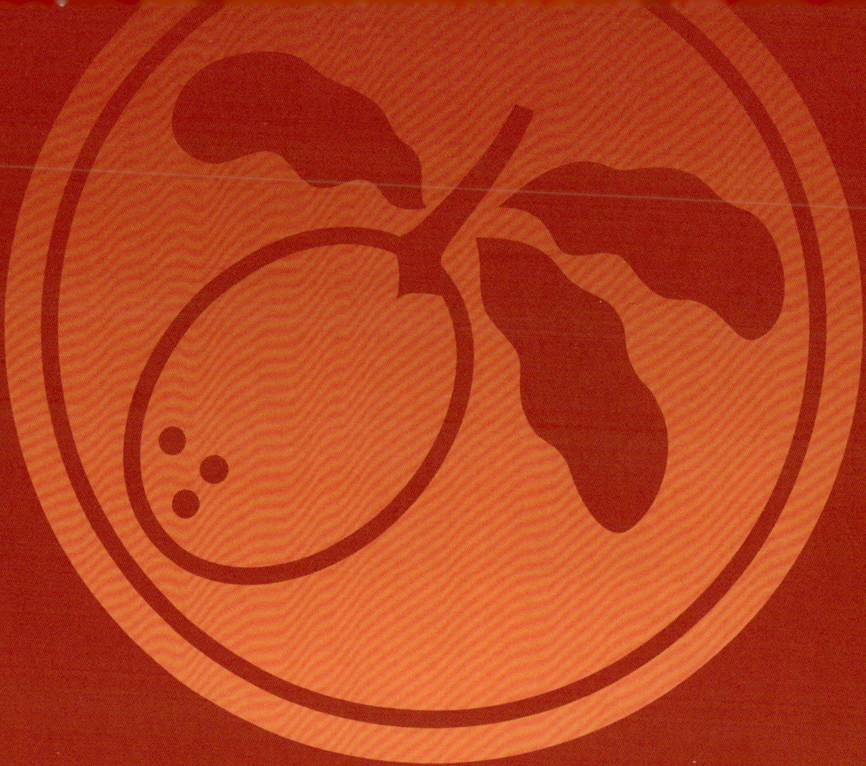

The HERO TWINS

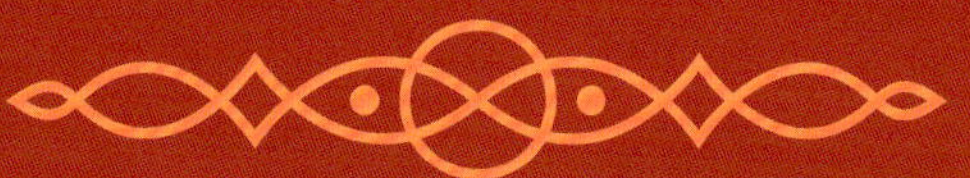

MAYAN MYTHOLOGY | GUATEMALA

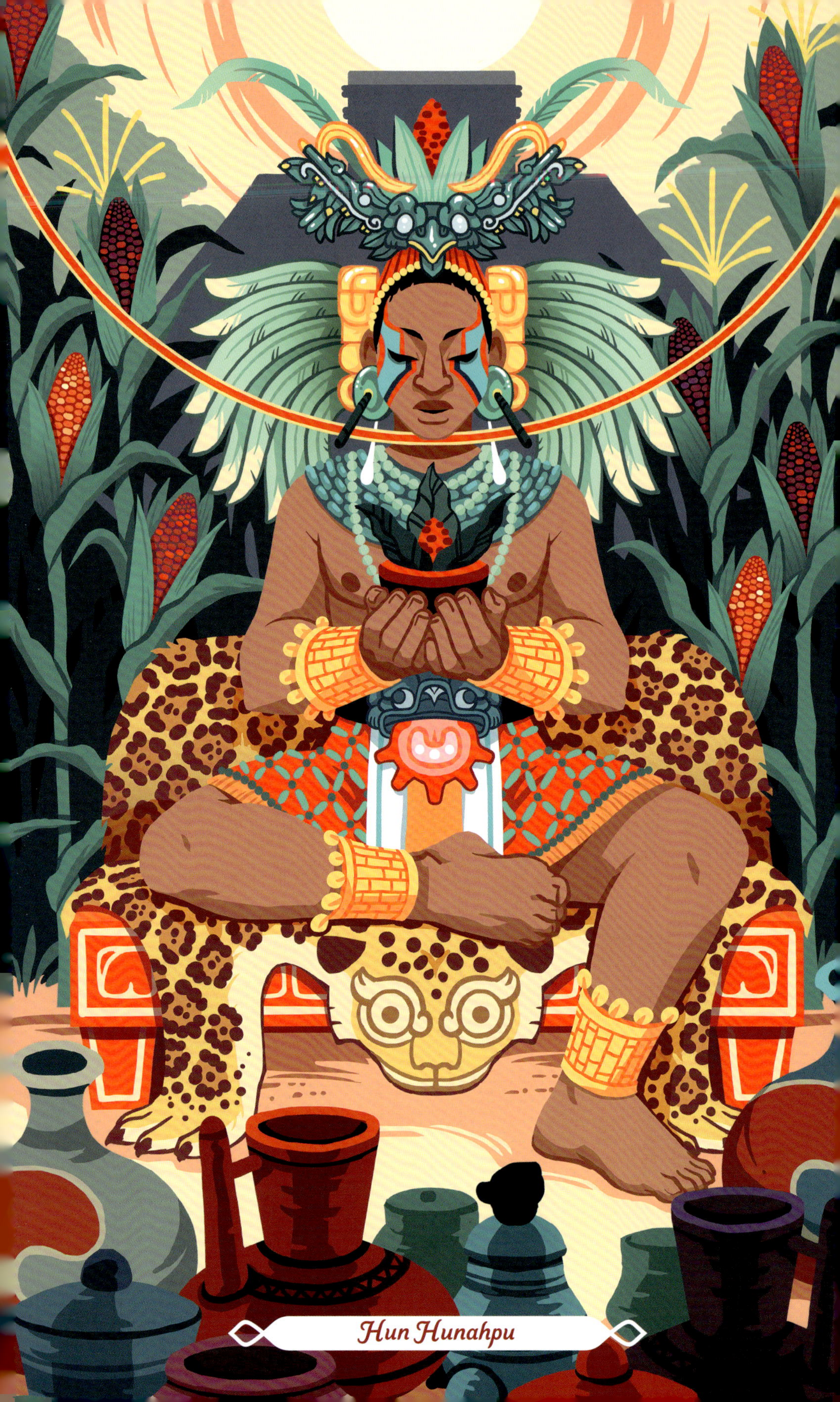
Hun Hunahpu

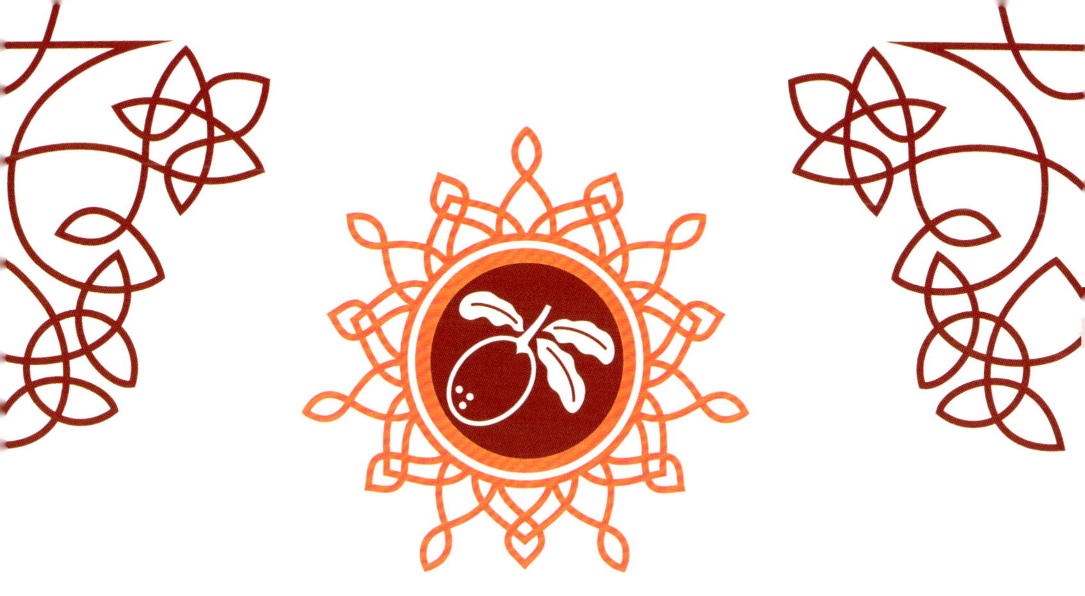

Long ago, the god Xpiyacoc and his wife the goddess Xmucane had two sons, the Gods of Maize Hun Hunahpu and Vucub Hunahpu. The sons loved to play pitz (or pok-ta-pok), loudly laughing, running, and bouncing the hard rubber ball in the court.

Unbeknownst to the brothers, their sport sounded like loud stomping on the ceiling of the underworld kingdom, Xibalba. The noise irritated the many gods of death and pestilence who lived there, especially Hun Came and Vucub Came, who began to scheme how to murder the two brothers.

When the lords of death invited Hun Hunahpu and Vucub Hunahpu to play pitz and other games in Xibalba, the unsuspecting brothers gladly accepted. They left Hun Hunahpu's sons, Hun Batz and Hun Chouen, in the care of their grandmother Xmucane and descended into the underworld. Unfortunately, all the games were rigged, and the brothers were repeatedly tricked with a burning bench, disguises, and frigid temperatures. Ultimately, they were defeated in the game of pitz and were executed. Both of their bodies were buried beneath the ball court,

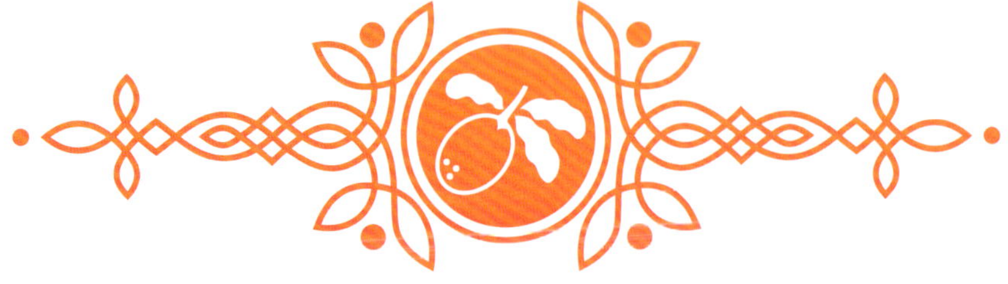

save for Hun Hunahpu's skull, which was hung in a calabash tree where it became just one fruit among many, hidden deep in the depths of Xibalba.

There he would have rotted for all time had not Xquic, daughter of the death god Cuchumaquic, heard rumors of the tree and how sweet the calabash fruit was. So great was her lust and desire for the decadent treat that she snuck to the tree in secret and outstretched her hand to the fruit. The fruit that was once Hun Hunahpu's skull spat nectar onto her palm, and she became pregnant with twins.

When the death gods discovered Xquic was expecting, they realized what had happened and demanded her execution. She had no choice but to escape, faking her death with the blood-red sap of the croton tree and fleeing to the earth's surface to her mother-in-law's house. Goddess Xmucane did not believe that Xquic was carrying Hun Hunahpu's sons until Xquic performed a miracle and harvested maize from barren crops.

Xquic gave birth to her twin sons Hunahpu and Xbalanque, and it quickly became clear that both were exceptionally clever and strong. Their talents caused their older half brothers, Hun Batz and Hun Chouen, to seethe with jealousy. They harassed the young twins endlessly, and with no father to protect them, the twins resorted to tricking their half brothers and turning them into howler monkeys. Free from the abuse of Hun Batz and Hun Chouen, the twins grew even more brilliant. They cleared forests with a single swing, defanged monsters, and slew gods. Until one day, they discovered their father and uncle's long-forgotten rubber ball.

Missing the father they never knew, the twins returned to the ball court their father and uncle had used long ago and began to play loudly. This noise once again roused the ire of the gods of death. Yet again, the lords of death invited two brothers down

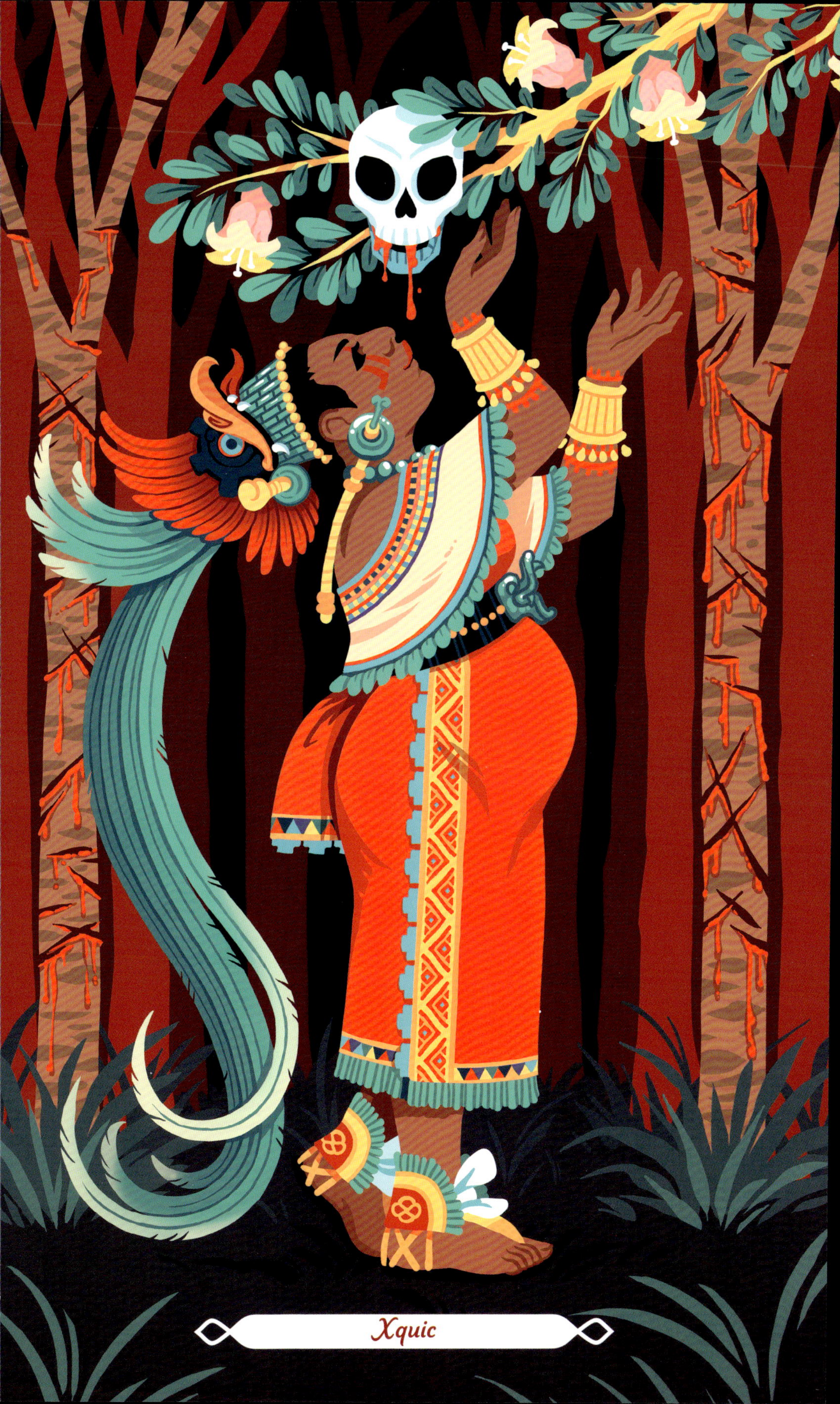
Xquic

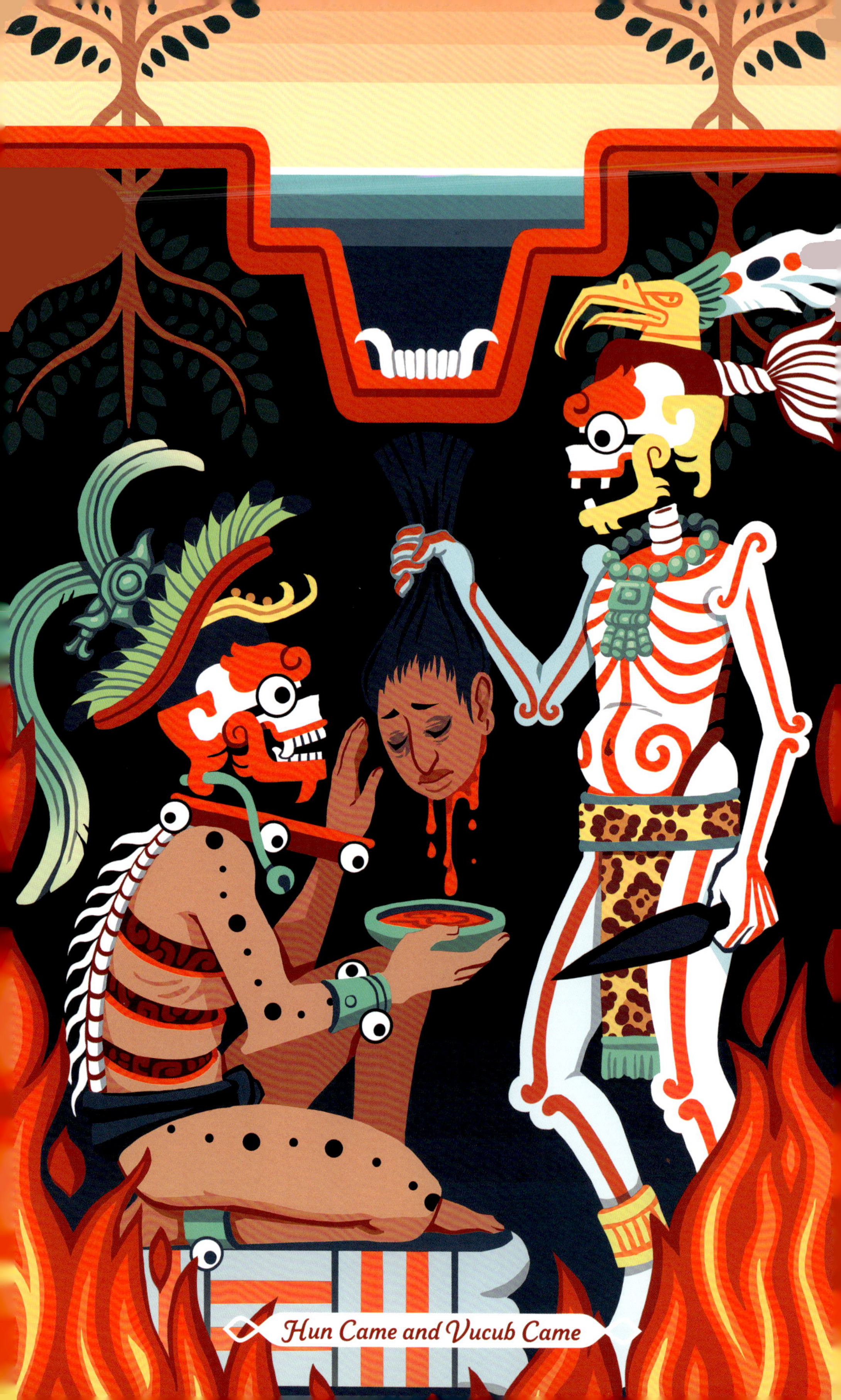
Hun Came and Vucub Came

into Xibalba with the intention of killing them. However, this time was different. Hunahpu and Xbalanque fell for none of Hun Came or Vucub Came's tricks. They avoided the benches, accurately identified the gods, and withstood the cold. All was going well for the twins until Hunahpu stuck his head out too early during a trial and was beheaded. The delighted gods of death began using his head as the ball in their game of pitz. Thinking quickly, Xbalanque carved a new head out of squash and placed it on his twin's body, who then rose and prepared to play. This confused the death gods long enough for the twins to steal back the true head. Whole once again, Hunahpu and Xbalanque defeated the lords of the underworld at their own ball game.

Fed up, Hun Came and Vucub Came tried one final trick to lure the twins into a giant oven. The twins, recognizing the trap, allowed themselves to be burned, and their ashes were scattered in the river. The gods of death thought they had finally won, but the twins regenerated as catfish, then transformed into men again. Amazed, the gods of death demanded to be shown how to resurrect. The twins agreed, but instead only slew them without bringing them back. The remaining Xibalbans shook with fear and begged the twins for mercy, showing them where the remains of their father and uncle lay. Hunahpu and Xbalanque took their bodies and cursed Xibalba to be a lesser realm, never to receive offerings from the world above.

The twins, having thoroughly avenged their father in the underworld and satiated their desire to adventure on earth, rose into the sky, where Hunahpu became the sun and Xbalanque became the moon.

THE STORY OF THE MAYAN Hero Twins, like many mythical epics, provides a window of insight into the culture that created it. Yet the destructive erasures of colonizing forces frustratingly obfuscate where pre-Columbian myth ends and Western influence begins. This confusion can be seen especially in the stories of the goddess Xquic and the hero twin Xbalanque. Xquic, depending on the translation, can be seen as a naïve young woman forced into motherhood or as an open-eyed intelligent woman who indulges her desires and gains her own independence. To a Western perspective, the story appears to be one of coercion with the skull-turned-calabash of Hun Hunahpu spitting on an unsuspecting, virginal Xquic. However, "eating the fruit" was a thinly veiled euphemism for sex in ancient Mesoamerica. Xquic's determined pursuit of the calabash places her as an active participant rather than a passive victim. Furthermore, Xquic is seen paying her own bride price by harvesting maize for her mother-in-law, after which she disappears from the story, apparently free from the authority of father or husband.

Xbalanque is equally enigmatic, with scholars debating for decades over the gender of the younger hero twin. While the most influential document, the *Popol Vuh*—an epic historical narrative authored by K'iche' Maya peoples in highland Guatemala, recorded in European script, and copied by a Dominican friar three hundred years later—records Xbalanque as male, the K'iche' document *El Título de Totonicapán* written in 1554 writes that Xbalanque is female. While all other twins in Mayan mythology are pairs of boys, Xbalanque becomes the moon, which is written as feminine in nearly all other Mayan myths. This detail has led some scholars to believe Xbalanque might be queer, transgender, or genderfluid. There might not be a single correct answer, with interpretation left to the worshipper.

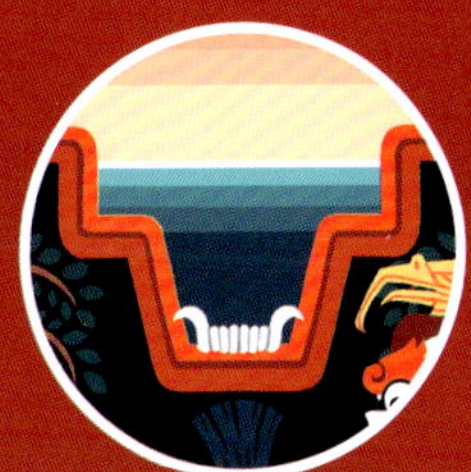

To the Mayans, caves and bodies of water such as lakes were considered passageways to the underworld. They were liminal places occupying a position in both the world of the living and the world of the dead.

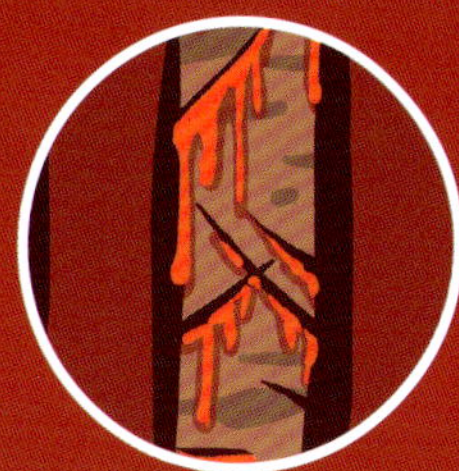

In order to escape her father, the goddess Xquic faked her death by making a false heart from the blood-red sap of a croton tree.

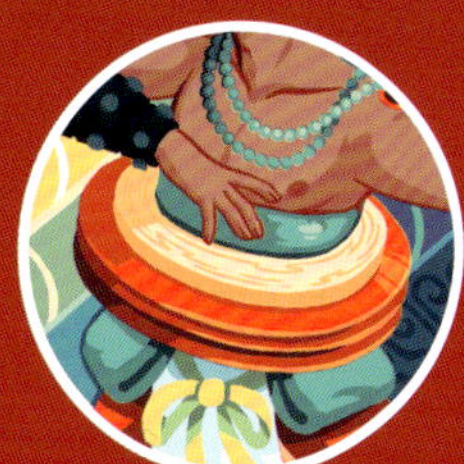

The Mayan ball game pitz featured a heavy hard solid rubber ball. With a ball capable of brutal damage, players wore a variety of different protections, including ample padding around the waist, arms, and legs.

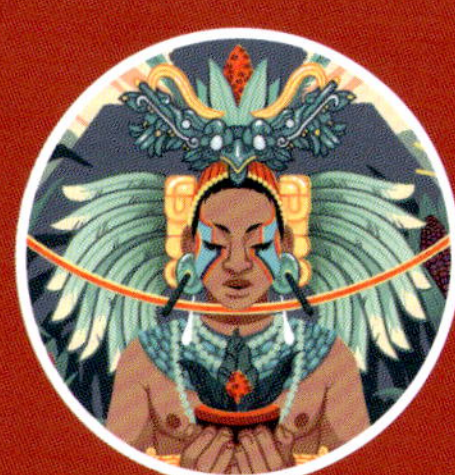

In Mayan society, the head was considered the core of a person, so elaborate and distinctive headdresses with feather and jade were necessary for high ranks and important ceremonies. In art, only captives were depicted nude without headgear.

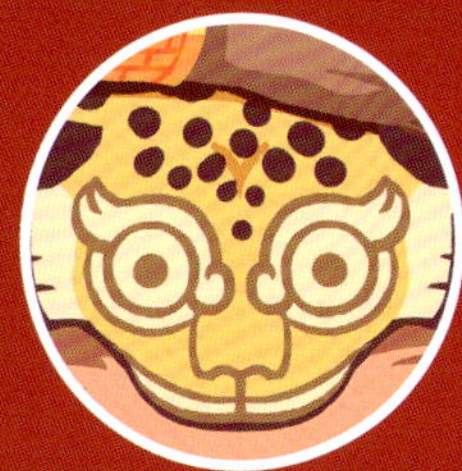

Jaguars are creatures of the night, symbols of death, rebirth, and transformation. On a throne, their pelts represent power and divine authority to those seated upon them.

THE DIVINE FRUIT

Divine Fruit often appear in myth and legend as powerful objects of desire that change the hero physically, spiritually, or mentally, often in unexpected ways.

In these stories, Divine Fruit are always superfluous. They are not needed to cure a dying princess or return life to a starving land. They are an indulgence whose consumption isn't necessary for the hero to live a happy and fulfilling life. Indeed, the Mayans believed that all fruit was hedonistic with little nutritional value. Because of this, Divine Fruit is always portrayed as something delicious, sweet, and dessert-like. Peaches, pomegranates, and apples are all examples of Divine Fruit.

In the Chinese epic *Journey to the West*, the Monkey King wishes to be respected by the gods and sneakily eats one of their peaches of immortality. This act, while turning him immortal, causes him to be chained to the will of a priest on a pilgrimage. The Greek goddess Persephone eats six pomegranate seeds of the underworld and ever after must spend six months of the year in the land of the dead. The Abrahamic Adam and Eve eat the one thing forbidden to them, the fruit—often depicted as an apple—from the Tree of Knowledge. The pair learns of good and evil, but are banished from paradise to live in pain on earth.

There are also times when a Trickster intentionally uses the pursuit of a Divine Fruit to cause chaos. In Greek myth, a golden apple is thrown into a wedding feast by Eris, the Goddess of Strife. This act sparks a beauty contest among three goddesses: Hera, Athena, and Aphrodite, ultimately leading to the events that cause the Trojan War. In a Korean folktale, the rabbit stops the tiger from eating him by telling the hunter that persimmons will turn him human. The tiger leaves the rabbit and consumes enough persimmons to make him sick. Although he does not become human, he does gain self-acceptance and enlightenment.

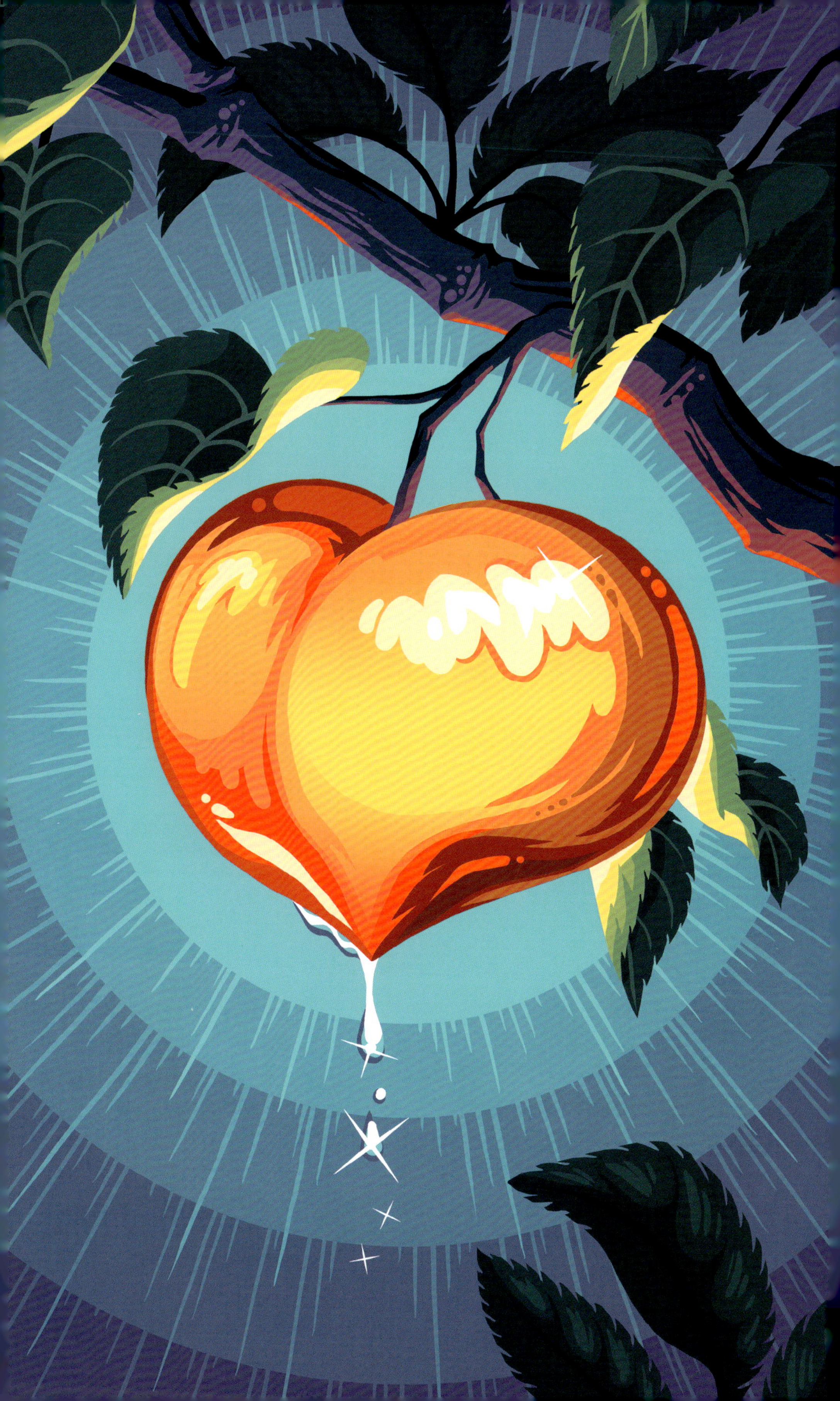

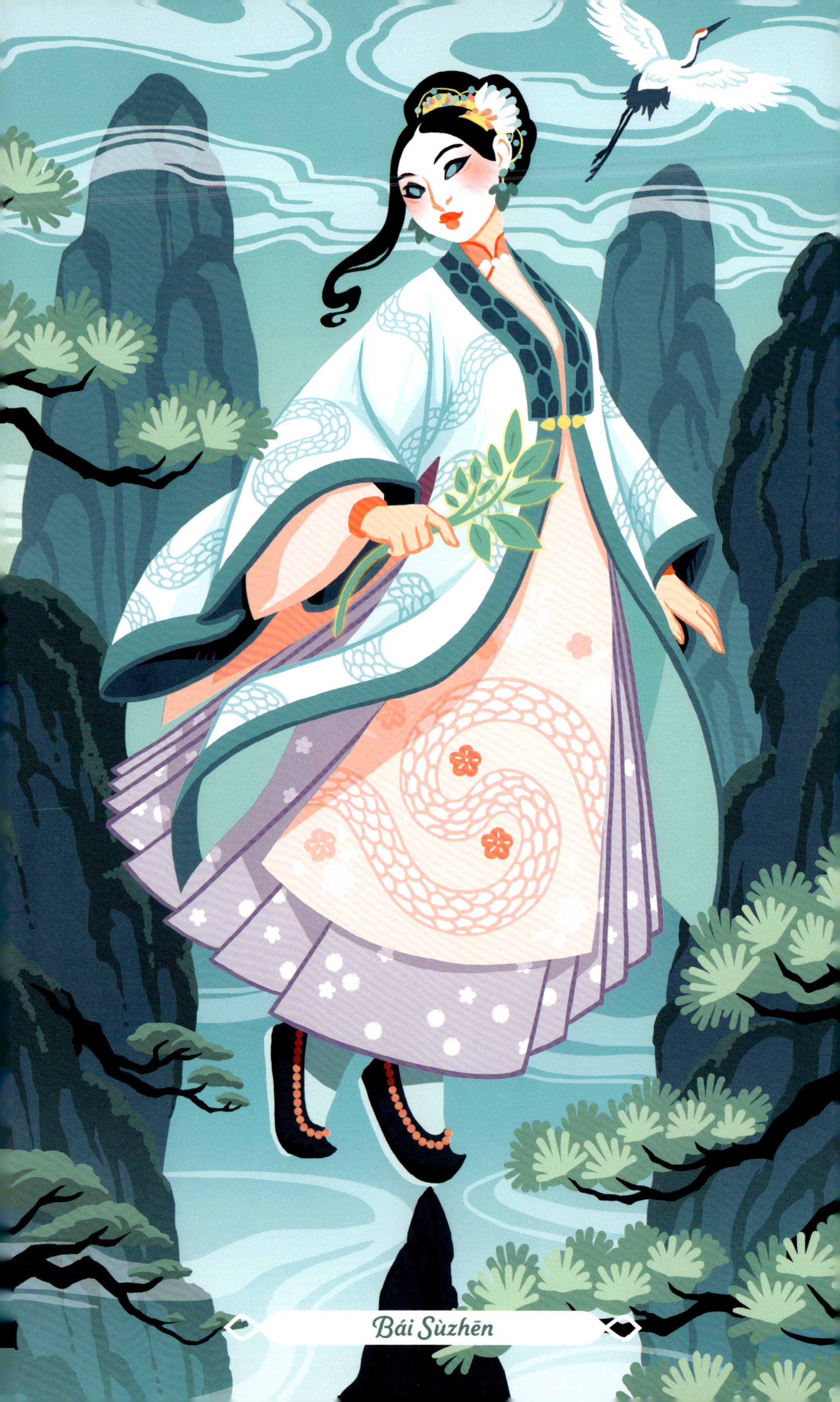
Bái Sùzhēn

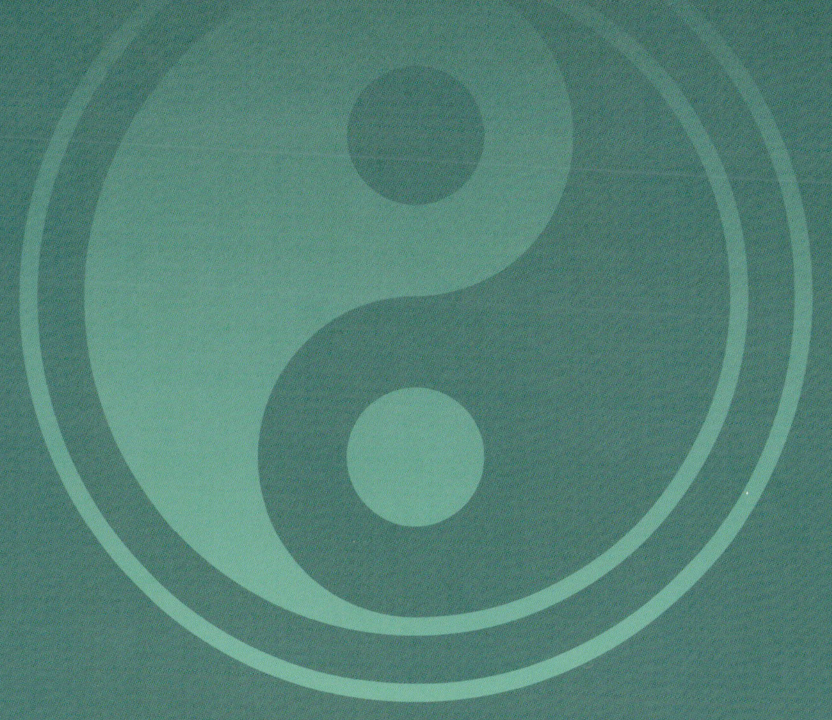

The Legend of the WHITE SNAKE

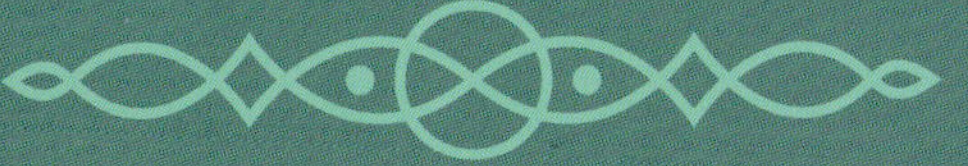

CHINESE LEGEND | CHINA

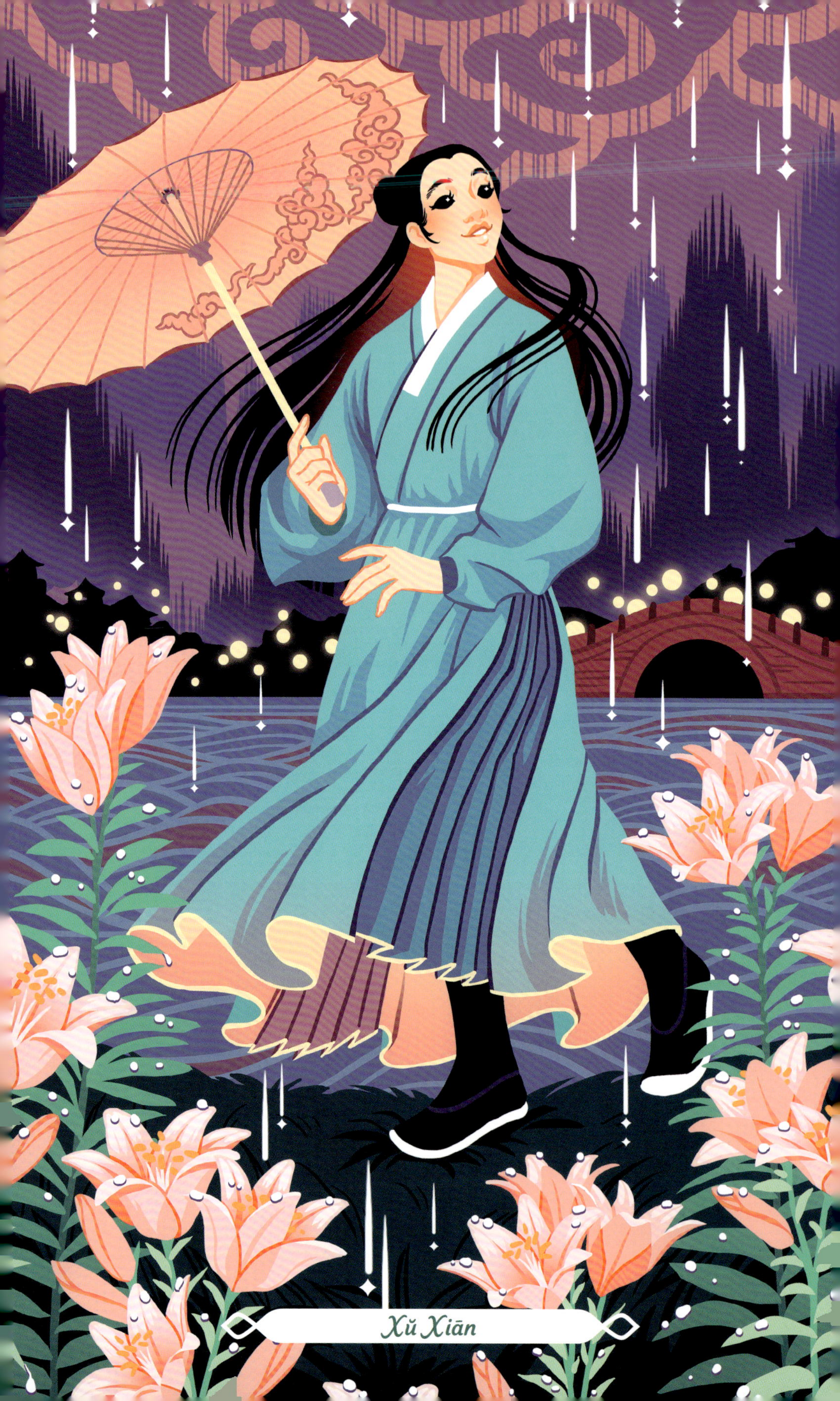
Xǔ Xiān

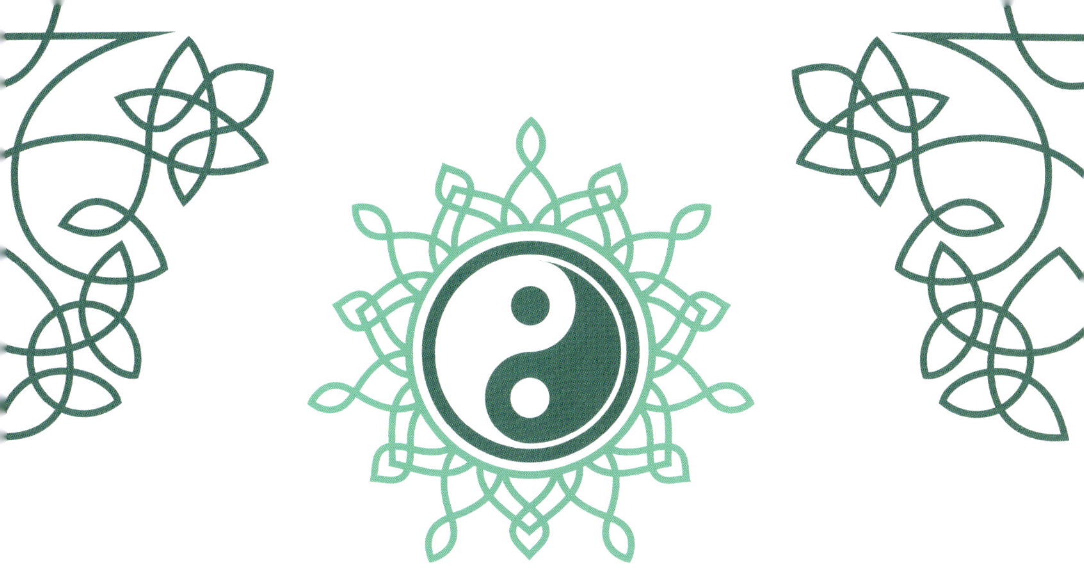

Once, a long time ago, a white snake was caught by a snake catcher. She was set to be eaten. But then a young boy came along, took pity on the sad snake, and freed her.

The snake, grateful for the boy's kindness, vowed to return the favor one day. Unfortunately, a small snake has no power, so she began to study Taoist magical arts of healing, transformation, and strength. She used her newfound knowledge and powers to save another snake, a young green one, from a cruel trap. Together they trained in Taoist martial arts, meditated for centuries, and cultivated their spiritual powers until they finally gained the ability to take on human forms. The two traveled the world as sisters, the white snake known as Bái Sùzhēn and the green as Xiǎoqīng.

One spring day, five hundred years later, the two snake-women were caught in a rainstorm while crossing the West Lake Bridge in the Hangzhou prefecture. A handsome young man offered them his umbrella. When Bái Sùzhēn saw his face, she instantly recognized him as the reincarnation of the boy who had saved her all those years ago. Their connection was immediate. He told her his name was Xǔ Xiān, and before long, love blossomed between them. Soon they were married and opened a medicine shop together.

Bái Sùzhēn never revealed her true nature, not even to Xǔ Xiān, and neither did her sister, Xiǎoqīng. Yet the abbot of the Buddhist Jinshan Temple, Fǎhǎi, a man of immense spiritual power, sensed that Xǔ Xiān's wife was unnatural. Convinced she was an evil demon in human form, he repeatedly warned Xǔ Xiān, but the young man refused to listen. Bái Sùzhēn was a good wife, and he loved her dearly.

At last, Fǎhǎi devised a cruel plan. The Dragon Boat Festival approached, when people traditionally drank realgar-laced wine to ward off disease and evil spirits. Knowing the wine was also poisonous to snakes, he urged Xǔ Xiān to persuade his wife to drink it.

The night of the festival, Bái Sùzhēn avoided the realgar-laced wine everyone else drank, but Xǔ Xiān, growing suspicious, secretly slipped her a cup. As soon as she drank it, she was temporarily stripped of all her magical powers. She fled to her chamber with Xǔ Xiān following. But when he opened the door, he saw not his beautiful wife but a massive and horrifying white serpent. Struck with terror, he collapsed and died of fright on the spot.

The heartbroken Bái Sùzhēn did not waste time mourning her husband but instead rushed to find a way to save him. Leaving Xiǎoqīng to guard his body, Bái Sùzhēn climbed Mount Emei to the home of Old Man Immortal, a man who had studied the Taoist arts and cultivated his spiritual practice and virtue enough to become immortal. There, she fought past his divine crane and deer guardians to steal Xiāncâo, the Immortal Herb. Returning home from her mission, she brewed a healing soup with Xiāncâo that brought Xǔ Xiān back to life. Husband and wife were reunited, and they lived together happily for a time. However, even though Bái Sùzhēn endured so much to save Xǔ Xiān, the shock of her revelation still haunted him, and her true form terrified him. In his unease, he turned once more to Fǎhǎi.

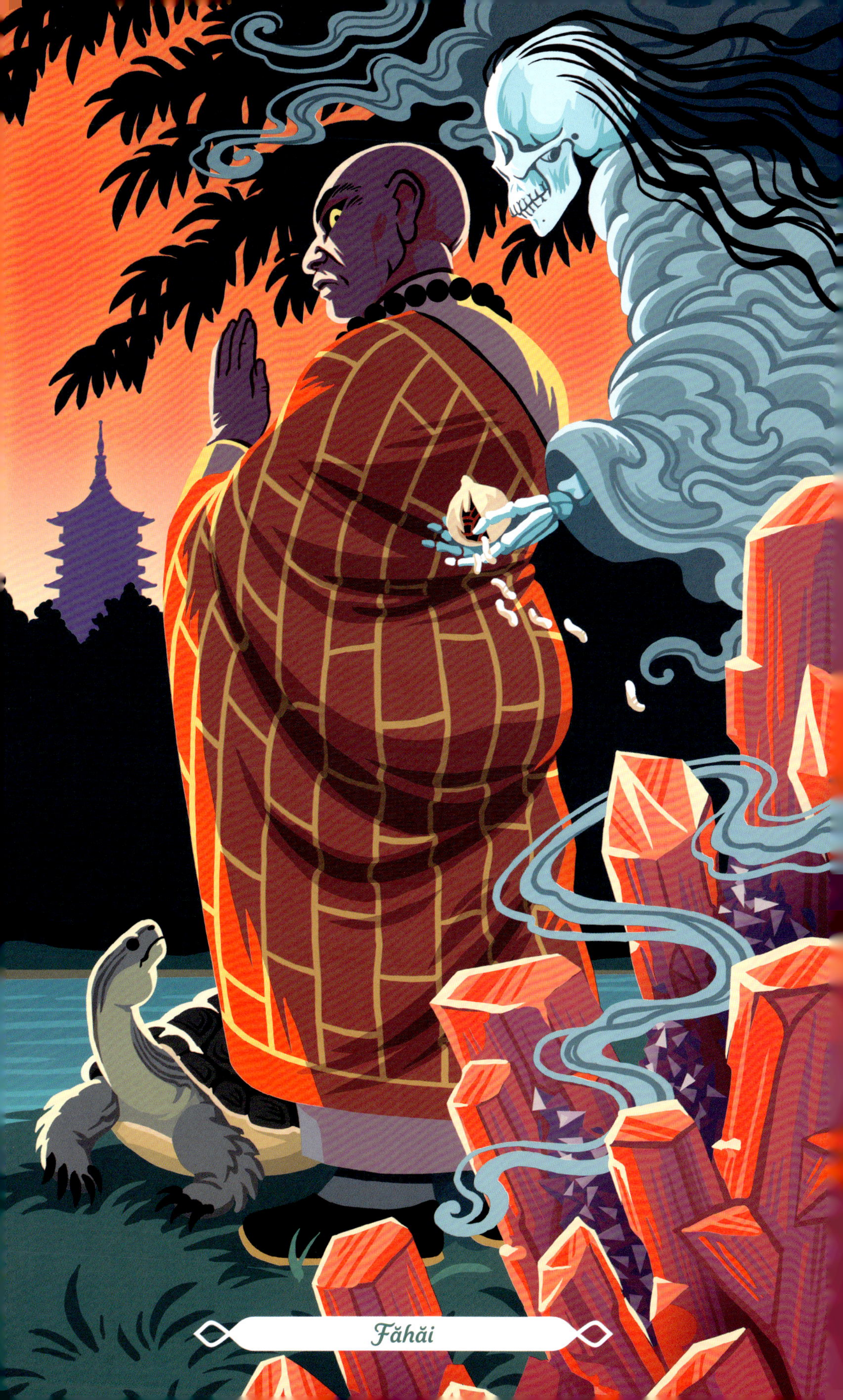
Făhăi

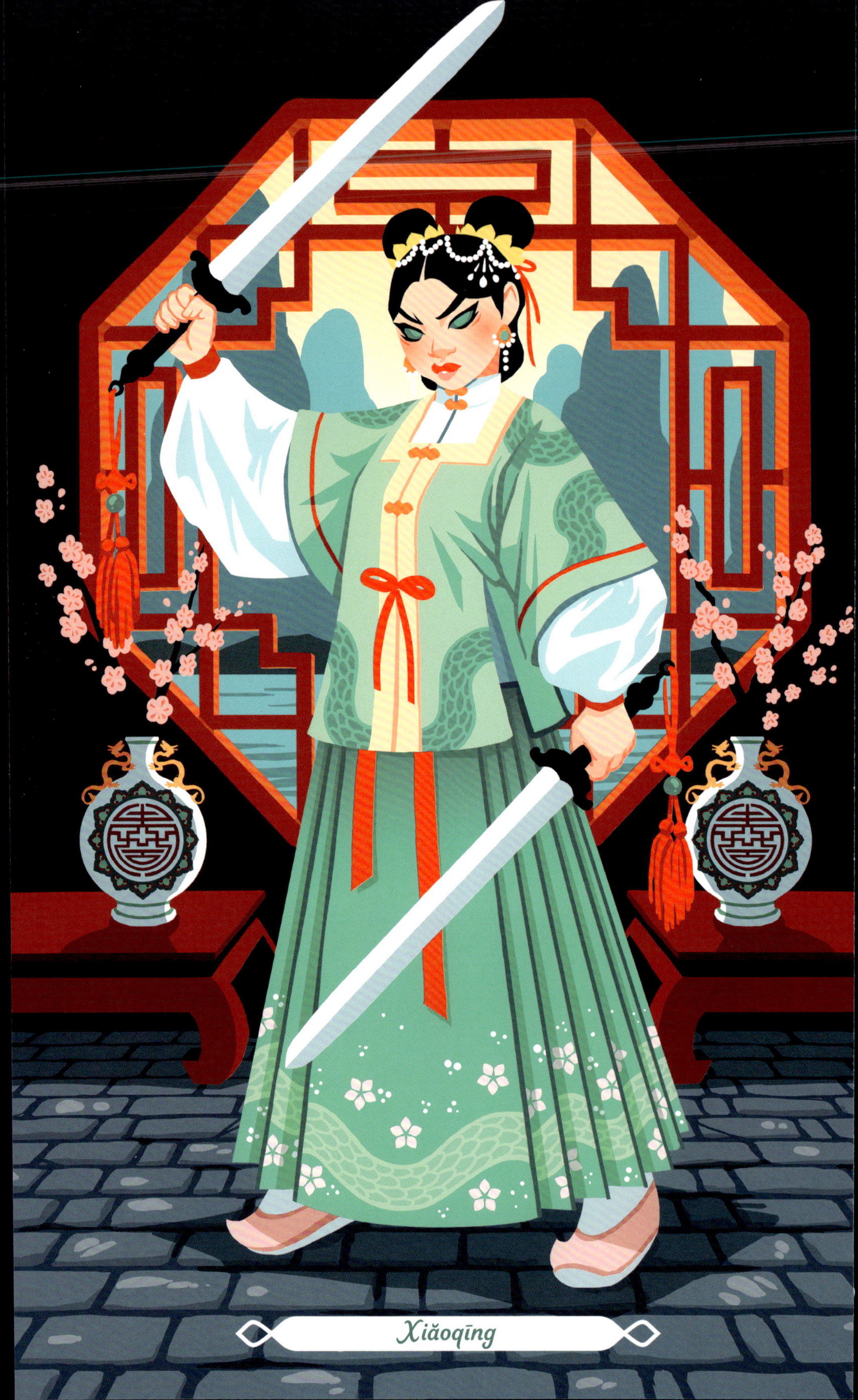
Xiǎoqīng

But Făhăi had no intention of helping Xŭ Xiān. Seizing his chance, he imprisoned the young man at Jinshan Temple to bait Bái Sùzhēn. When Bái Sùzhēn charged in to free her husband, Făhăi summoned the Buddhist guardians Skanda and Sangharama to defeat her. Under normal circumstances, Bái Sùzhēn would have easily won, but she was pregnant with Xŭ Xiān's child, and her powers were limited. In desperation, she flooded the temple and surrounding area, killing hundreds of innocent people in collateral damage, and still failed to free Xŭ Xiān. She was forced to retreat home to gave birth to her son, Xŭ Mèngjiāo.

In the confusion of the chaos, Xŭ Xiān managed to escape the temple and return home. During his time as a captive, he realized his wife's love was genuine, and at last he accepted her true nature. He begged his wife to forgive him, she accepted, and together they happily held their son.

But heaven would not forgive. For the crime of killing so many innocents and breaking heavenly law by using demonic powers on sacred ground, the Jade Emperor, Supreme Ruler of Heaven, stripped Bái Sùzhēn of her strength. Făhăi returned and easily captured the powerless Bái Sùzhēn, imprisoning her under the Leifeng Pagoda in the Hangzhou prefecture.

Bái Sùzhēn's snake sister Xiăoqīng vowed to avenge her. For the next twenty years, she raised Xŭ Mèngjiāo with Xŭ Xiān, and together they trained ferociously in Taoist martial arts. When Xŭ Mèngjiāo came of age, he excelled in the imperial examinations and gained a prestigious post. With her duty as guardian fulfilled, Xiăoqīng finally confronted Făhăi. Armed with decades of training, she defeated the abbot and shattered his hold over Bái Sùzhēn, allowing the family of four to be reunited once again.

THE EARLIEST RECORDINGS of the Legend of the White Snake appear sometime in the ninth century, but the original story is vastly different from the more popular versions shared today. In the beginning, a beautiful woman appears before a young man and, after seducing him, drains the life from him, only to be revealed she is not a woman but a giant demonic white snake. Later versions introduced a Taoist exorcist, who is able to save the young man in time and imprison the woman, who is actually a white snake, and her daughter, who is actually a black chicken, under stone pagodas. Over time, the story continued to change, transforming the once lustful snake into a meditative and thoughtful woman who would defy the heavens to be with her one true love. A conniving daughter became the faithful sister. A lecherous young man became a true and honest husband who runs a respectable medicine shop. A righteous exorcist became a suspicious and jealous terrapin-turned-monk bent on destroying the white snake. A purification ritual became a doctrinal battle between Taoism and Buddhism. These changes recast the story from a cautionary monster tale into one of forbidden love, where the very universe is trying to tear the romantic couple apart. Lastly, the setting changed. Starting as a simple tale that took place in a nameless village, it grew into a drama rooted in larger mythology and real physical places, such as the West Lake Bridge in the Hangzhou prefecture. When the actual Leifeng Pagoda collapsed in 1924, residents claimed to have seen a giant white snake fly into the sky: Bái Sùzhēn was freed after nearly a century of imprisonment.

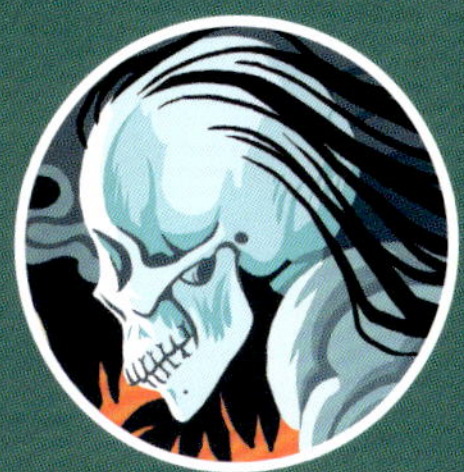

Baigujing was a shape-shifting demoness whose true form as a skeleton only the Monkey King Sun Wukong could see. To everyone else, she was an innocent who fed heroes delicious food.

Realgar is an arsenic sulfide mineral sprinkled as a repellent against snakes and insects. Added to wine, it is considered a protection against evil spirits.

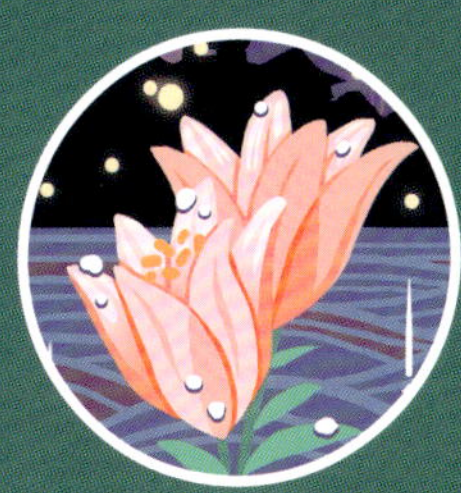

In Chinese, *bǎi hé* is lily, which sounds like part of the proverb *bǎi nián hǎo hé*, or "happy union for one hundred years."

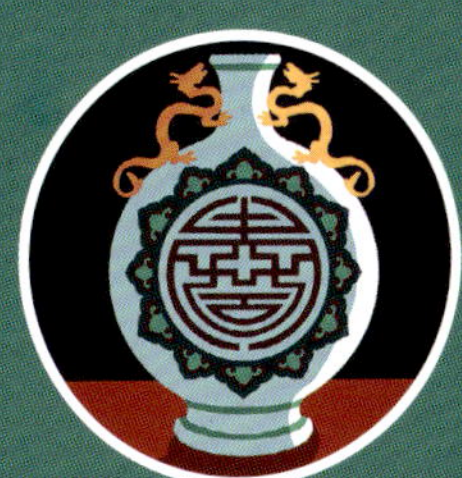

A stylized *shou*, this Chinese character means "longevity, good fortune, and well-being." It is used as a blessing on many everyday items.

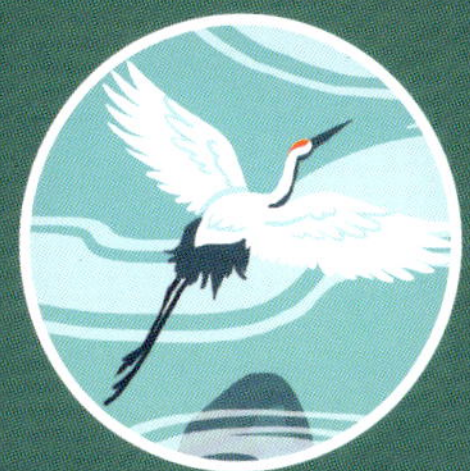

Cranes represent enlightenment, meditative discipline, immortality, and spiritual purity. In Taoism, cranes are animals that connect the earthly world to the heavens.

THE MAGIC SKIN

The Magic Skin is an enchanted garment—fur, feather, scale, or skin—that by donning or shedding allows a being to transform between two states of existence: animal and human, divine and mortal, or wild and gentle.

The Magic Skin is not a disguise, but a representation of the duality of identity. The skin is both boundary and bridge, allowing its wearer to be harmoniously both untouchable and deeply vulnerable, wholly other and intimately familiar, subtly masculine and overtly feminine. Unlike tales of curses or forced enchantments, the conflict often arises not from transformation itself, but from the means of transformation being controlled or stolen.

In the Selkie tales of Celtic lore, seal-women are trapped in human form when their seal skins are taken and hidden away. They live among humans, marry, raise families—but always long for the sea. When the skin is found, they return to their true form and escape back to the ocean, never to return. In the Japanese tale *Hagoromo,* a mortal fisherman steals the feathered robe of a divine celestial maiden, making her mortal and preventing her from flying back to the heavens. Only after she dances for him does he return her robe and allow her to fly home. In the Norse story of Völund, he and his two brothers discover three swan maidens bathing by a lake with their swan skins drying nearby. The brothers steal the skins and marry the women. After seven years, the swan maidens find their skins and fly away, returning to their mysterious otherworld.

To have the skin is to access power and freedom; to lose it is to feel the ache of the divided self, exile, or entrapment. These stories explore the tension between captivity and liberation, concealment and revelation, surface and soul.

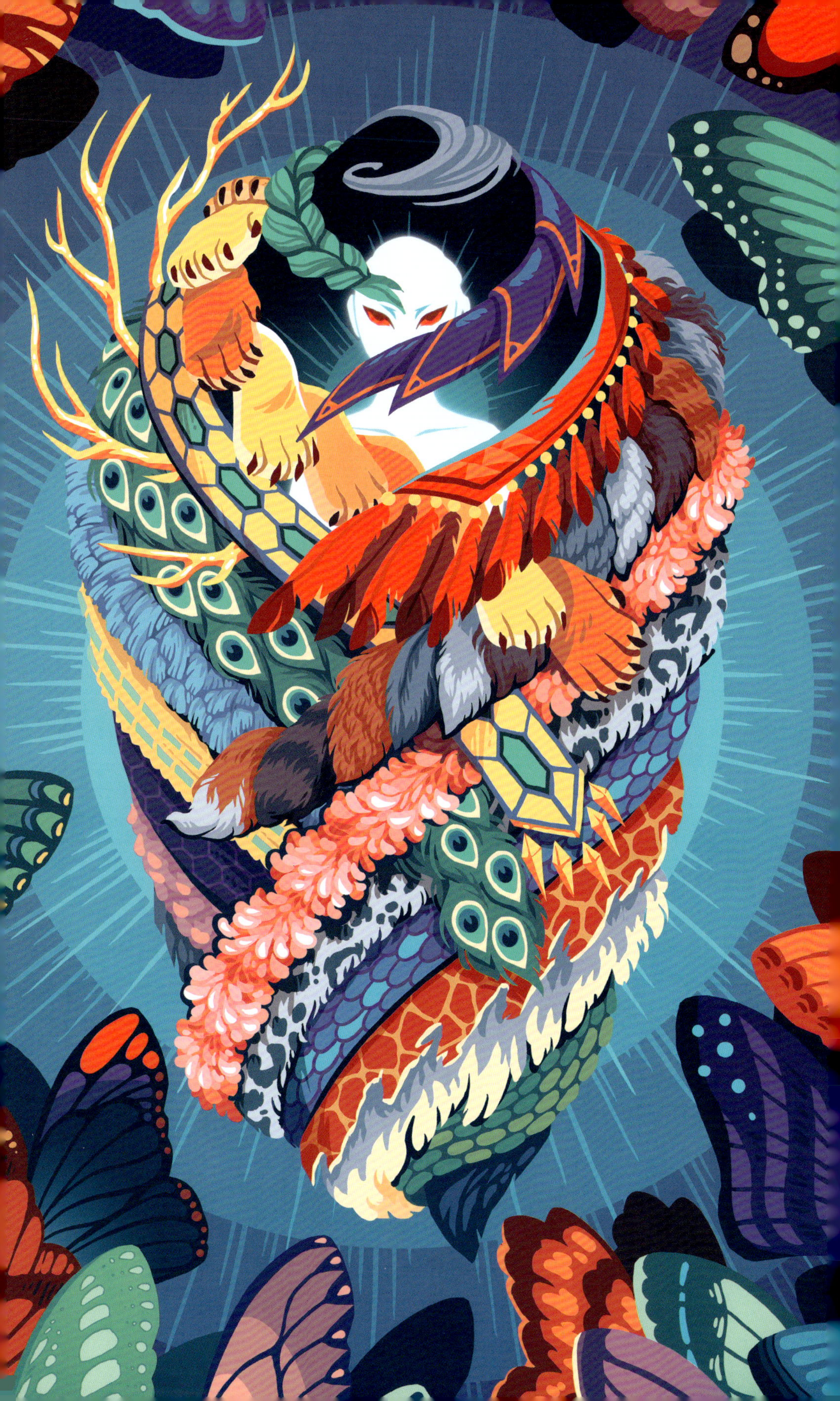

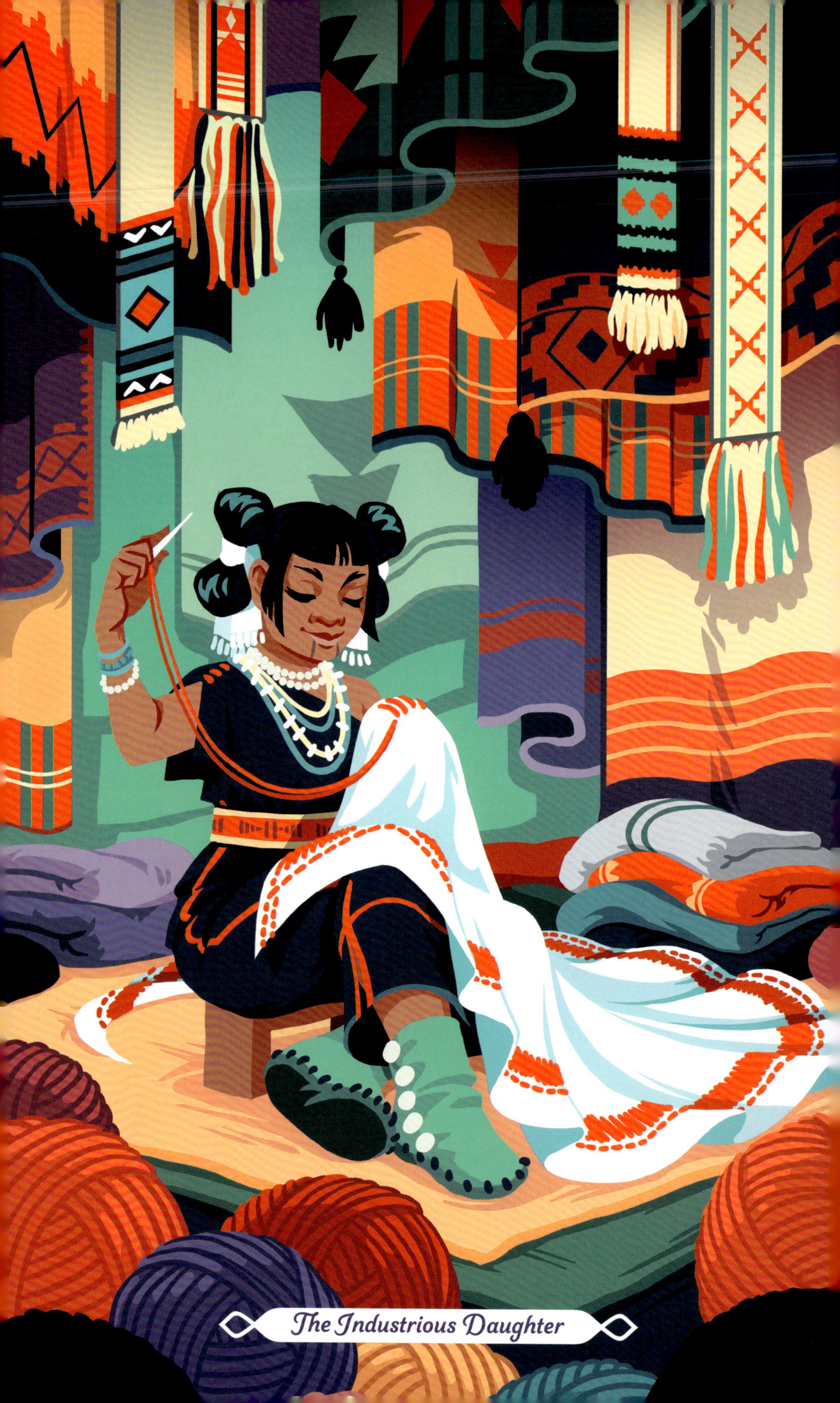
The Industrious Daughter

The INDUSTRIOUS DAUGHTER

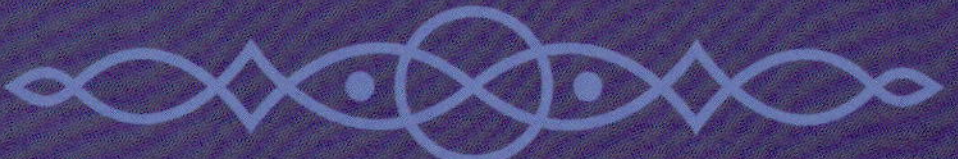

COCHITI LEGEND | NEW MEXICO

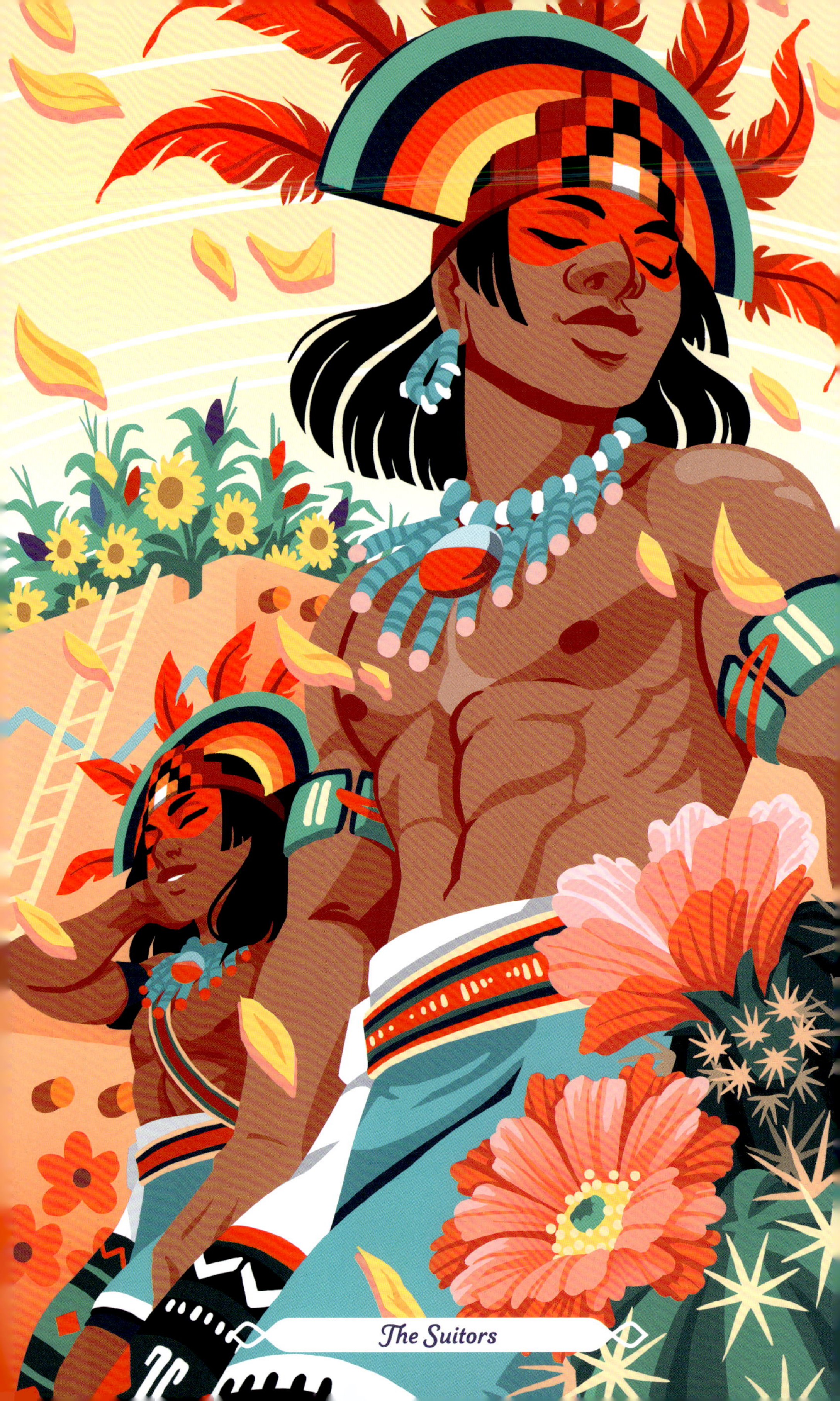
The Suitors

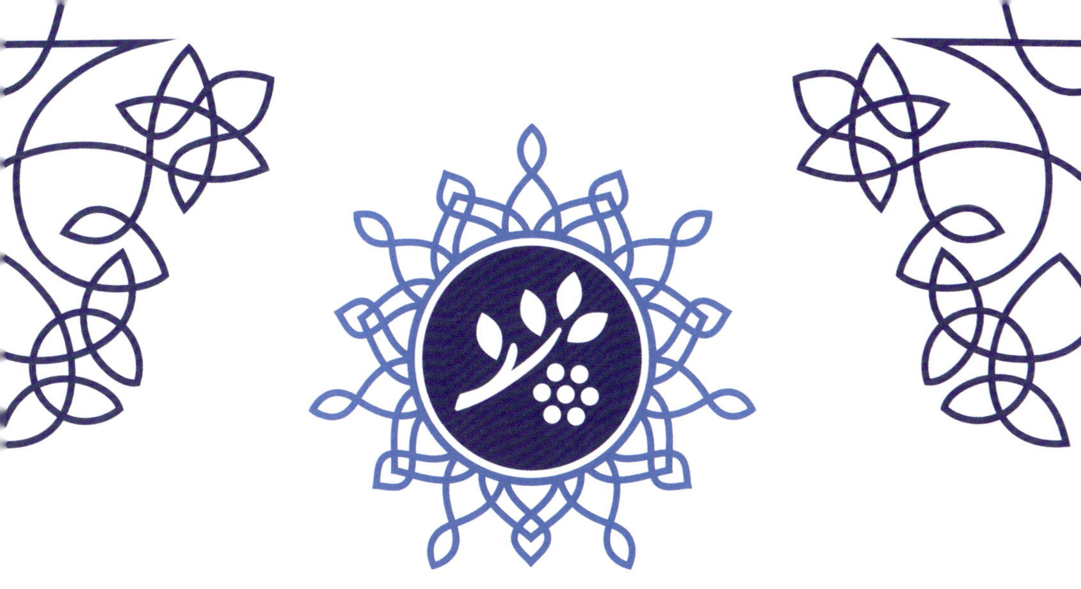

There once was a poor village couple who had a daughter quite late in life. The daughter grew up and began to think to herself, "My parents are very old. What shall I do to take care of them myself?"

The girl began by picking up the scraps of discarded cotton from around her home and village. She combed them, spun them into yarn, and rolled the yarn into a ball. When she had enough yarn to knit a pair of footless stockings, she did. Satisfied with her work, she went out and gathered more cotton fragments to roll into more balls of yarn. With this yarn, she threaded her loom and wove a white manta shirt that she then embroidered. Her parents were pleased with what she had made, so she continued. She dyed and pulled more yarn across the rafters of her home to dry straight so it wouldn't stretch, then she wove it into a belt. The girl and her parents admired her artistry.

"Take these," the girl said to her parents, handing them the stockings, shirt, and belt, "and see if you can sell them." Her parents took what she had created into the village and sold them all.

With this encouraging success, the industrious daughter wove more. She created large mantas, ball-fringed sashes, openwork stockings, and more. Soon everyone in the village wore her pieces and each had a complete dancing outfit.

By this time, the girl had grown into a handsome and prosperous young woman, and all the young men of the village gathered before her house to dance the rainbow dance and flirt with her, vying with one another to marry her. But the young woman didn't stop spinning her yarn to look up at any of them, so the men went home dejected.

The next day, the young men each brought her gifts of beautifully woven mantas and belts. But the young woman just scoffed, "Thank you, but I can make these myself. I know how to make what I want." And in saying so, she returned to her weaving as the men again went home discouraged.

The day after, the young men painted their houses and decorated them with sunflowers and colorful varieties of corn to lure her in. However, the young woman said, "I take care of my parents and live well. I don't need anything more. I don't want to marry." She didn't stir from her embroidery as the men went home angry, and they didn't waste any more time on her.

The village began to gossip about the young woman, calling her conceited and arrogant, and her parents began to worry. Her father tried to encourage her to rest. Her mother tried to entice her to go outside, but the industrious daughter shook them off. "I can't help working," she replied. "I like it."

This gossip was how Coyote, living in his large hole in the High Bank, heard of the young woman. "See this," said Coyote. "I shan't offer her treasures or charms, and still she will go with me." And so saying, he fetched a branch of black currants from the mountains.

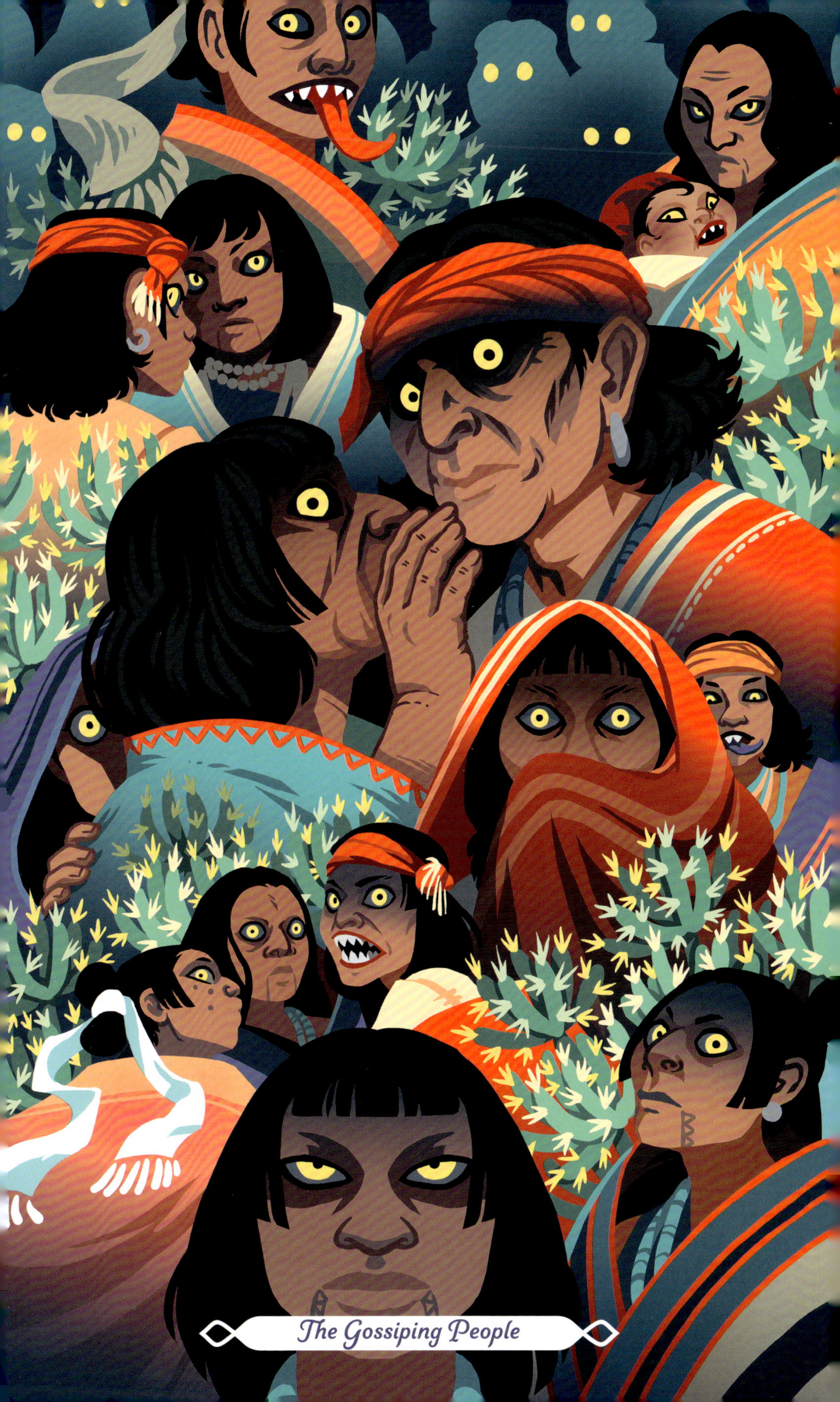
The Gossiping People

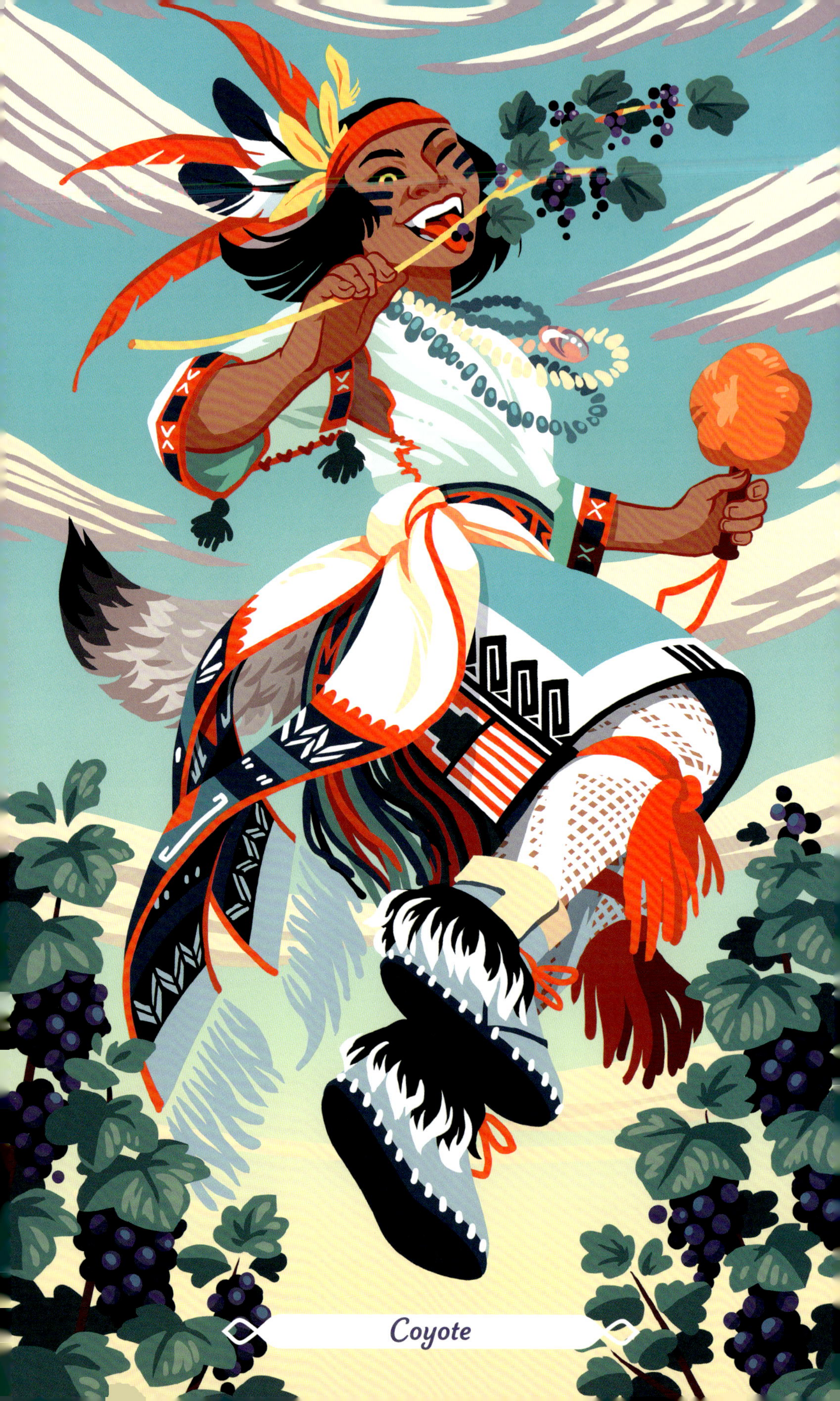
Coyote

Down in the village, Coyote put on his dancing clothes, buckskin moccasins, skunk skin tied to his ankles, lace stockings, white manta shirt, embroidered kilt, woven belt, white bead and abalone shell necklace, and long and short parrot feathers. Then he stamped his foot four times and said, "Do I look pretty? Yes, I look pretty!" He grabbed the branch of black currants and his gourd rattle and danced, not in front of the young woman's house, but in the middle of the village plaza.

The young woman heard his singing and the sound of his rattle and looked up from her loom. "What a fine-looking young man," she said as she went outside, leaving her work behind to admire him. Then she spotted the black currants, of which she was very fond, and said, "Give me the branch of black currants, and I'll invite you into my home."

The boys of the village sneered at her and called her a dirty, miserable girl to reject their lavish gifts for nothing but a handful of berries. Her mother bemoaned her daughter's actions and her father paled, but the young woman was happy and soon gave birth to little coyotes. She was a fine-looking industrious young woman, but no one in the village cared for that anymore.

Coyote turned to the old parents, who were now affluent, and said, "I shall take my wife and children back to my own home." And so he did, and the young woman found that the hole in the High Bank led into a large home richly supplied with beautiful mantas, and she was happy thereafter.

OFTEN, LEGENDS AND FOLKTALES are stories told to reaffirm a culture's beliefs and values. They can serve as a window into the ways societies assigned roles in the past. Trickster characters, like Coyote, throw a wrench in this process. By their very nature, Tricksters are unpredictable. Stories that involve them can show the repercussions, and just as likely the benefits, of breaking the rules. The effects of Tricksters can be seen when comparing the Cochiti tale of the Industrious Daughter to another Cochiti legend: the Rabbit Huntress, who also has to care for her aging parents. Without any previous experience, the Rabbit Huntress decides to go hunting and take on "the duties of men." Natural elements punish her for transgressing against her role as a woman, so she is forced to return home and become a dutiful wife to a male hunter.

The Industrious Daughter, by comparison, methodically develops her own skills. Even though she applies herself to culturally gender-appropriate tasks, she gains enough wealth independently in doing so that she can escape her community's expectations for her. When Coyote enters the story, instead of offering her the gifts that her society deems worthy, he gives her the gifts and lifestyle that she desires. Rather than emphasizing the need to stay within social norms like the Rabbit Huntress story does, the Industrious Daughter shows someone who breaks with tradition to live the life that makes her happiest.

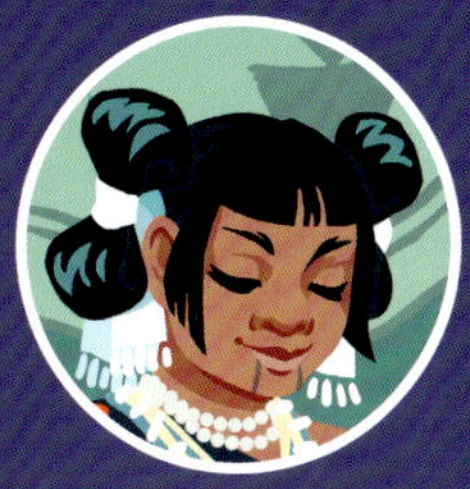

Among the Cochiti, as well as other Pueblo people, bangs and elaborate hairstyles were preferred for young unmarried women.

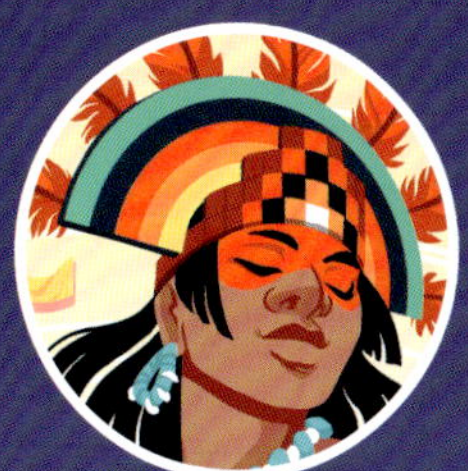

The rainbow dance is loud and joyous, with dancers in bright outfits accompanied by drums and chanting to celebrate rain, crop growth, fertility, the changing of the seasons, and the beauty of the world.

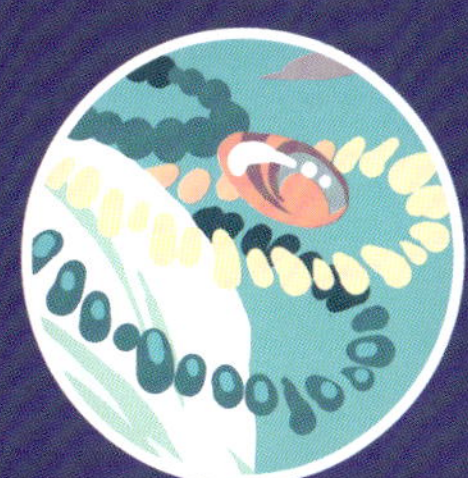

The Cochiti favor iridescent abalone shells in jewelry and pottery. Living hundreds of miles from the California coast, the Cochiti traditionally obtained the shells through extensive trade and paired them with locally mined turquoise.

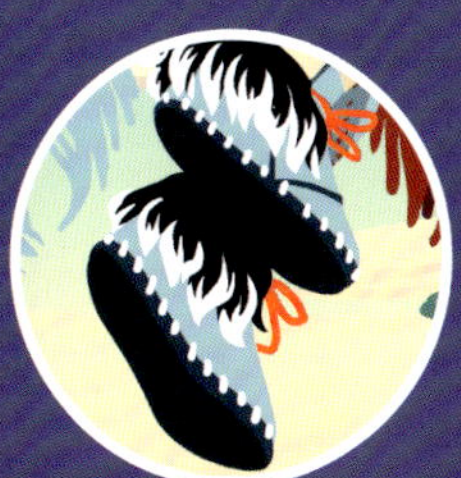

Pueblo moccasins are made of deer or elk hide. In ceremonies or other special occasions, skunk fur may be tied around the ankles to provide protection and ward off evil energies.

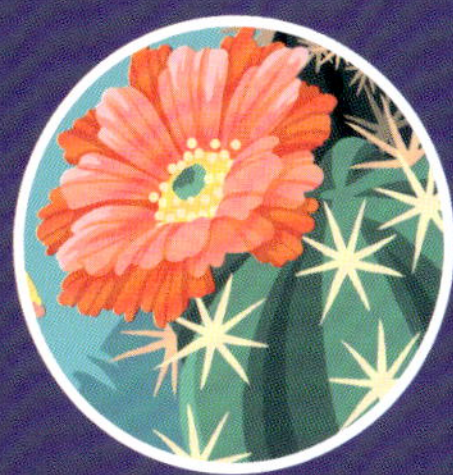

Spiny cholla is a dangerous cactus indigenous to the American Southwest. With spines that easily detach and rapidly burrow into the skin, removal is delicate and painful.

THE MONSTER MARRIAGE

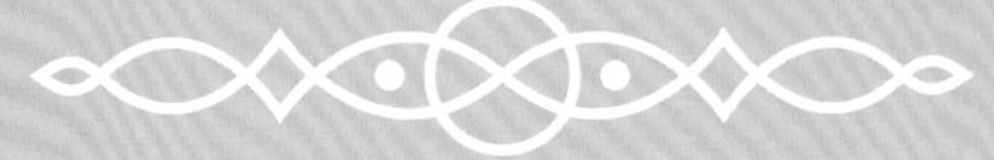

The Monster Marriage is a story trope that centers on a union of a human and a partner who is grotesque, magical, or morally ambiguous.

This motif embodies the fear of entering the unknown, mirroring the anxiety of marrying into a strange family or culture, worries over intimacy, and loss of independence. These tales question the limits of compassion and the conditions under which transformation—of the self or the other—is possible. They ask whether love can survive revulsion, mystery, or conflicting ethics. They challenge characters to look past surface horror to what lies within—but also to recognize when the monstrous is irredeemable.

Often such stories cast monstrosity and humanity as opposing forces that must come into balance for a happily ever after. In the French fairy tale *Beauty and the Beast*, the heroine learns to love the Beast not despite his monstrous form, but because of the goodness within it. The transformation is mutual—he becomes human, and she gains wisdom, courage, and compassion. In the Danish fairy tale *King Lindworm*, a cursed prince born as a serpent demands a bride. Only a woman daring enough to peel away his outer layers, both literal and emotional, can break his curse and turn him human.

But not all monster marriages offer redemption. In the French folktale *Bluebeard*, the husband is charming but hides a terrible secret—that he has murdered his past wives. His monstrosity is not physical, but moral. The heroine's survival depends not on acceptance, but resistance and escape.

Monster Marriage tales explore the peril and promise of loving the unfamiliar. Some monsters become men; some men are revealed to be monsters. The cost of love lies in knowing the difference.

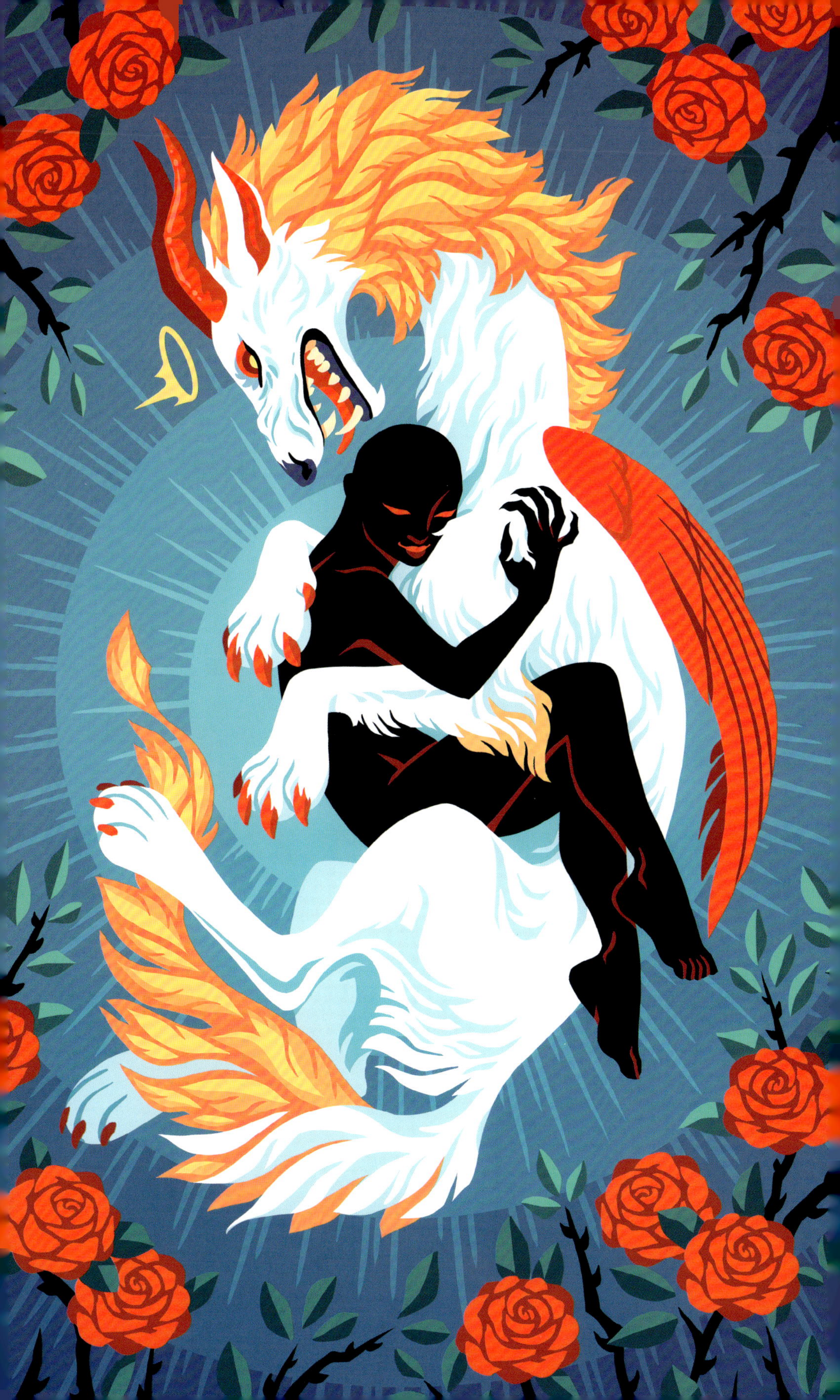

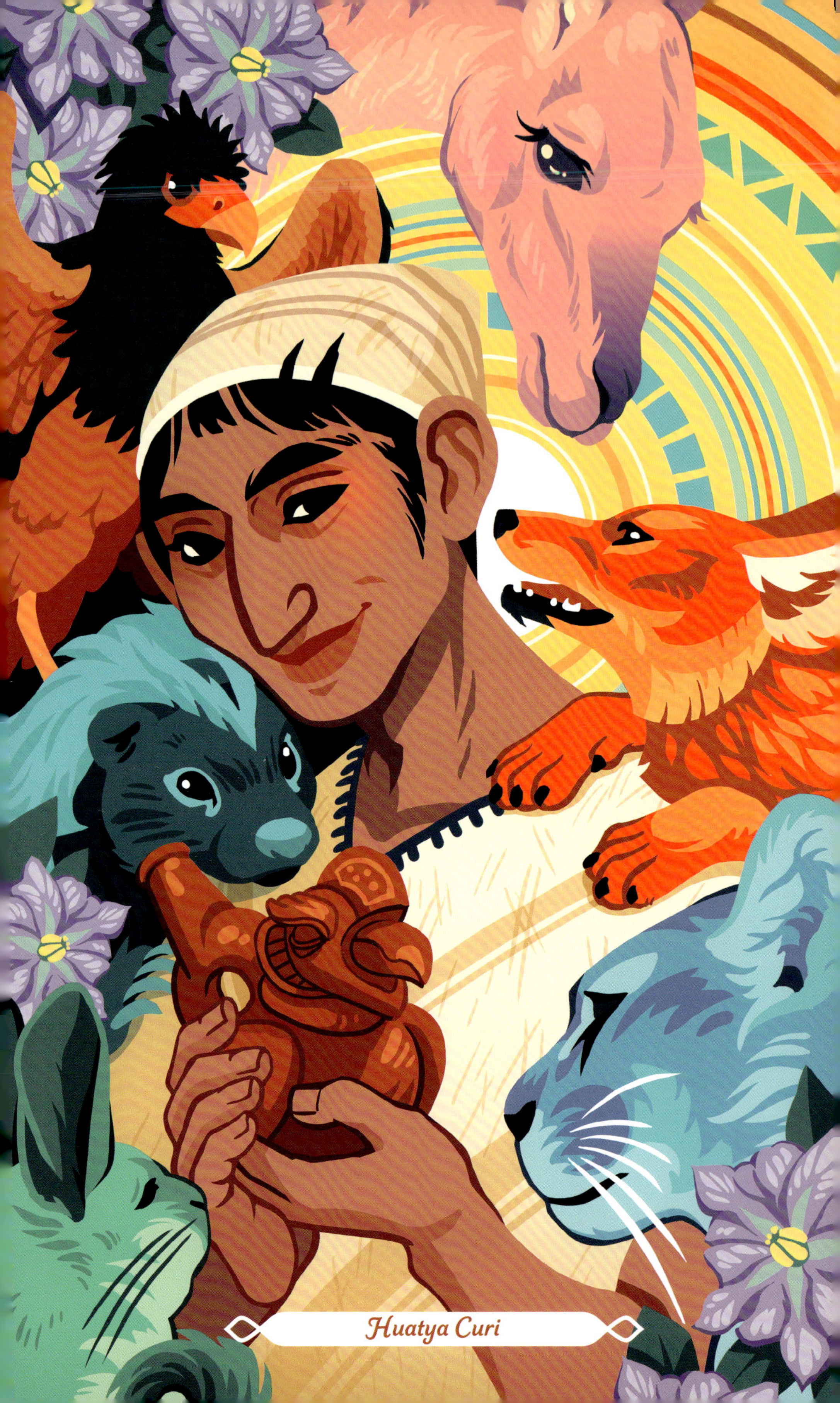
Huatya Curi

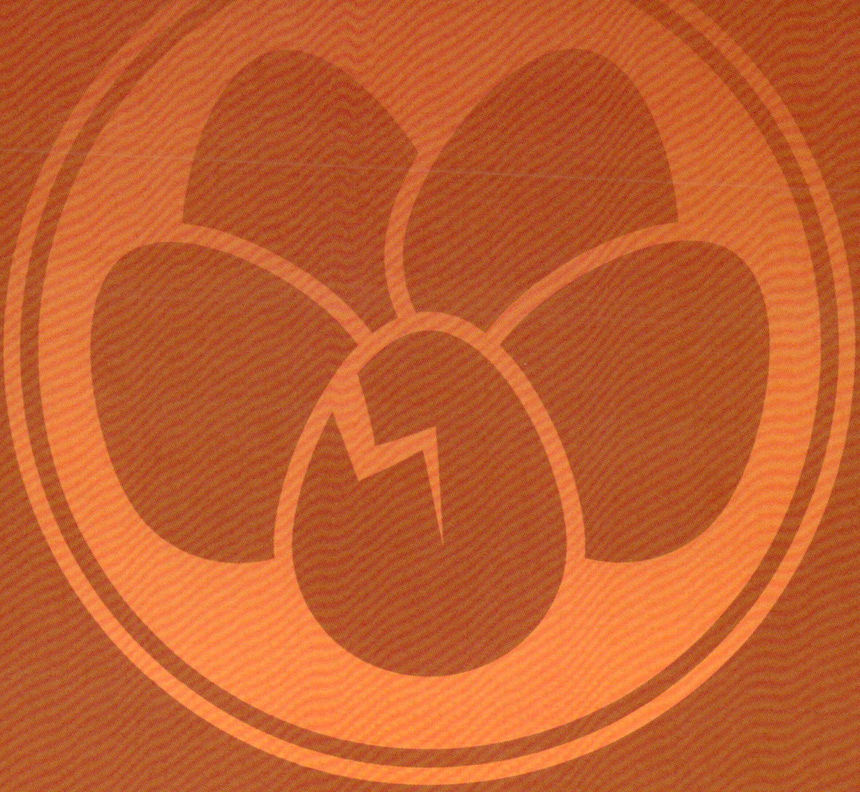

HUATYA CURI
and the Five Condors

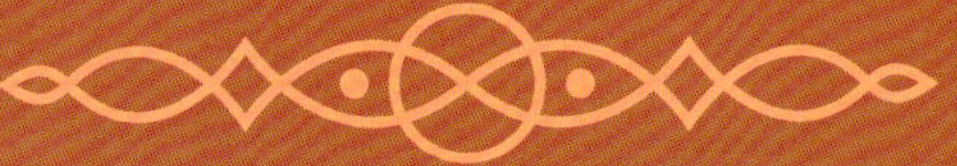

HUAROCHIRÍ MYTHOLOGY | PERU

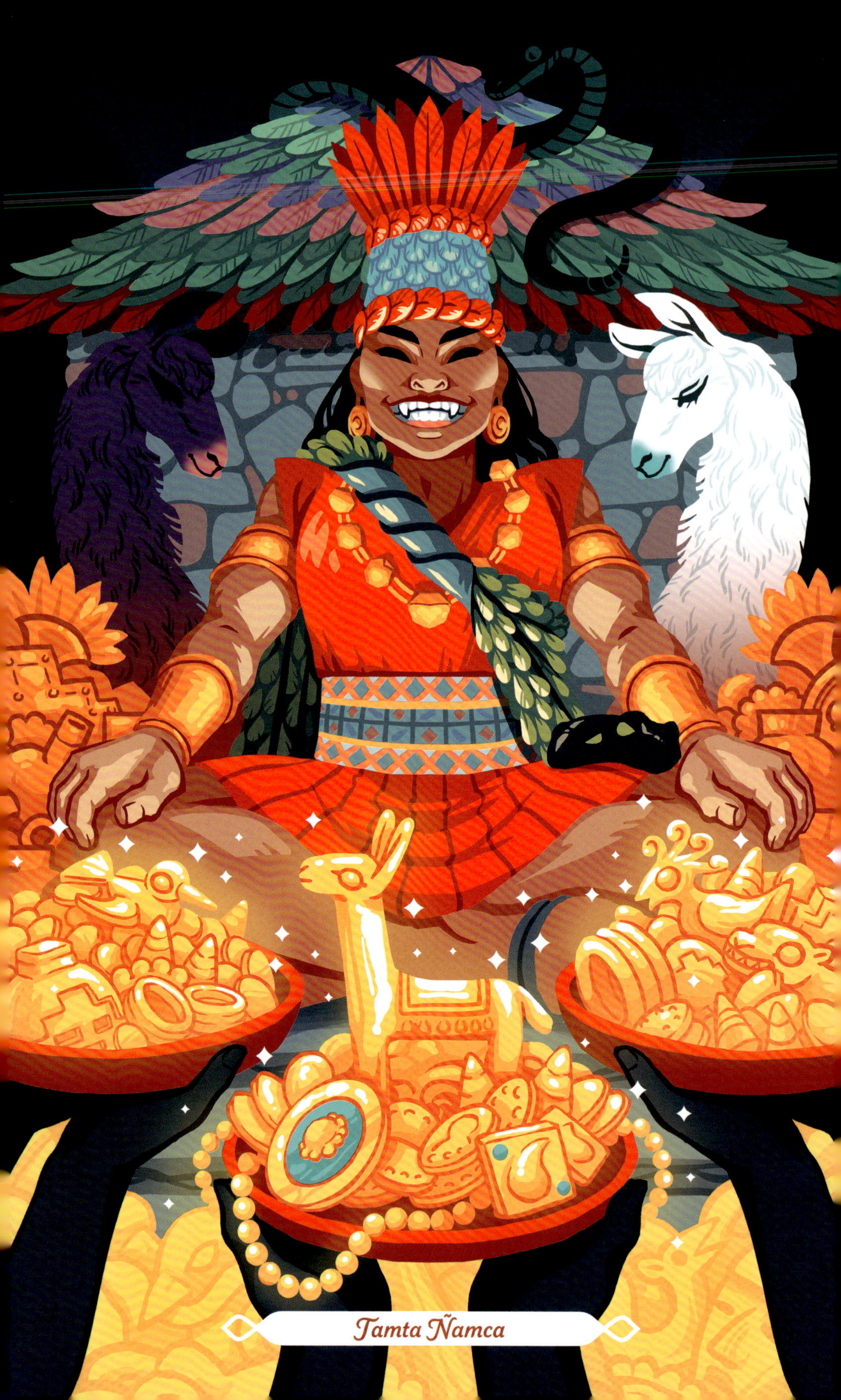
Tamta Ñamca

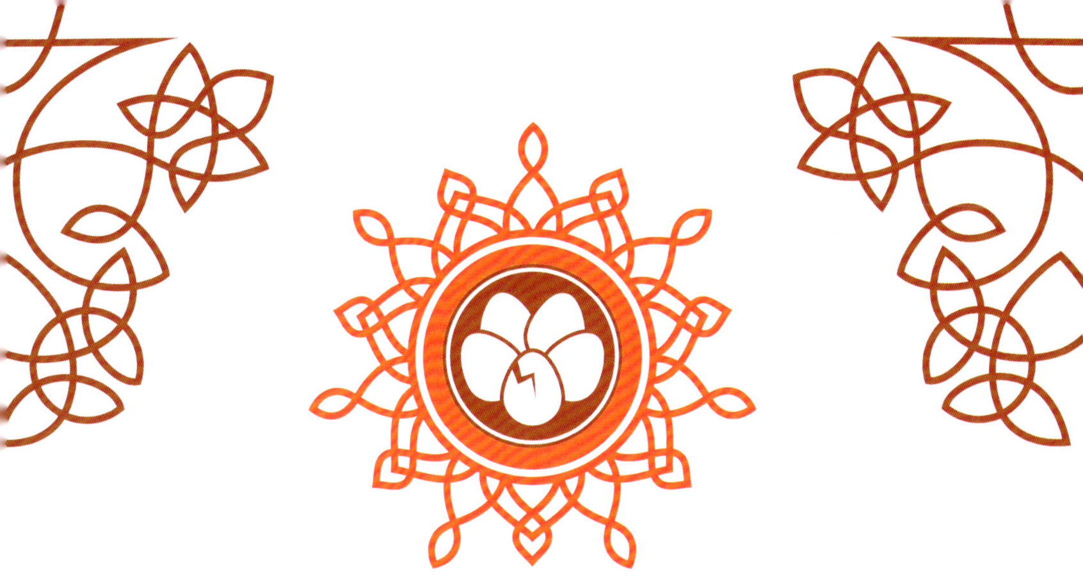

This story begins right before the birth of the great god Paria Caca, who exists here in the form of five condor eggs nestled at the top of a mountain. No one knew he was about to hatch except his son, Huatya Curi.

Huatya Curi was a very poor and friendless man because he did not yet have the support of his father. He spent his days wandering and digging for potatoes, that being all he could afford, which is how he came to overhear two foxes gossiping.

The two foxes spoke of a man named Tamta Ñamca, who was so rich that he owned llamas of every hue and the roofs of his many houses were thatched with the wings of birds. He was so rich that his neighbors had begun regarding him as a god. He pretended to be wise and gave them advice on things he knew nothing about.

But now, Tamta Ñamca had fallen ill with a horrible disease that no amount of money could cure. Even promising the hand of his beautiful sister Chaupi Ñamca to whoever could heal him yielded no remedy—neither doctor nor shaman could find a cure. One of the foxes laughed as he revealed the cause of the disease: Tamta Ñamca's wife had fed tainted maize to a visitor, a taboo

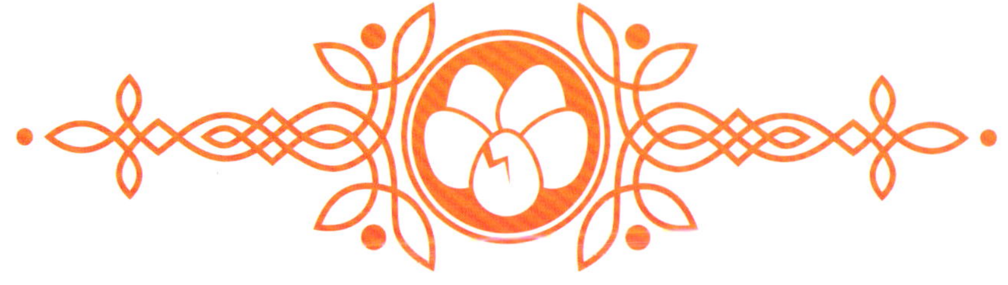

act that resulted in their home being cursed with two poisonous snakes living in their roof and a two-headed toad hiding under their grinding stone. But no one in the family knew of these venomous animals.

Upon overhearing this story, Huatya Curi hurried to Tamta Ñamca's house and offered to cure him in exchange for his sister Chaupi Ñamca's hand in marriage. Tamta Ñamca scoffed at the destitute Huatya Curi but was desperate enough to agree. Then Huatya Curi purged the house of vermin, killing the snakes in the roof and the two-headed toad under the grinding stone. He bade Tamta Ñamca's wife to be more careful, scolded Tamta Ñamca for pretending to be a god, and told them all to worship instead the soon to be born great god Paria Caca.

Chaupi Ñamca saw the goodness in Huatya Curi and happily married him. After they wed, Chaupi Ñamca revealed to Huatya Curi that she was a piece of a five-part great goddess of fertility. While her four other faces roamed the world as four other women living in promiscuity or solitude as they saw fit, this part of Chaupi Ñamca was happy to be a wife to Huatya Curi and live simply with him.

The newlyweds would have lived happily ever after. Unfortunately, as soon as Tamta Ñamca was fully recovered, he came to his senses and realized he did not want to be related to a poor beggar with no friends and family. So the rich man devised a plot to run Huatya Curi off. He challenged him to see who could throw the better party, a competition meant to utterly humiliate the penniless Huatya Curi while also showing off Tamta Ñamca's excessive luxuries. Huatya Curi knew he could not win on his own, so he climbed the mountain and asked the five condor eggs that were his father for guidance. Paria Caca advised his son to steal a beer jug from a fox and a drum from a skunk, which Huatya Curi quickly accomplished.

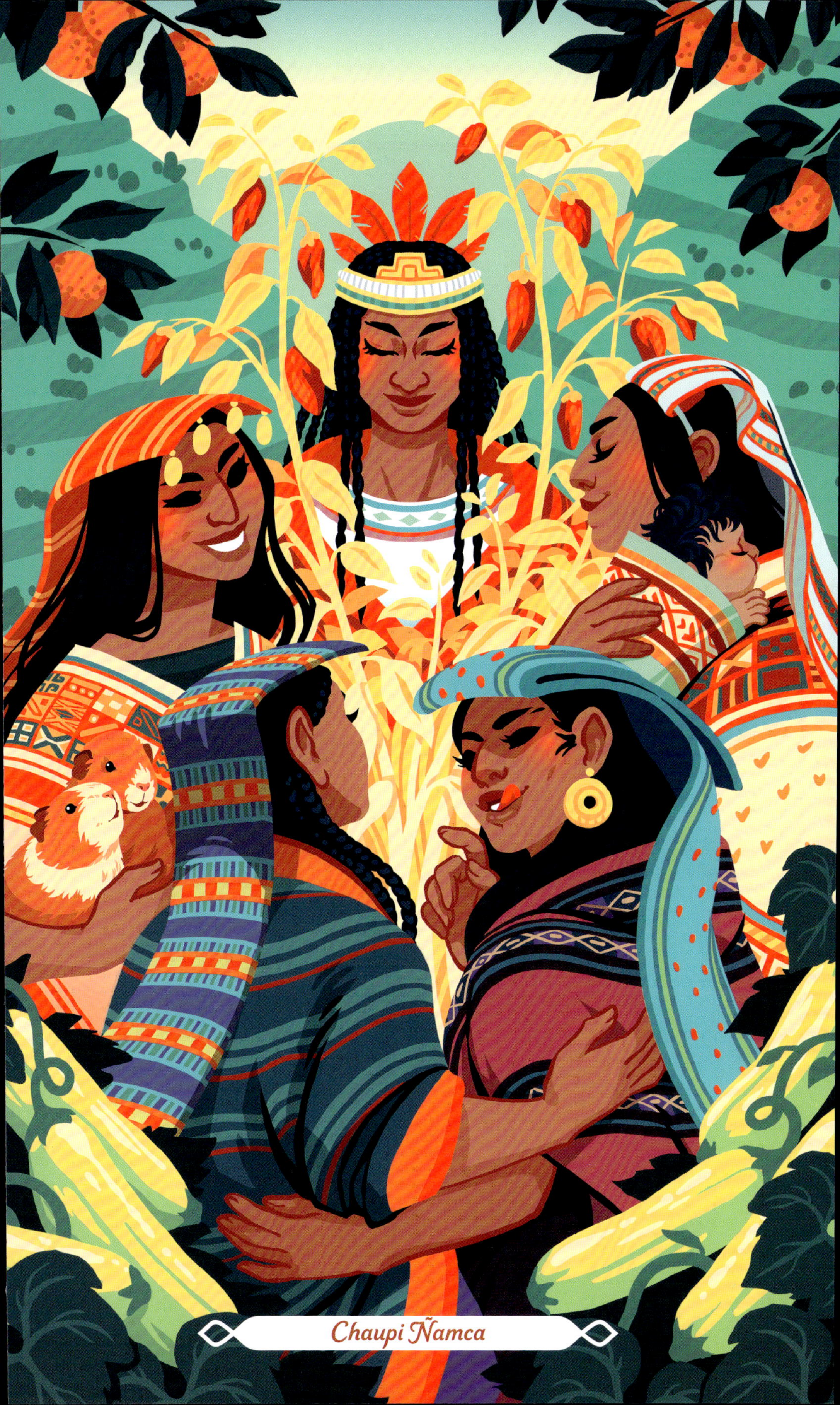
Chaupi Ñamca

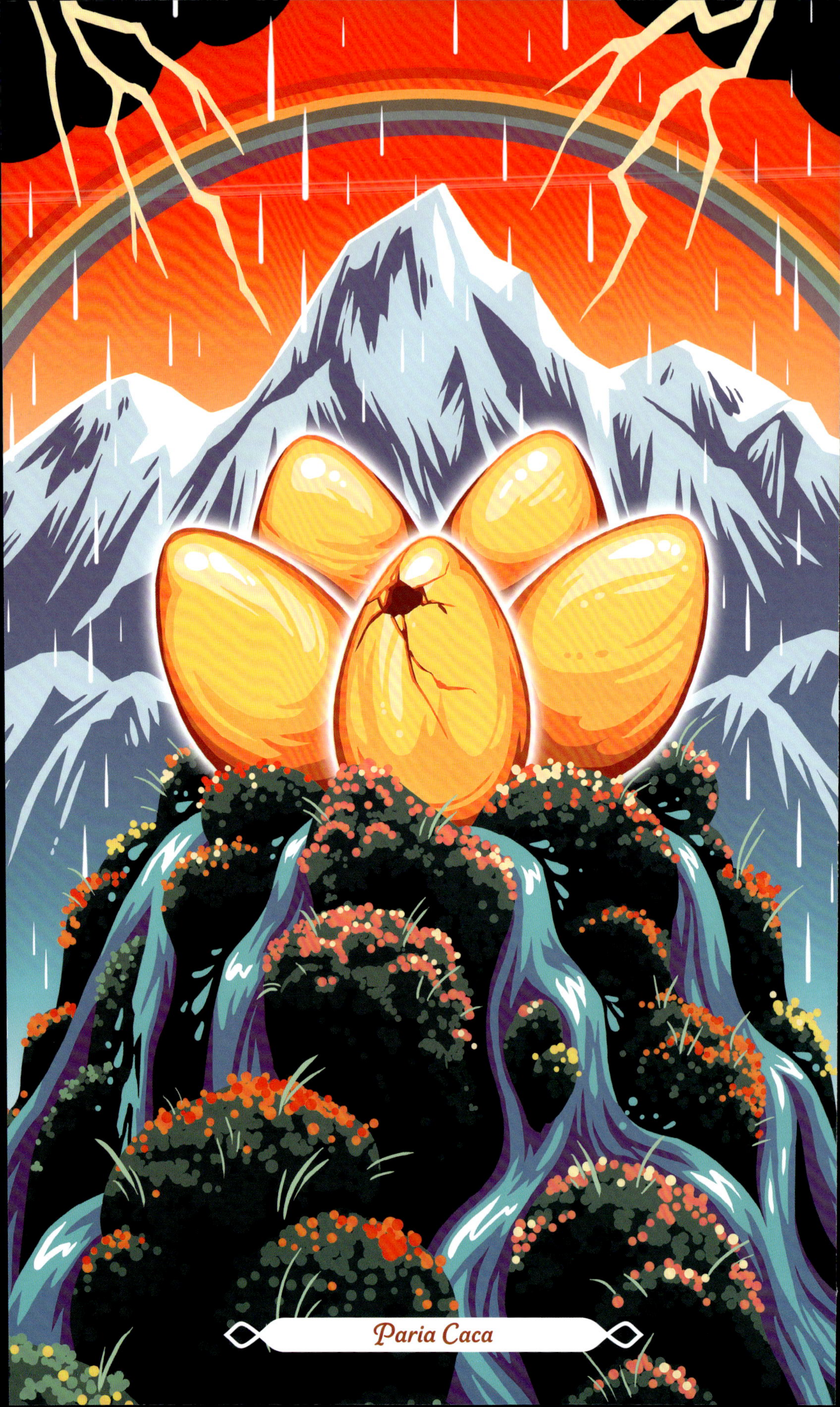
Paria Caca

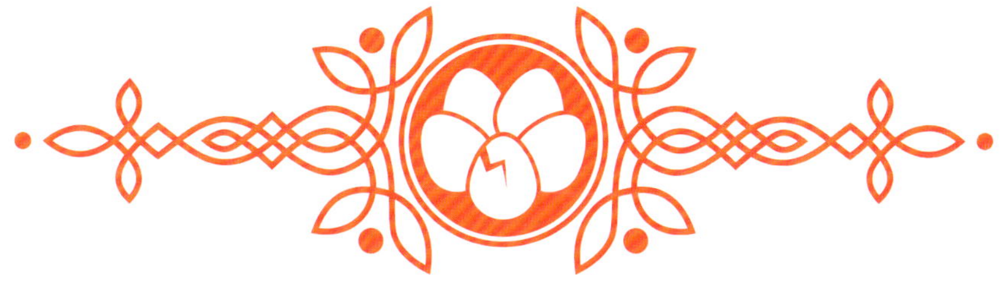

Back in the village, the contest commenced with the rich man bringing out his two hundred wives to dance with him and serve large barrels of beer. At Huatya Curi's turn, only he and Chaupi Ñamca danced, but the skunk drum boomed until the very earth danced. He had only a tiny beer jug, but it never emptied, and the entire village drank until they collapsed.

Next, the rich man challenged Huatya Curi to a clothing contest. He wore garments resplendent head to toe in beautiful and expensive feathers. Huatya Curi again visited Paria Caca, who gave him clothes made from snow, so piercingly white that they blinded all who looked upon them. Then the rich man challenged Huatya Curi to a building contest and hired many laborers to finish constructing a whole house in a day and a half. Huatya Curi spent the day strolling about with his wife. In the evening, he consulted Paria Caca, who contracted all the animals of the land to complete the home in a single night.

Tamta Ñamca seethed, but Huatya Curi had also had enough of the games. This time, he challenged the rich man to a dancing contest. Tamta Ñamca agreed. As he began to dance, Huatya Curi charged at him screaming and scared him so badly that he transformed into a brocket deer as he fled, never to be seen again. With Tamta Ñamca gone, Huatya Curi settled happily with his wife for the rest of his days.

INDIGENOUS HUAROCHIRÍ MYTHOLOGY, unlike the Incan mythology that eventually conquered the region, contains little cosmological worship. Instead, the Huarochirí venerate *huacas*, which can be any physical thing that manifests as superhuman: peaks, springs, lakes, caves, ancient ruins, effigies, mummies of ancestors, twins, a perfect flower, or a tree split by lightning. The god Paria Caca is the Pariacaca Mountain, and the goddess Chaupi Ñamca the Chaupihuaranga River. The Huarochirí religion is inseparably tied to the land itself.

Much of what is known today of pre-Inca and pre-colonial Peruvian Huarochirí belief comes from the Huarochirí Manuscript, a document both beautiful and horrific in its creation and use. Compiled over many years, it seems to have been directed by a Catholic priest intent on erasing the very traditions he recorded. Knowledge from the manuscript was weaponized against the people, leading to atrocities against the heart of Huarochirí culture. On December 20, 1609, a mass burning of huacas was carried out and believers were publicly whipped. The wound of this destruction still lingers today, generations later. Yet the manuscript itself is not wholly corrupt. While sections were shaped under colonial oversight, others appear to come directly from Indigenous voices, including Hernando Paucar, once a priest of the goddess Chaupi Ñamca. These passages preserve rare authenticity, capturing the religion as it was lived.

Thus, the Huarochirí Manuscript stands in paradox: a colonial tool of suppression but also a vessel of survival. These preserved portions are clearly meant for future generations of Andeans to read with pride in their past, and it is with this intention that the tale of Huatya Curi is shared.

A potato flower. Among the Huarochirí people, "Potato-Eater" was an insult for people who were too poor to eat maize and had to resort to foraging for potatoes from the Earth.

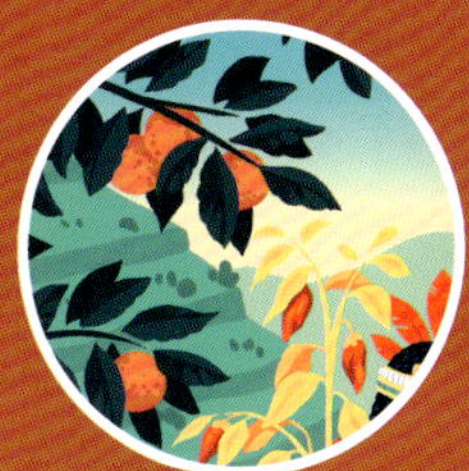

The goddess Chaupi Ñamca is associated with valleys, the low-altitude and hot parts of Huarochirí where citrus fruit and squash are grown. These areas are watered by the lakes found higher up in the mountains.

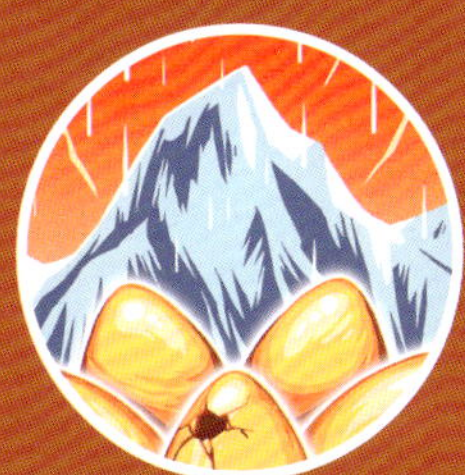

All Huarochirí *huacas* (gods, spirits, or sacred things) are associated with a tangible object, particular person, or specific place. The god Paria Caca is the mountain Pariacaca located in the Lima region of Peru.

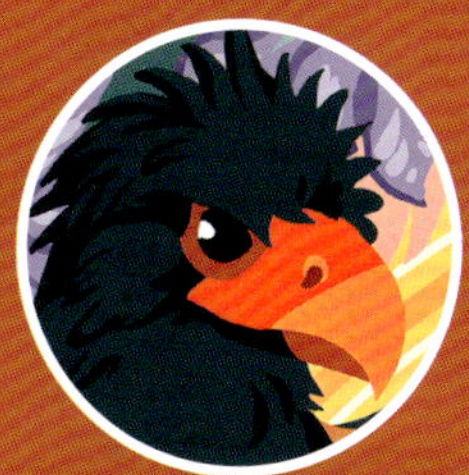

The mountain caracara is revered as a sacred bird that connects the physical and spiritual worlds. It is believed to carry messages between the gods and humans, acting as a divine intermediary.

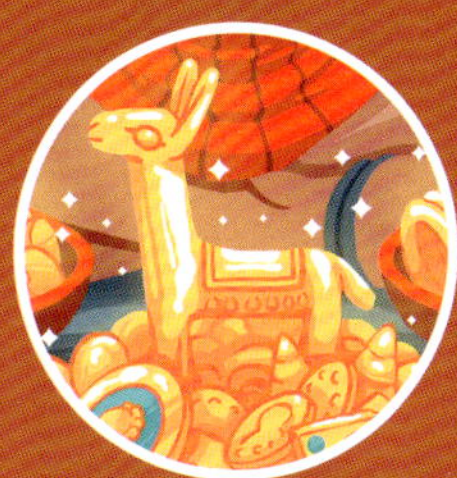

Used for transport, food, wool, and dung fuel, llamas are symbols of wealth and prosperity. Traditionally they were used as tribute payment, and a large healthy herd indicated high status.

THE FLOOD

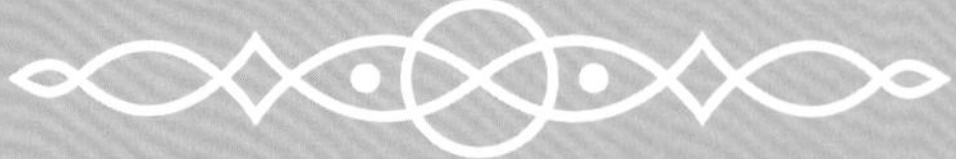

The Flood myth always begins with a prophecy, vision, or divine message warning of an impending disaster. Most ignore it, but the few who listen are able to escape the catastrophe and rebuild.

Unlike stories that focus on the chaos of destruction, Flood myths emphasize the preparation and discipline during the time before catastrophe strikes. They celebrate the wisdom to heed advice, work beforehand, and to know when to leave. The Flood becomes a force of purification, sweeping away arrogance, ignorance, and corruption. What remains is clarity, awareness, and the foundation for renewal. The tragedy lies not in the Flood itself, but in the failure to act when forewarned. This theme underscores that disaster, though uncontrollable, is often foreseeable.

Many early civilizations lived near rivers and coasts, making them especially vulnerable to floods. Even today, floods are among the most common and devastating natural disasters globally. It's no surprise, then, that numerous Flood myths are found across cultures. In the Mesopotamian tale of Utnapishtim, the gods decide to cleanse the world, but one man is warned and preserves life aboard a great boat. In the Abrahamic tradition, Noah receives a divine command and survives by building an ark filled with his family and two of each animal in the world. In Hindu myth, the god Vishnu appears as a fish to warn Manu, who saves seeds, animals, and the sages of wisdom aboard a giant vessel. In Andean Huarochirí legend, the storm god Paria Caca, disguised as a beggar, warns only those who are kind to him of a coming flood that destroys the valley and village.

The Flood is associated with themes of preparedness, caution, and responsibility. It teaches that destruction is survivable, but only for those willing to recognize warning signs. The survivors don't just escape; they also rebuild and pass their wisdom on to the next generation.

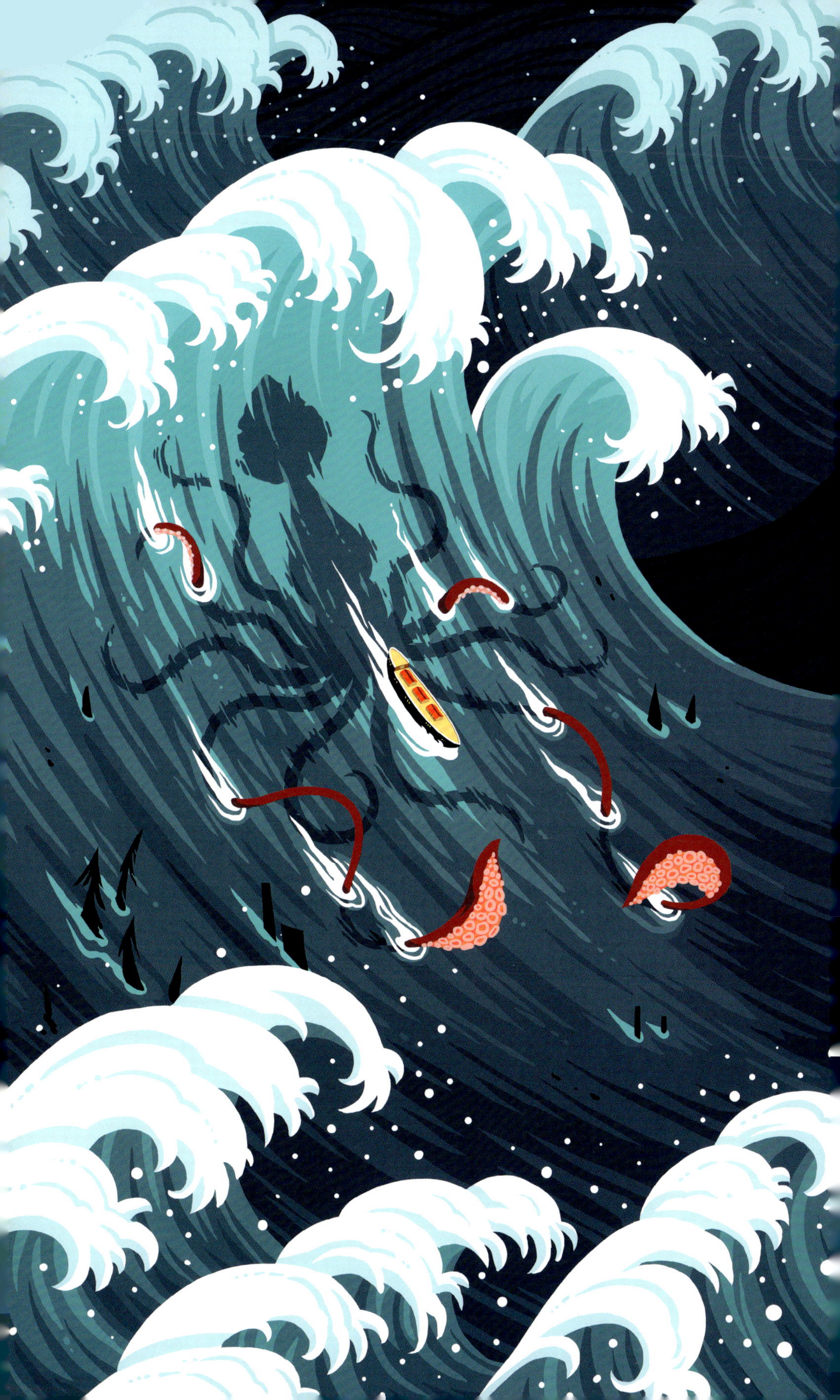

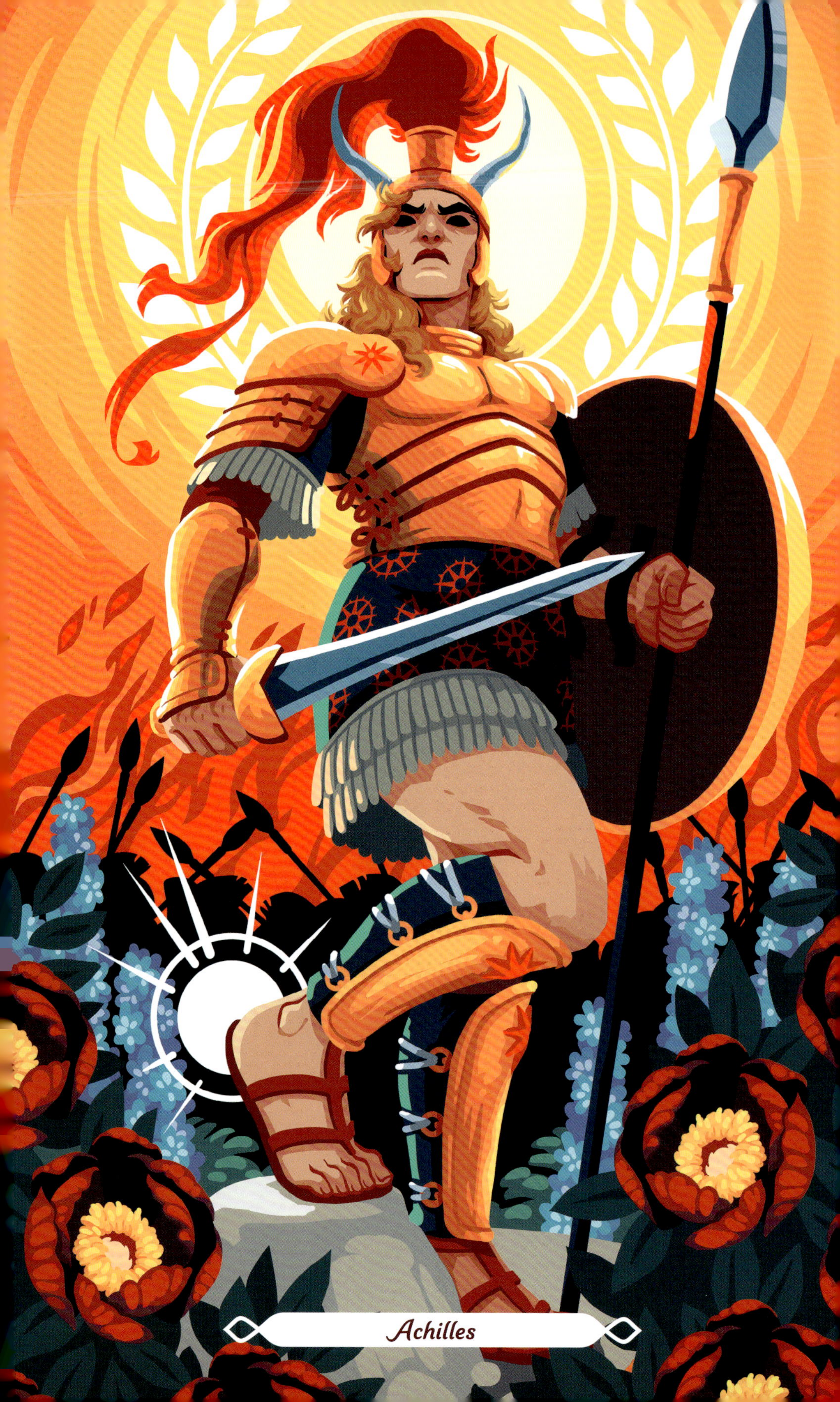
Achilles

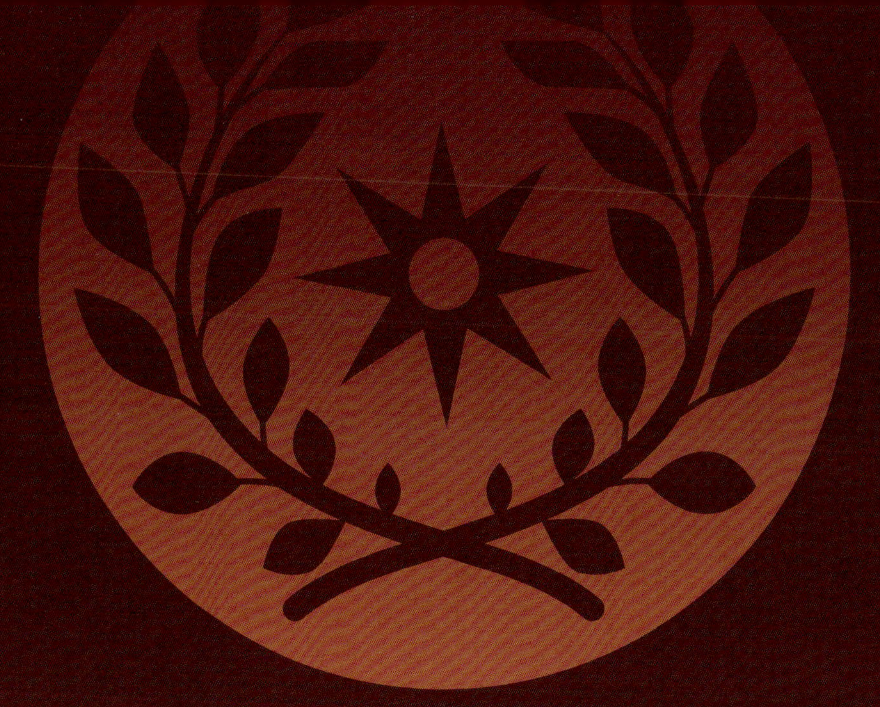

The TROJAN WAR

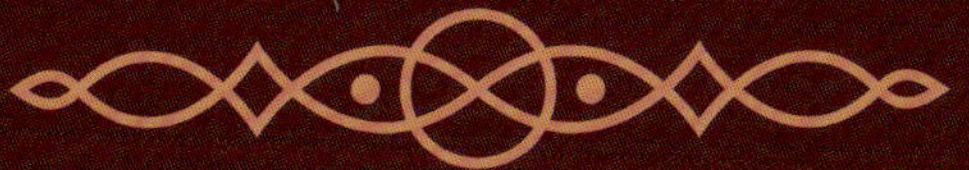

GREEK MYTHOLOGY | GREECE

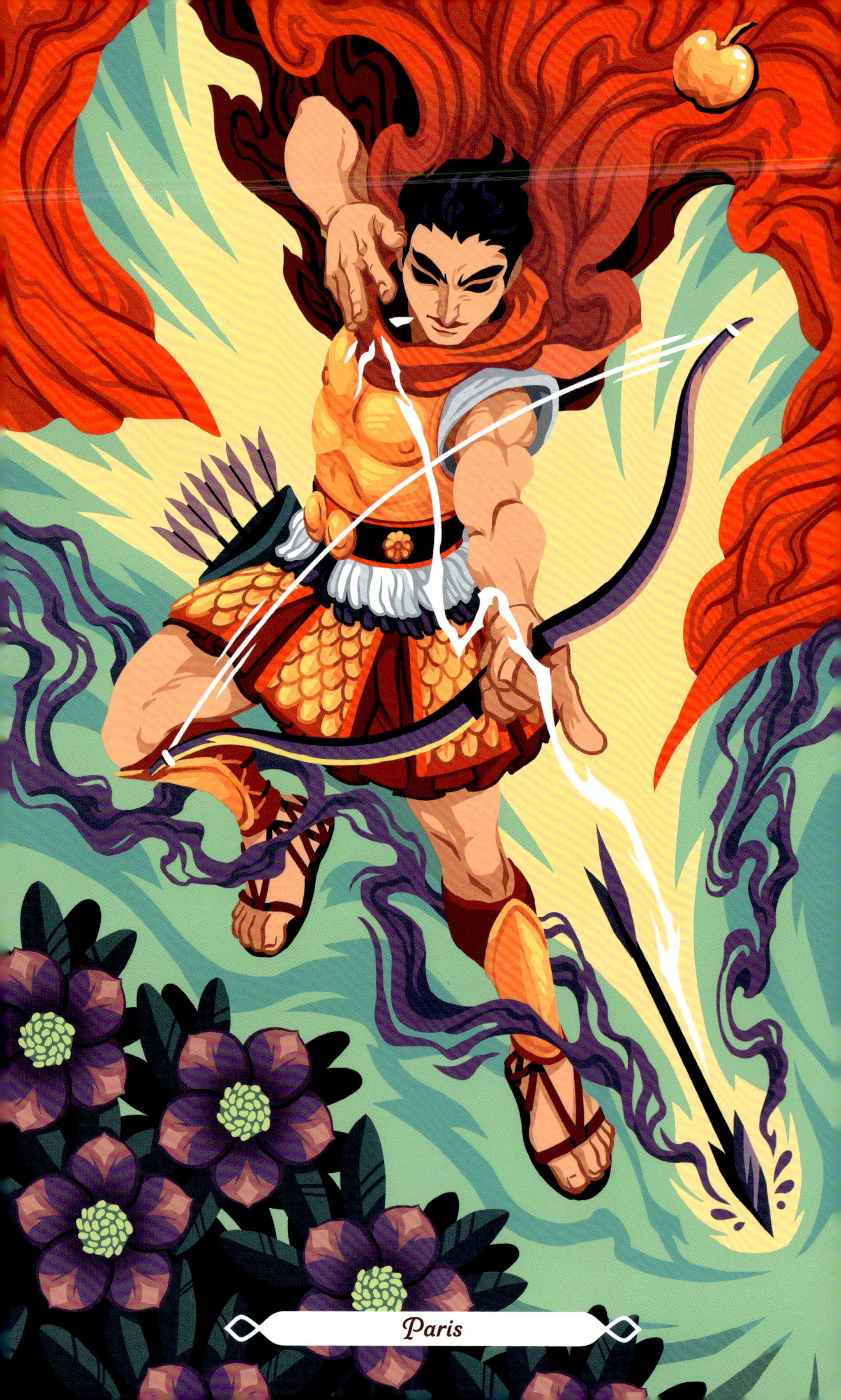
Paris

Eris, Goddess of Strife, was not invited to the divine wedding of King Peleus and the sea nymph Thetis. As revenge, she tossed an apple with the inscription "For the most beautiful." Eris cackled as she watched the goddesses Hera, Athena, and Aphrodite fight to claim it.

Fearing the goddesses' wrath, the god Zeus appointed the Trojan prince Paris to judge who was the most beautiful and deserved the apple, as he had been fair in a previous contest with the god Ares. However, Paris could not decide, as all three goddesses were equally beautiful. So the goddesses attempted to bribe him. Hera offered ownership of Europe and Asia, Athena offered the skills of a legendary warrior, and Aphrodite offered the love of the most beautiful woman on earth. Blinded by lust, Paris chose Aphrodite's gift. But what Aphrodite had failed to mention was that Helen, the world's most beautiful woman, was already married to King Menelaus of Sparta. Eager to claim his prize, impulsive Paris stole Helen, and spirited her back to his kingdom of Troy. This kidnapping infuriated the Spartans and the rest of the Achaeans, igniting the great Trojan War.

Meanwhile, King Peleus and Thetis gave birth to a son named Achilles. Thetis, wishing to protect her son, held him by his heel and dipped him in the magical waters of the River Styx. This ritual granted him invulnerability everywhere except that single heel. Then Peleus handed Achilles to the centaur Chiron to raise. Chiron, unlike other centaurs who are driven by beastly instincts, was a wise and thoughtful scholar who lived secluded from his brethren on Mount Pelion. He bestowed upon Achilles a wide breadth of knowledge, ranging from practical skills such as hunting, medicine, and battle to intellectual skills such as music, astrology, and divination.

When Achilles grew to be a young man, his mother Thetis received a prophecy that her son would either die young in glory or live a long life in obscurity. Attempting to assure the latter, she took him from Chiron and disguised him as a noble girl in the court of King Lycomedes of Skyros. He might have remained there all his life had not the Achaean hero Odysseus received his own prophecy. The prophet Calchas told Odysseus that the Achaeans would be unable to capture Troy without the warrior Achilles, who currently hid in the king's court on the island of Skyros. With such advice, Odysseus quickly discovered Achilles and successfully enticed him with tales of glory and fame to join the war against the Trojans.

Although Achilles was young and hopeful when he first arrived on Trojan shores commanding fifty Myrmidon ships, the decade-long war with losses on both sides aged him into a fierce and seasoned warrior. In between battles for control of various cities, Achilles took comfort in his childhood friend turned companion Patroclus, with whom he shared a tent and played the lyre.

The war appeared evenly matched until the gods became involved. The change began when King Agamemnon, who commanded the Achaeans, robbed a temple of Apollo while besieging

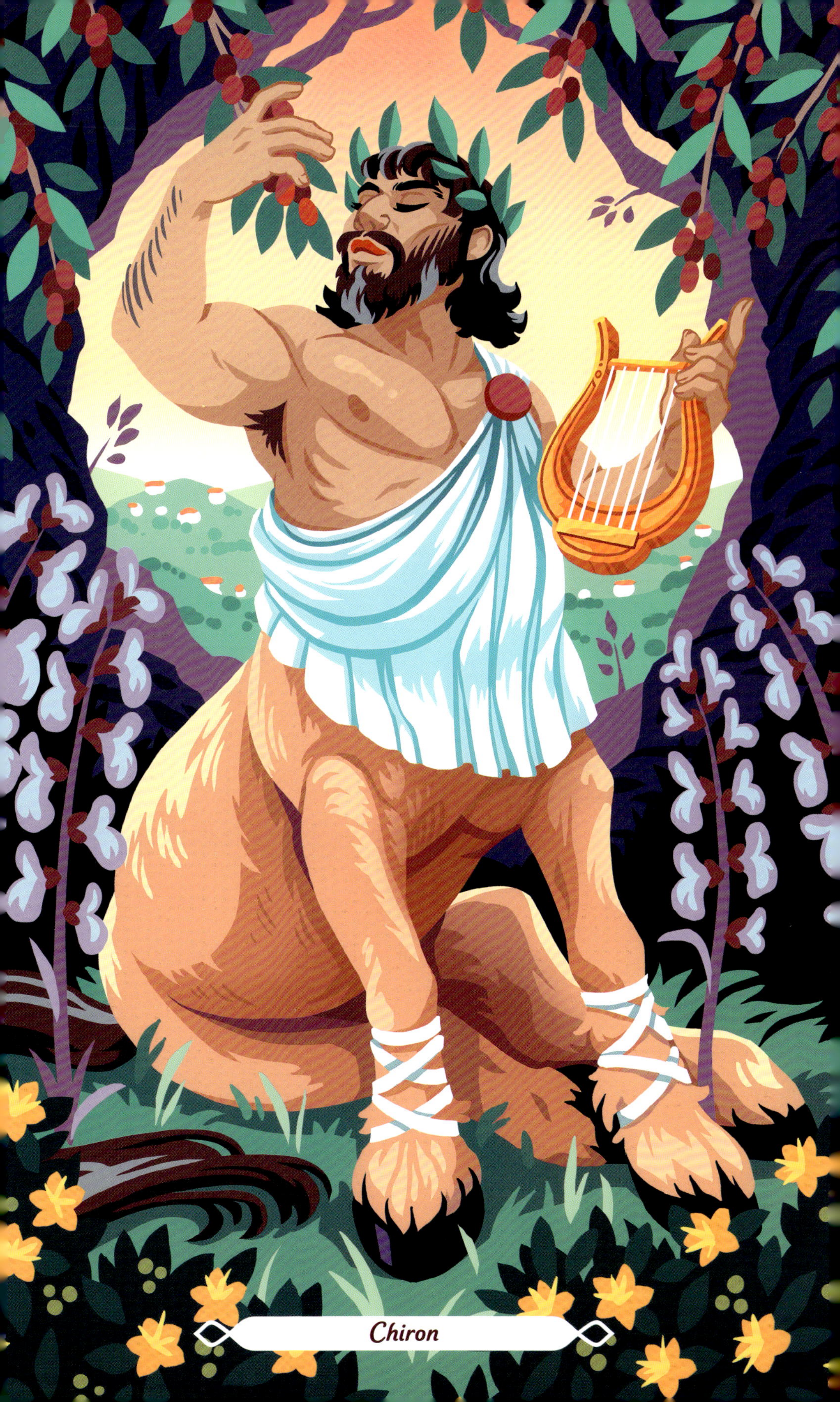
Chiron

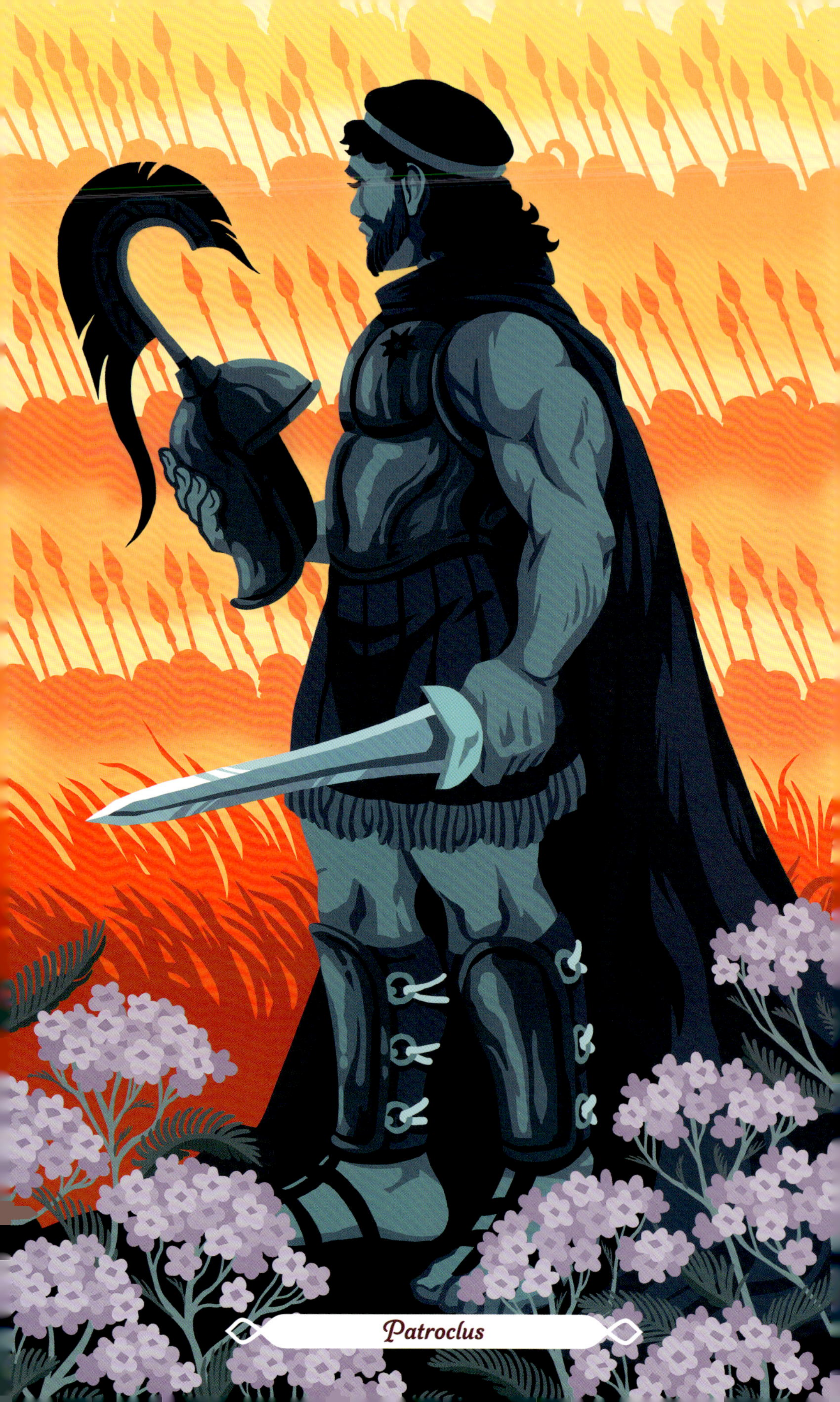
Patroclus

a Trojan city. This theft angered Apollo, who sent a plague against the Achaeans. Achilles demanded Agamemnon return what he stole, which he sullenly did, but only after replacing his lost goods with Achilles' belongings as punishment for commanding him. While Apollo was appeased, Achilles was enraged and begged his mother to ask Zeus to punish the Achaeans. Zeus agreed, and the weakened Achaeans were forced back to the very shores of Troy. Even then Achilles refused to help, his pride too injured. Instead, Patroclus saw it as his duty to save the Achaeans. He donned Achilles' armor and pretended to be him, using the legend of Achilles to rally the troops.

The Achaeans, thinking Achilles had rejoined them, took heart and pushed back the Trojans. Unfortunately, the greatest warrior of the Trojans, Prince Hector, also believing Patroclus was the prophesied Achilles, slew him. When Achilles was told his beloved Patroclus was dead, he forgot his anger at Agamemnon and rejoined the war, chasing down Hector, killing him, and desecrating his body. Achilles' mistreatment of Prince Hector's corpse re-angered Apollo, who directed Hector's brother Paris to sneakily shoot an arrow into Achilles' one vulnerability, his heel.

After Achilles died, his ashes and the ashes of his beloved Patroclus were combined in a single golden urn, together for the rest of time.

The Trojan War continued without Achilles, but his triumphs changed the tide of the conflict. Eventually the decisive victory came from Odysseus and the ruse of the giant wooden Trojan Horse. The Greeks won, and Helen was reunited with her husband Menelaus. The Achaeans began the long journey home, but that is another epic entirely.

THE TROJAN WAR, one of the central conflicts in Greek mythology, may be loosely rooted in historical events from the twelfth century B.C. While Homer's *Iliad* and subsequently *The Odyssey*, which describe Odysseus's journey back home from battle, are the most famous surviving account, the epic was originally an oral tradition. It circulated for centuries through poems, plays, and decorative art, many of which still survive. Because of this, there is no single definitive narrative.

The warrior Achilles' own chronicle is equally contradictory. Most sources agree that he was born to King Peleus and Thetis, was taught by Chiron, fought alongside Patroclus during the Trojan War, and died from an arrow fired by Paris. Yet the details shift depending on the storyteller. In some accounts, Achilles is nearly invulnerable, blessed with divine strength; in others, he is an exceptionally skilled but still mortal fighter. In some plays, Achilles and Patroclus are seen to have a deep and loyal friendship; in others, it is common knowledge that they are lovers. Part of this ambiguity may reflect the cultural context, as ancient Greek did not strictly separate heterosexual and homosexual attraction, seeing desire for both genders as ordinary. Even his death resists a single telling. In some versions Paris shoots a poisoned arrow into Achilles' heel on the battlefield; in others, it is a divine arrow in the dark of a temple; still others have Apollo disguising himself as Paris, ensnaring Achilles with an arrow before another blow fells him.

The larger war is equally expansive, filled with hundreds of mortal and divine figures whose interwoven stories often begin generations earlier. These cameos would have been familiar to an ancient Greek audience and been an anticipated part of any retelling.

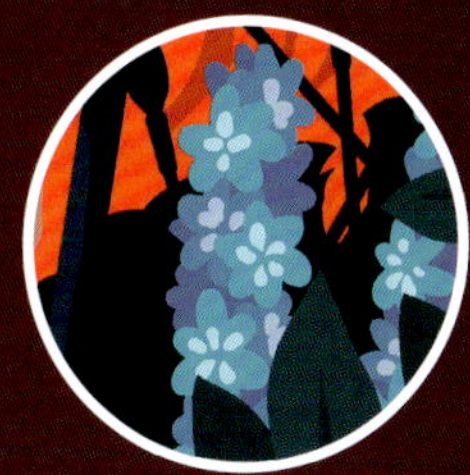

After Achilles died, the Greek warrior Ajax desired his armor, but it was instead given to Odysseus. In his rage, Ajax slaughtered his enemies before falling on his own sword. From his blood sprang delphinium flowers.

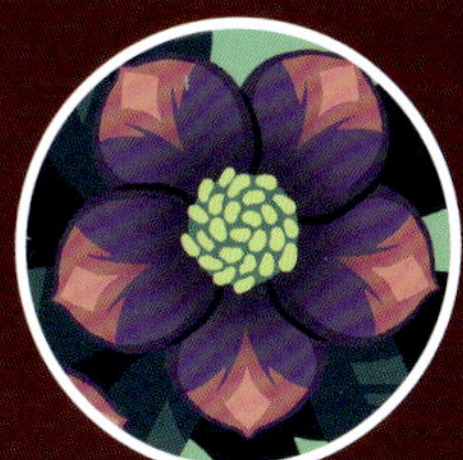

Black hellebore is a toxic plant used by the ancient Greeks for medicine and to poison arrow tips. While not all versions of Paris's story have him using poison to shoot Achilles, he might have used this.

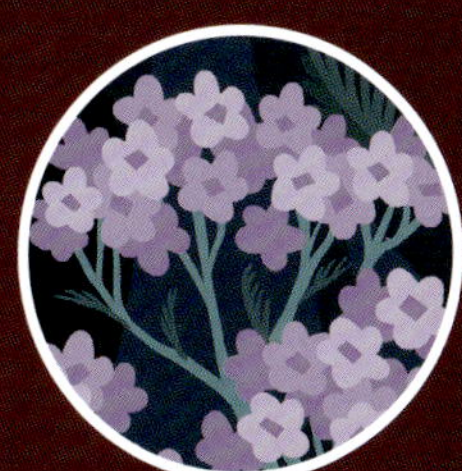

Yarrow, also known as Achillea because Achilles used this plant to help stanch the blood of his companions' wounds. It was also believed that sleeping with it under the pillow would cause one to dream of love.

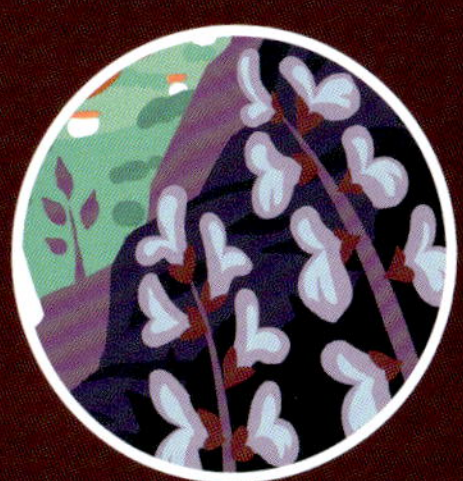

The ancient Greeks believed that sage protected one from evil and conferred wisdom. A symbol of fertility, good health, and a long life, it was consumed as a tea to improve digestion and applied externally to treat venomous snake bites.

Hypericum, or St. John's wort, was used by the ancient Greeks to treat emotional or spiritual turmoil such as melancholy and other nervous conditions. Additionally, it was used to reduce inflammation, bruises, and swelling.

THE SACRED SWORD

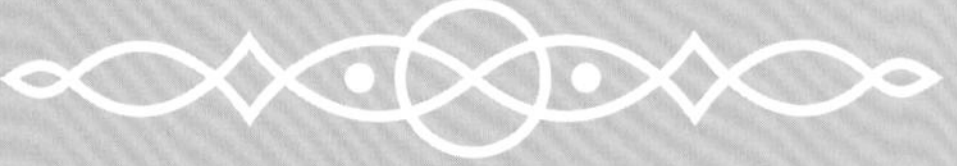

Sacred Swords are divine weapons of power, purpose, and judgment. Whether pulled from stone, forged by gods, or gifted through prophecy, they represent honor, destiny, and resolve. Although often swords, they can also appear as other weaponry such as spears, axes, lightning bolts, or even antlers. Their commonality is not their form but their role as instruments of divine will.

These weapons represent decisive action. Their appearance in a story moves the narrative forward by bestowing upon their wielder the power to unite a fractious people, to pierce the armor of an impenetrable monster, and to cut to the heart of a complex matter.

Sacred Swords are distinct in that they choose their wielder, judging them worthy in heart or purpose. In Arthurian legend, only Arthur is capable of pulling the sword from the stone, proving him the rightful king. In Japanese mythology, the Kusanagi-no-Tsurugi sword is drawn from a slain serpent's tail, becoming one of the imperial regalia and a symbol of heavenly authorized rule. In Shia Islamic tradition, the bifurcated blade Zulfiqar, given to Ali by the Prophet Muhammad, represents divinely sanctioned leadership.

In other instances, these divine blades are used not as mere instruments of violence but as weapons to inflict justice and restore cosmic order. In Hindu mythology, Nandaka, the sword of Vishnu, cuts through the demons of ignorance and chaos to restore knowledge. In Norse mythology, Mjölnir, the hammer of Thor, is used to protect gods and humans, and to beat back the hostile Jötnar giants.

Sacred Swords are legendary weapons that embody divine intent and legitimacy. Wielded by the worthy, they exist not merely to conquer, but also to restore, preserve balance, and dispel darkness.

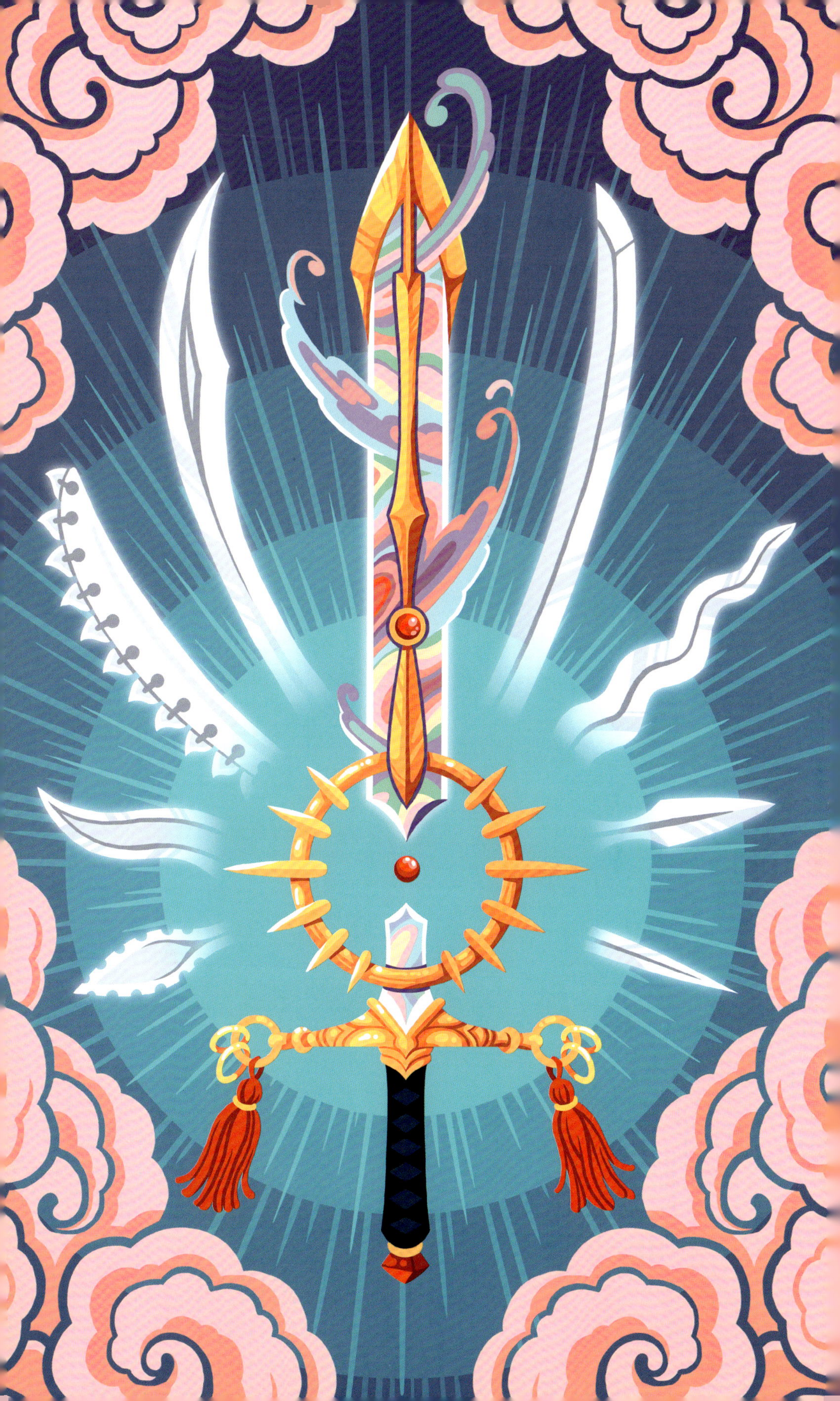

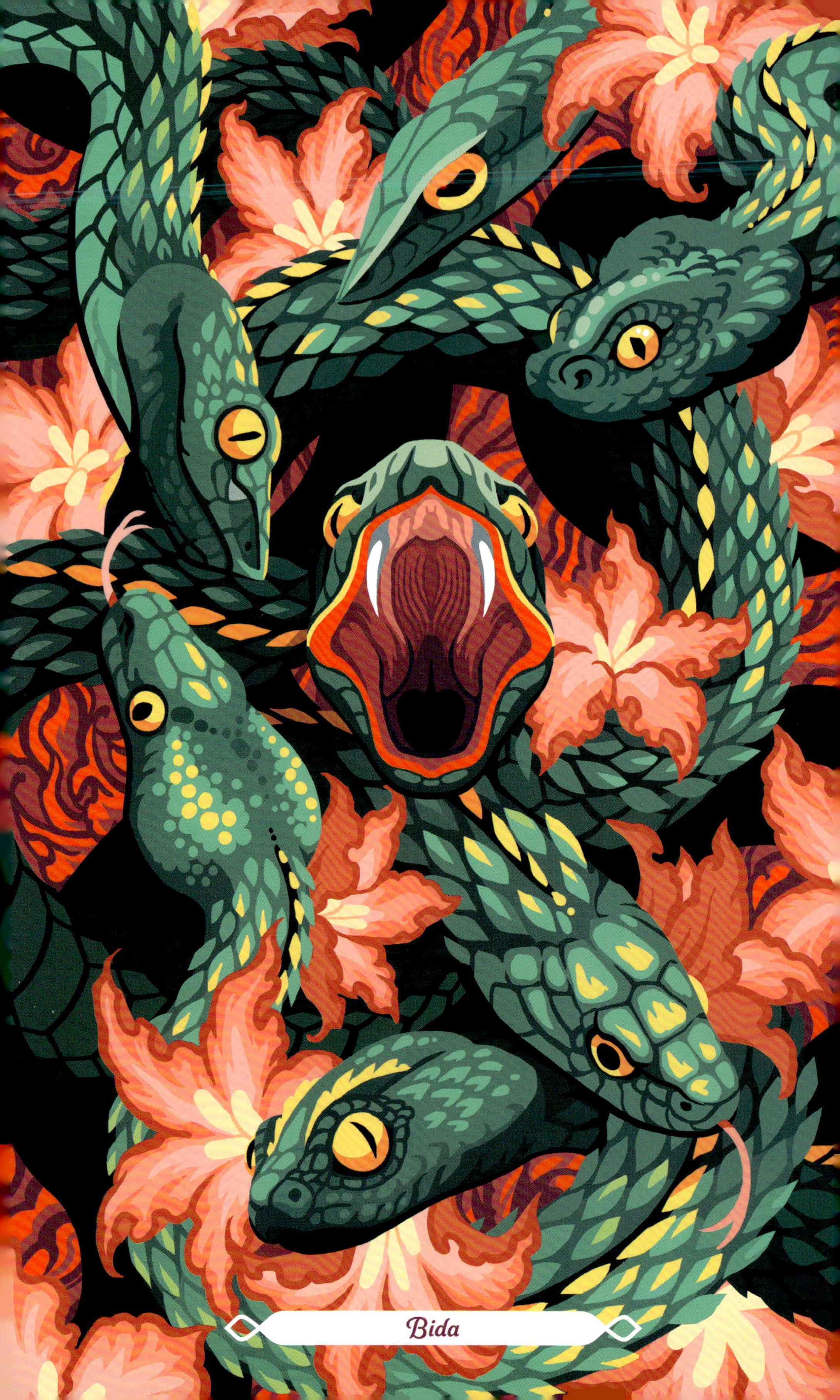
Bida

The Snake OF WAGADU

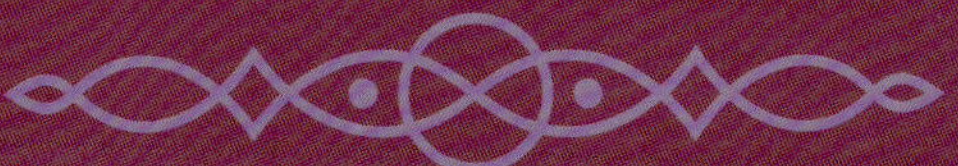

SONINKE MYTHOLOGY | WEST AFRICA

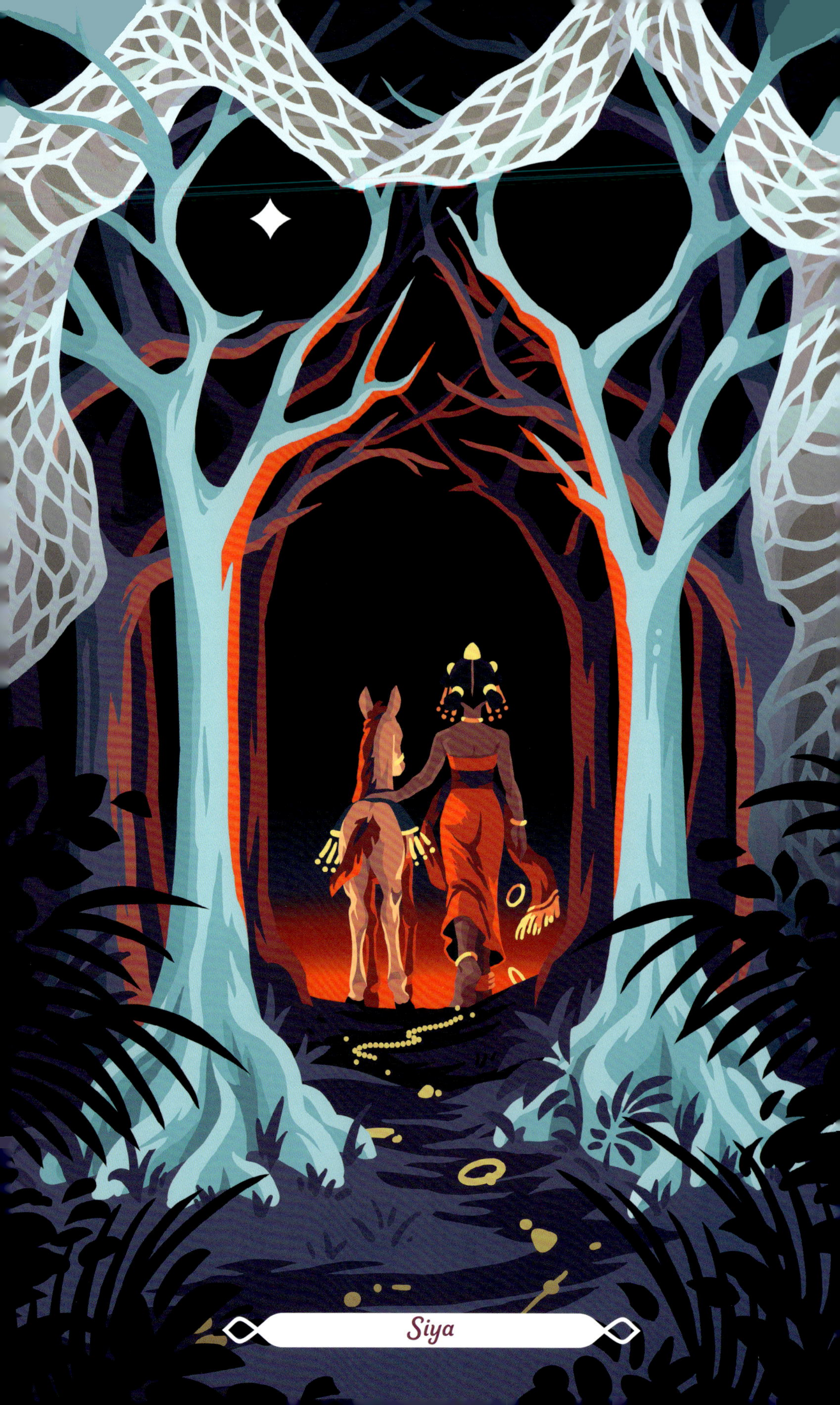
Siya

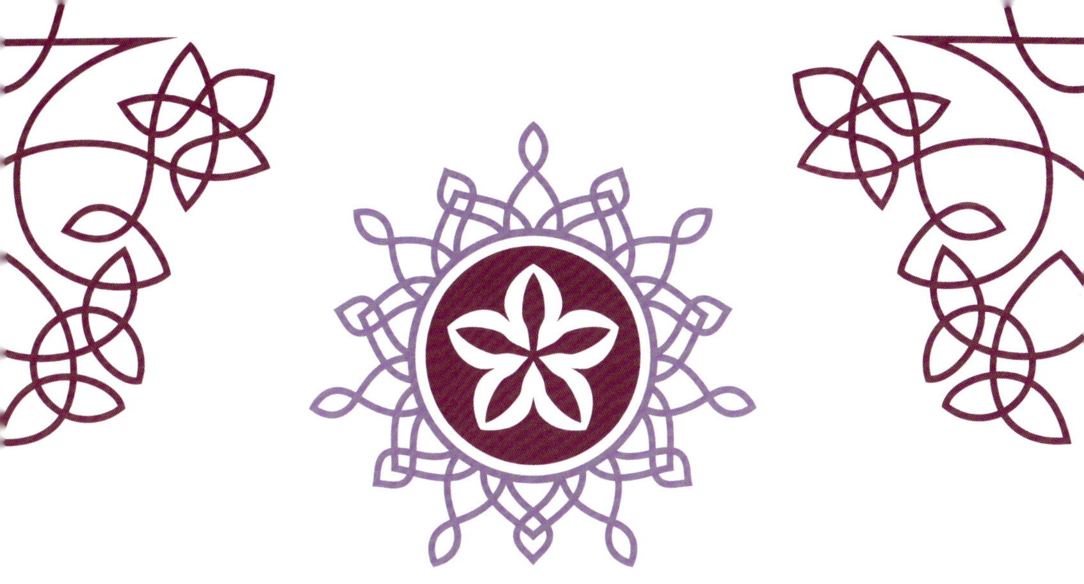

Long ago, the wise leader Dinga Cissé dreamed of a prosperous land for his people. After an arduous search, he discovered a dry well in a barren land. At its bottom lay a seven-headed snake named Bida.

Sensing Dinga Cissé's purpose, Bida spoke and offered him a pact: If Dinga and his descendants would sacrifice a pure maiden and a healthy young foal to the serpent each year, Bida would reward them. He would cause rain to fall, nourish the earth, and draw gold from the ground. Dinga Cissé agreed, and it was from this agreement that the great kingdom of Wagadu was born.

Generations passed, and the kingdom flourished. Wagadu became one of the richest and most powerful empires in the world. Its fields overflowed with crops, its rivers ran clear, and its people wore gold like cloth. But each year, the people upheld their end of the ancient bargain: One maiden and one foal were taken to Bida's well and never returned.

Although the sacrifices were mourned, they were accepted as the price of the kingdom's fortune. Parents wept for their daughters, but the people believed the serpent's blessing was too valuable to lose.

Then came the year when a young woman named Siya Yatabéré was chosen as the purest offering. She was beautiful, kind, and deeply loved—especially by her betrothed, the brilliant warrior and tactician Maadi. Upon hearing of Siya's selection, Maadi was devastated. Siya herself wept—not for her life, but for the life she would never live. Yet, in the end, she accepted her fate, believing her death would repay the sacrifices others had made before her.

Maadi, however, could not. Determined to save her, he went to his mother, the wise and respected Djamere Soukhounou, and told her he planned to kill Bida. Djamere warned him that if the serpent died, so too would Wagadu's blessings. The rains would stop. The gold would vanish. The empire would crumble.

But Maadi had made up his mind. He would rather lose the kingdom than lose Siya.

Seeing his resolve, Djamere gave him her blessing.

Knowing Siya would oppose his plan, Maadi said nothing to her. On the day of the sacrifice, as Siya walked solemnly toward Bida's well with the foal, Maadi followed in secret. When the seven-headed serpent rose from the depths, Maadi leapt from his hiding place and attacked. One by one, he struck down each of Bida's heads with his sword.

As the last head fell, Bida cried out a terrible curse. The serpent condemned Wagadu to drought and famine, its rivers to turn to sand and its gold to turn to dust. The kingdom was cursed to vanish from the earth and be remembered only in sorrow.

Maadi grabbed a shocked Siya's hand and fled. The people, horrified by what had been done, rose in outrage. A furious mob chased the couple through the city, blaming them for dooming the empire.

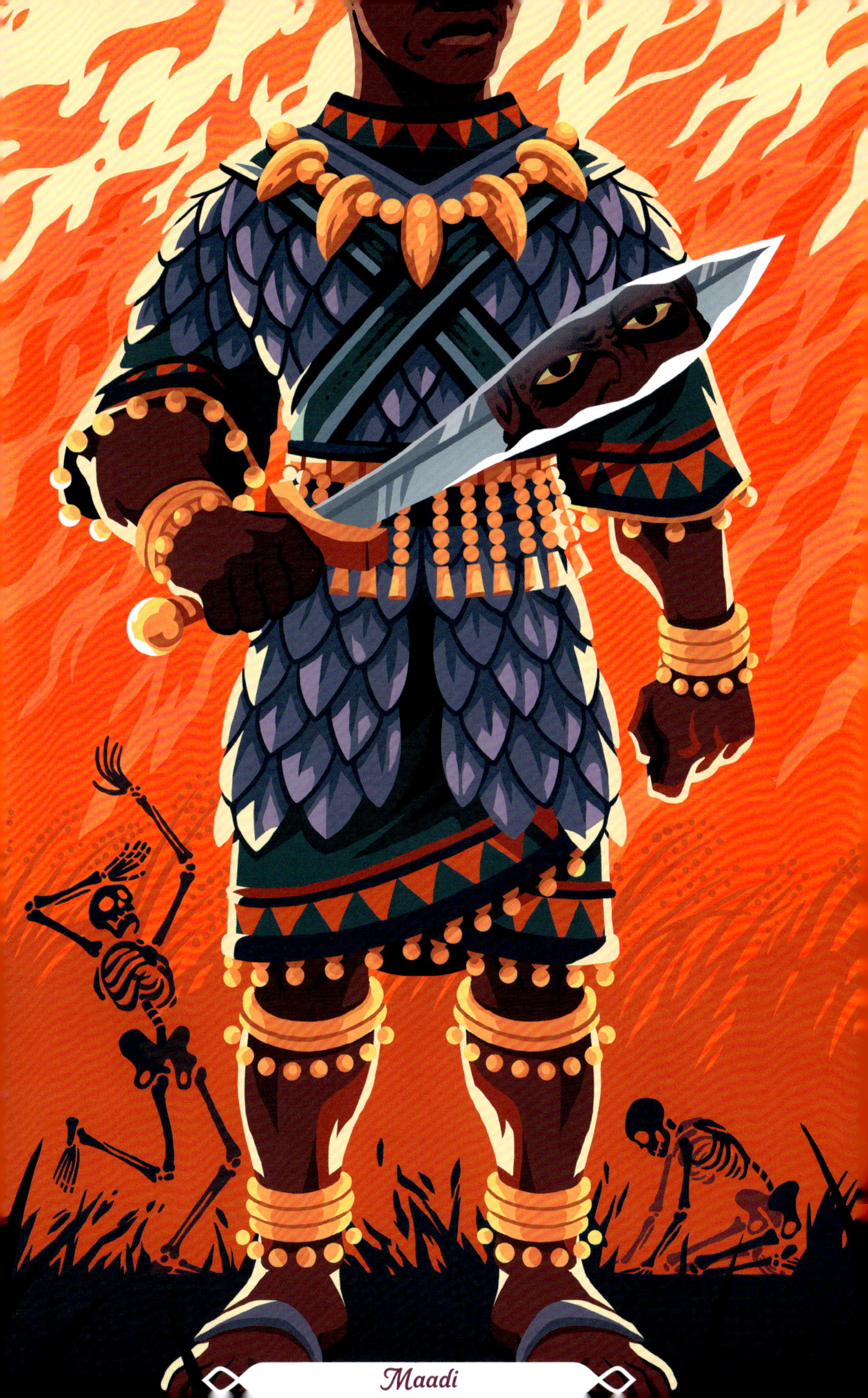
Maadi

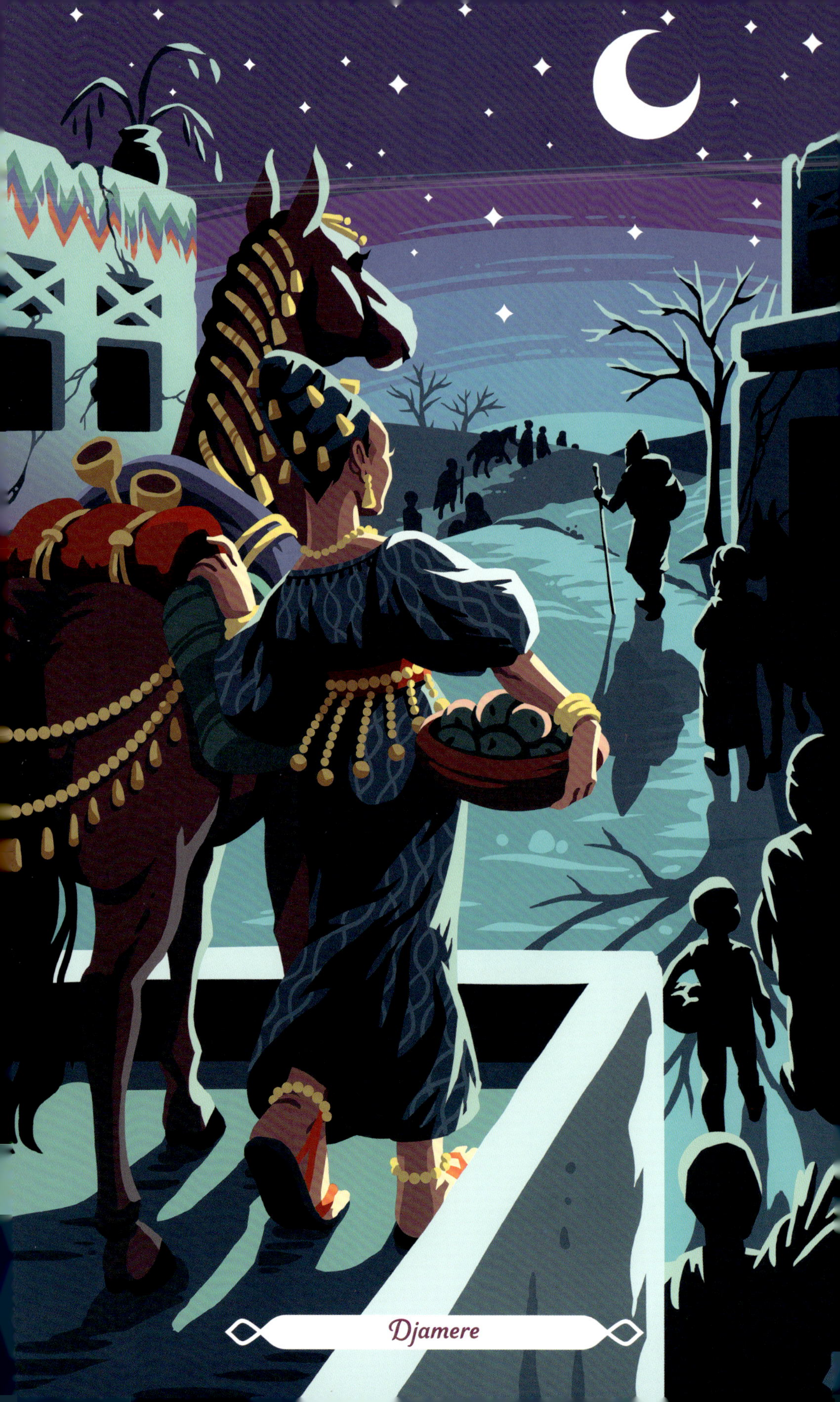
Djamere

The pair ran to the home of Djamere, who sheltered them from the crowd. Then she stepped outside to face the people. Calm and resolute, she took responsibility for her son's actions, knowing what they had cost. She promised to care for and protect all the people of the kingdom.

As the curse took hold, Wagadu withered. The rain stopped falling. The gold mines collapsed. The once proud empire crumbled into dust. Djamere led the people away from the dying land, guiding them in search of a new home.

Wagadu was no more.

But though it vanished from the earth, it was never forgotten. The name of Wagadu lived on in songs, in stories passed from elders to children, and in the hearts of the people scattered far and wide across the land.

As for Siya and Maadi, the storytellers disagree. Some say they escaped and built a new life together, far from the ruins of Wagadu. Others say that Siya, heartbroken by the destruction Maadi had caused, and furious that he did not consult her, never forgave him—and that they never married at all.

But all agree on this: The death of Bida ended an era, and with it, the golden age of Wagadu.

THE LEGEND OF WAGADU and the snake Bida is central to the cultural heritage of the Soninke people, the original inhabitants of the ancient Ghana Empire, also known as Wagadu. More than just a myth, the story serves as an allegory for the rise, wealth, and eventual fall of one of West Africa's most influential empires.

The Ghana Empire flourished between the sixth and thirteenth centuries, centered in what is now southeastern Mauritania and western Mali. Renowned for its vast gold reserves, intricate trade networks, and powerful rulers, it controlled the flow of gold and salt across the Sahara. Arab scholars such as Al-Bakri described a city so rich that gold adorned the royal court and even the dogs wore golden collars.

The tale of Bida, the seven-headed serpent who demanded annual sacrifices in exchange for rain and gold, symbolically explains this golden age. The story reflects an understanding of spiritual reciprocity—that prosperity comes with a cost, often in the form of communal sacrifice. The eventual killing of Bida by Maadi, out of love for Siya Yatabéré, is a turning point that results in drought and ruin, mirroring the historical decline of the Ghana Empire due to changing trade routes, internal strife, and external pressures such as the Almoravid invasions.

For the Soninke people, the legend is a unifying myth preserving their collective memory. It explains past greatness while offering moral lessons about duty, loyalty, resilience, and the dangers of disrupting sacred order. Civilizations built on morally questionable foundations are fragile, and prosperity without justice is temporary.

Although Wagadu vanished, the legend remains alive in books, movies, and oral tradition.

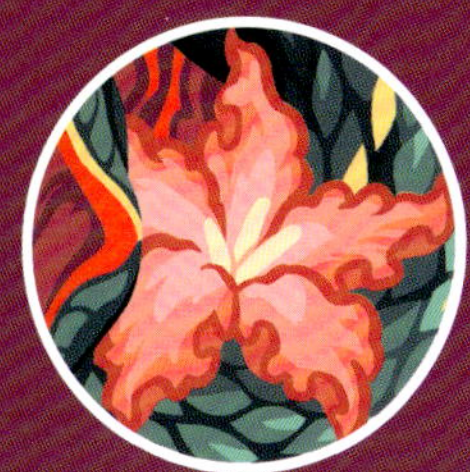

The impala lily is a small, succulent tree whose bark and fleshy parts of the trunk are used to make poison to catch fish, tip arrows, and inflict magical harm.

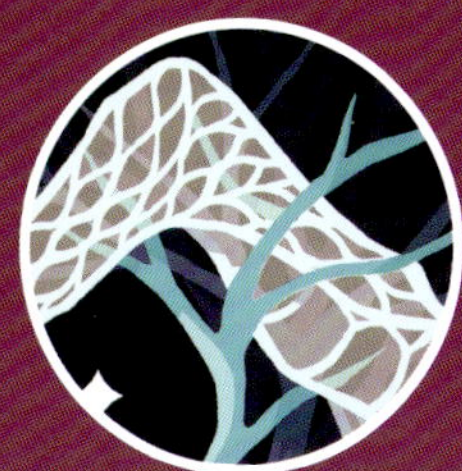

A shed snakeskin symbolizes transformation and leaving an old life behind. In this way, snakes represent immortality and healing.

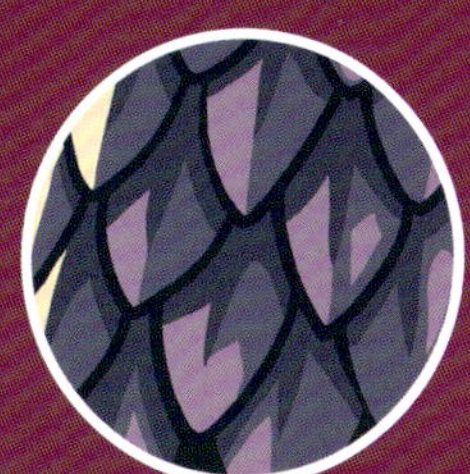

While no examples of Wagadu armor remain, art from the Benin Empire, which overlapped in time with the Wagadu Empire, depicts scaled armor resembling pangolin hides, potentially made of tanned hide or bronze.

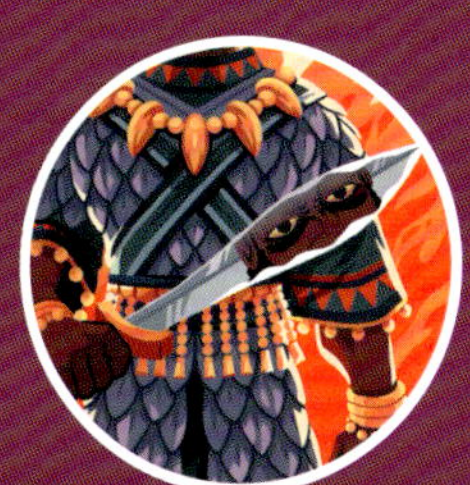

The Wagadu Empire was renowned for its mastery of ironworking, with its warriors wielding powerful iron swords. The shape of the swords is unknown but may have resembled the leaf-shaped Yoruba swords.

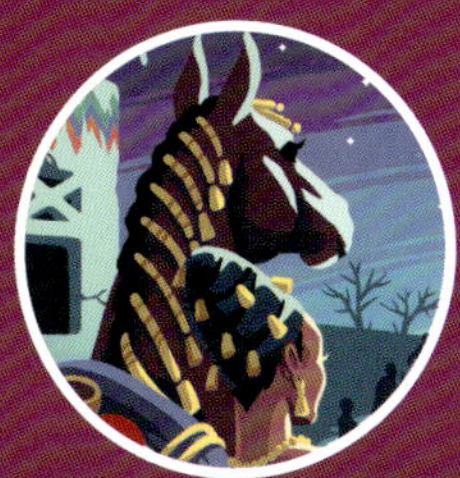

According to the eleventh-century Andalusian Muslim historian and geographer Al-Bakri, the empire of Wagadu was so wealthy that even their horses were covered with gold.

THE FORBIDDEN

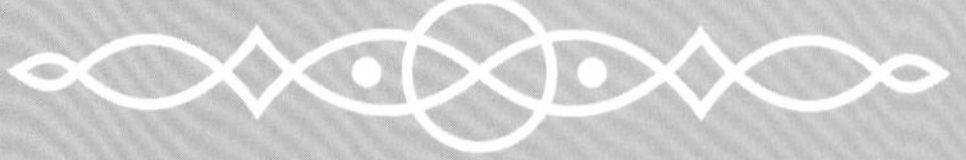

The Forbidden is an object, place, or action that must not be touched, opened, or known—often under dire warning. In stories and myth, the Forbidden sets boundaries of perceived safety, and crossing these lines leaves the hero without protection against the dangers of the world. While these tales caution against temptation, they also represent the naïveté of complacency and the insight that comes from the consequence of disobedience, suggesting that some knowledge comes only through loss. These stories are about curiosity and the deeply human urge to know.

Often this theme marks a rite of passage, representing the shift from childhood innocence to adult worldliness. In the Greek myth of Pandora, Pandora opens the forbidden box, unleashing suffering, evil, and misfortune into the world—a metaphor for the awakening of consciousness and the difficult truths that come with maturity. In the Norse-influenced fairy tale *The White Bear King Valemon,* the heroine is forbidden to look upon her husband. When she does, he vanishes, and she must undergo a long, painful quest to regain him. Her life before her transgression was sweet, but it was based in ignorance and deception. Disobedience is necessary for her to gain her own agency and power.

Sometimes, the Forbidden symbolizes taboo and the loss of control that comes from breaking the rules. In the Japanese tale *Urashima Tarō*, the hero is given a magical box and told never to open it. When he does, he instantly ages centuries, losing his place in the world. In the Italian story *Sleeping Beauty,* simply pricking a forbidden spindle causes the princess to fall into a cursed sleep—a passive, irreversible consequence of disobedience.

Ultimately, the Forbidden explores the high cost of venturing into the unknown—whether for love, knowledge, or truth—and the transformation, tragic or necessary, that follows.

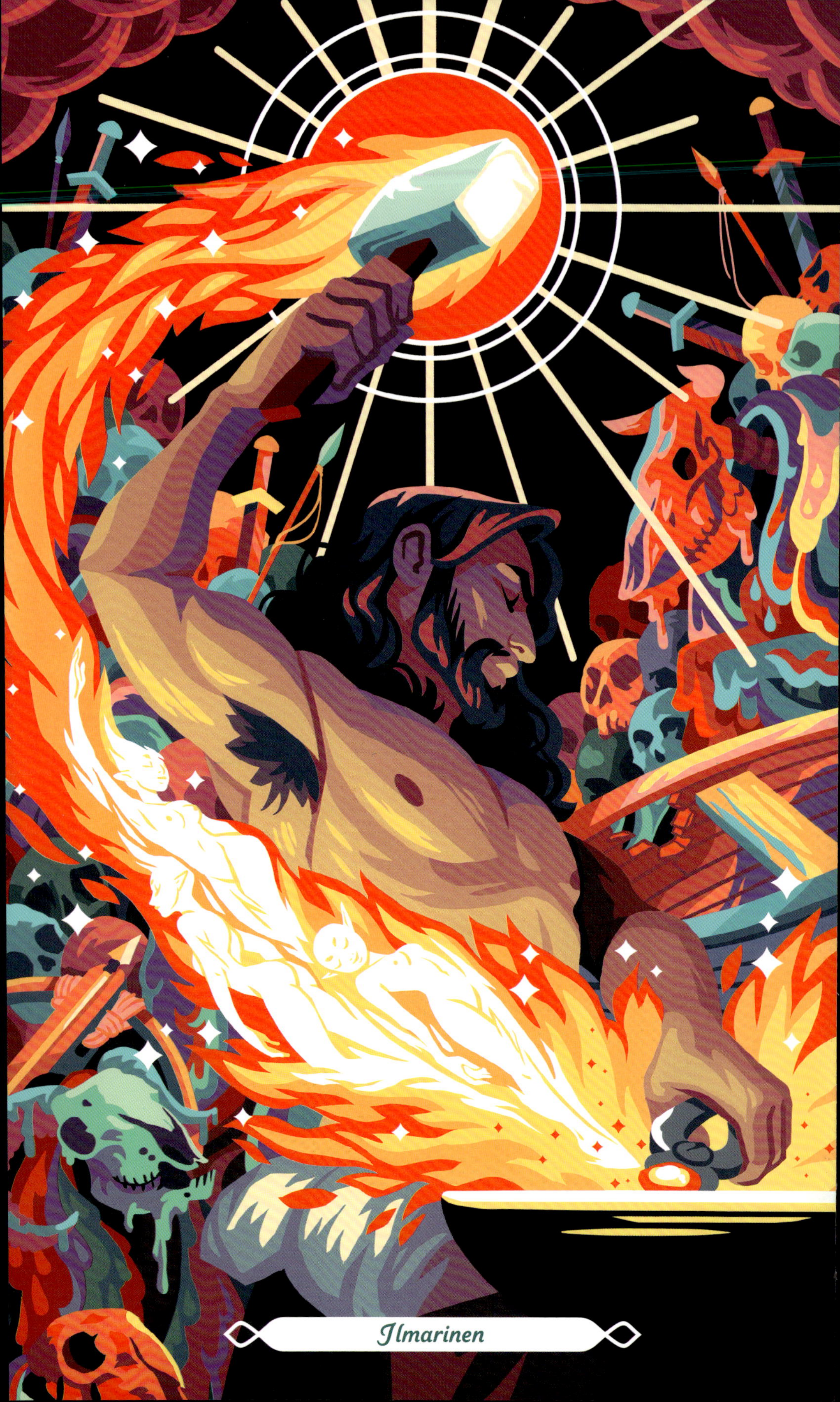
Ilmarinen

KALEVALA

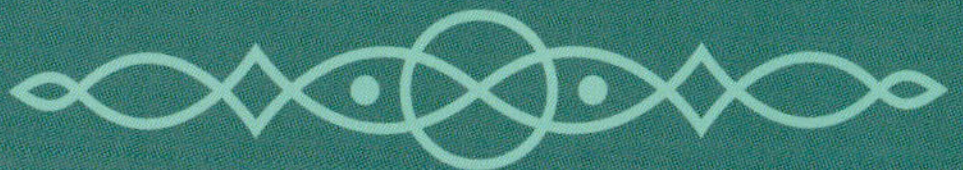

KARELIAN AND FINNISH MYTHOLOGY | FINLAND

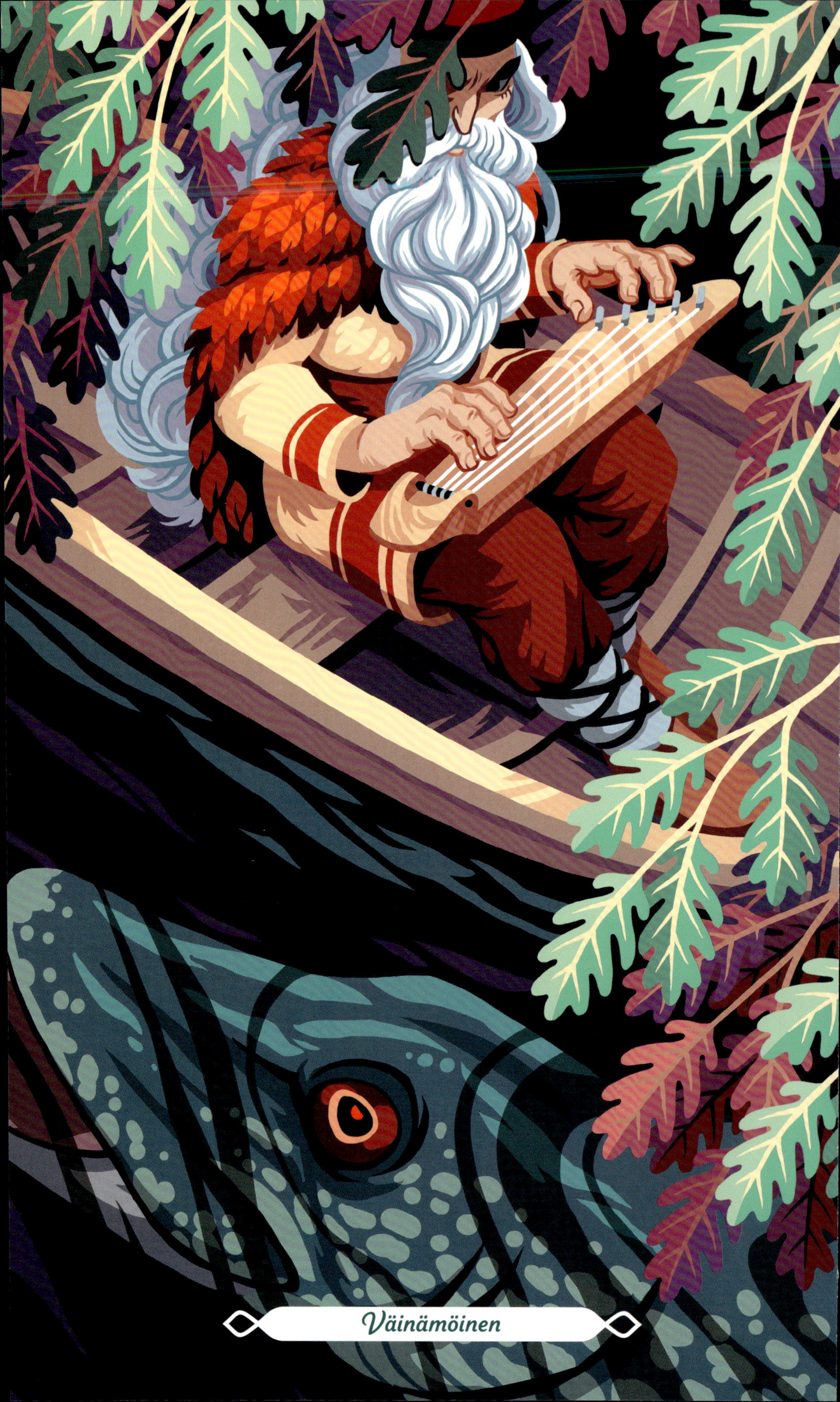
Väinämöinen

Far to the north lay the freezing land of Pohjola, where its wicked mistress Louhi had two beautiful daughters. The eldest she pledged to whoever could bring her the Sampo, a magical object capable of generating endless wealth and prosperity.

In the southern land of Kalevala lived Väinämöinen, an immortal magician who had been born old but never married, who longed to have Louhi's daughter as his wife. Unfortunately, although he was rich, strong in magic, and wise in song, the Sampo did not yet exist, and he was incapable of making it. Instead, he used his clever wiles and tricked his neighbor the poor blacksmith Ilmarinen into creating the Sampo by promising him Louhi's daughter while intending to steal credit for himself. Ilmarinen, young and hale, was also unmarried. When he saw Louhi's eldest daughter, he became smitten and agreed to attempt to make the Sampo.

Ilmarinen forged wondrous creations—a crossbow, ship, heifer, and plough—but each proved ill-mannered, bloodthirsty, and destructive. Disappointed, he melted them all back into scraps, seeking something true and good from his forge.

Finally, Ilmarinen began to forge a bright lid and a cauldron-shaped object and knew his work was good. When completed, the Sampo was a corn mill on one side, a salt mill on another, and a money mill on the third. By twilight, it had ground a full bin of corn to eat, a bin of salt to sell, and a bin of money to store at home.

Väinämöinen brought Ilmarinen to Louhi, and they presented her the finished Sampo. Extremely pleased with the result, the mistress of Pohjola took the Sampo and bade her daughter marry Väinämöinen. But the daughter refused to marry the old and ugly magician, regardless of his riches. Instead, she wanted to marry the handsome and youthful Ilmarinen, despite the fact that he was poor.

Louhi was displeased by her daughter's choice of the soot-smeared Ilmarinen. She challenged the smith to three impossible tasks to try to dissuade him. First, he must plough a field of serpents; second, bind legendary beasts; and third, catch the Pike of Tuonela without a net. Armed with enchanted tools and secretly guided by the daughter's whispered advice, Ilmarinen triumphed, shaping miracles from silver, steel, and fire.

Louhi finally conceded and threw a loud and lavish wedding for the couple. Väinämöinen bitterly admitted defeat, realizing wealth could not compete with youth and vigor.

Ilmarinen returned south to his homeland of Kalevala with his wife, and they lived happily for a time. But unfortunately, she tried to trick the wrong farmhand and was mauled to death by bears soon after. Ilmarinen was devastated, weeping endlessly day and night. In his grief, he attempted to make himself a new perfect wife out of the most beautiful metals in the world: silver and gold. In his first two forgings, he made a golden ewe and then a golden horse. Although delightful, they were not a wife, and he pushed them back into the forge. On his third attempt, Ilmarinen hammered

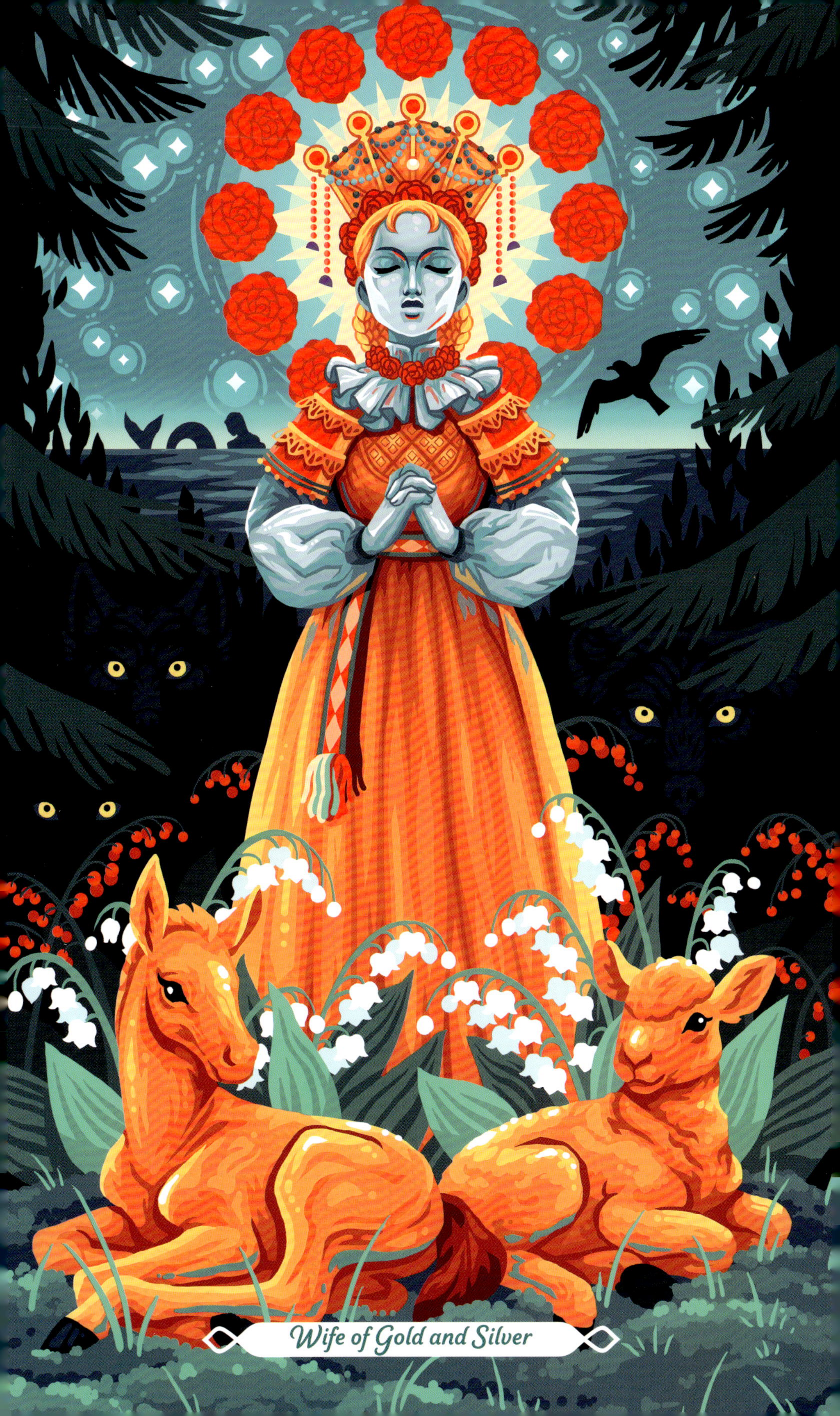
Wife of Gold and Silver

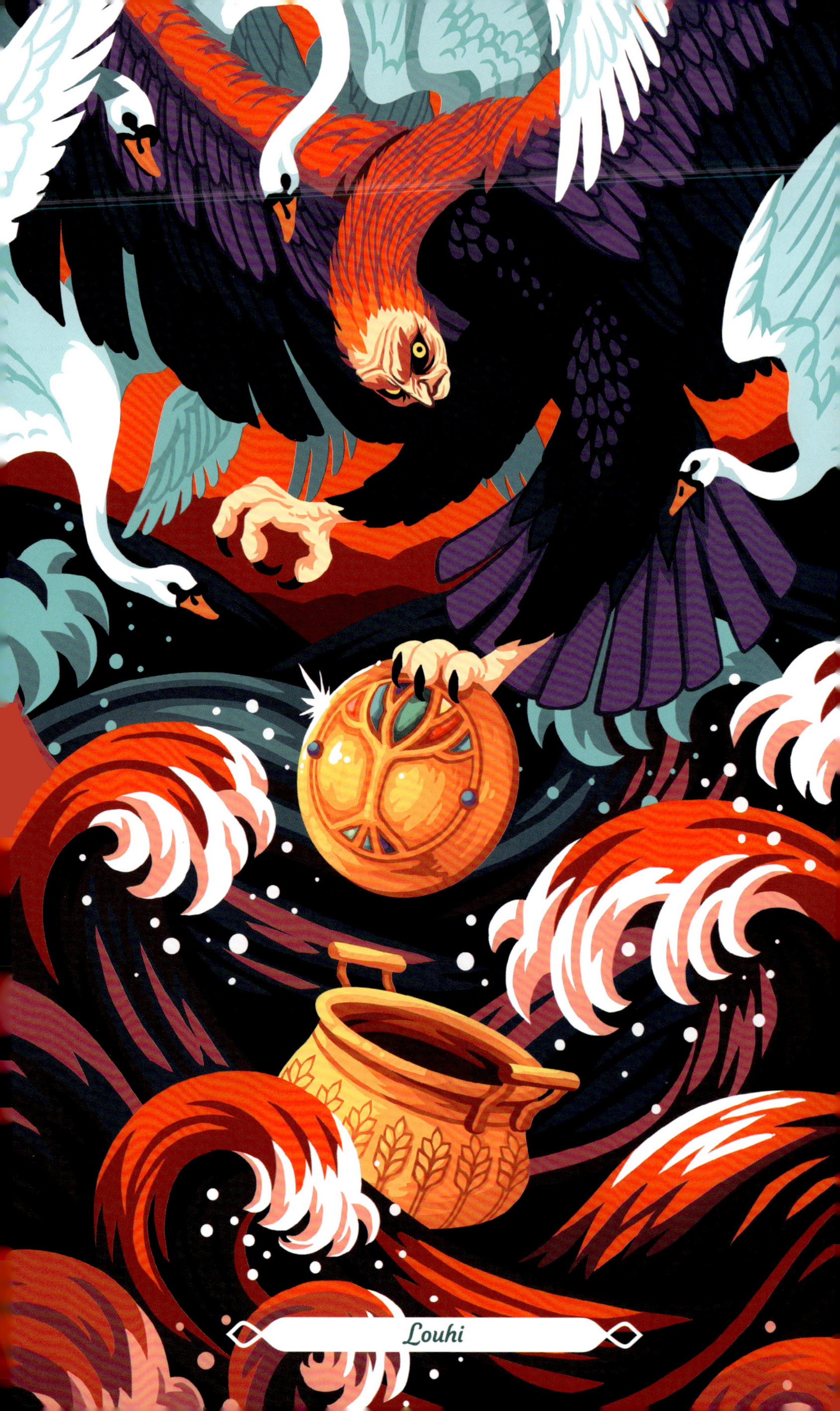
Louhi

a maid of silver skin and golden curls. Although she was beautiful perfection, she could not talk, she could not listen, and she could not see. She had no will and was cold to the touch. Disturbed, Ilmarinen cast her from his house.

Still wishing to remarry, Ilmarinen traveled back to Pohjola. The northern land had changed since Ilmarinen had last been there. Although still cold, the endless riches of the Sampo had turned Pohjola into a thriving land full of growing fields and bountiful good luck. He journeyed up to Louhi's doorstep and proposed to her younger daughter. The daughter was dismayed to learn of the death of her older sister. She outright refused to marry the husband who could not protect her, peppering her rejection with a variety of insults. Ilmarinen returned to Kalevala without a wife, but with a new desire to possess the prosperity of the Sampo.

Ilmarinen told Väinämöinen of the bounty the Sampo was delivering to Pohjola, and the two plotted how to gain this largess for their own southern country. The pair soon returned to the north with an army of ships and demanded Louhi give Kalevala half of the Sampo's yield, or they would take the Sampo itself by force. Louhi refused their demands, and Väinämöinen played a song on his kantele that put all of Pohjola to sleep. The invading army grabbed the Sampo and began to sail their boats back to Kalevala.

When Ilmarinen and Väinämöinen were only partway home, Louhi woke up. She summoned a terrible storm, transformed into a giant eagle, and tried to retrieve the Sampo. Unfortunately, in the chaos, she was only able to grab the lid of the Sampo, and the main part sank beneath the waves, never to be seen from again. The life of endless ease was lost forever.

IN 1849, FINNISH PHYSICIAN Elias Lönnrot published the *New Kalevala*, an expanded and revised edition of his earlier 1835 *Old Kalevala*, which he promoted as the national epic of Finland. This compilation of Finnish folklore, rooted in centuries of oral tradition, played a crucial role in cultivating a distinct national identity in a country long dominated by Swedish, and later Russian, rule since the 1200s. By highlighting a culture that was both unique and independent, the *Kalevala* became a cultural touchstone, helping lay the foundation for Finnish national pride and, ultimately, contributing to Finland's Declaration of Independence in 1917.

Before Lönnrot, there was no unified epic or structured pantheon of Finnish gods. Instead, the tradition consisted of *runoja*—runic songs sung by ordinary people and shared across generations through family, neighbors, and traveling singers. These oral poems ranged from heroic tales of characters like Väinämöinen and Ilmarinen to practical charms, lullabies, and personal laments. By the early nineteenth century, the practice was fading, prompting Lönnrot to make eleven field trips to rural villages to record and preserve this cultural heritage.

He later stitched these individual pieces into a single epic, the *Kalevala*. Some of the material dates back thousands of years, while other parts were edited, modernized, or invented by Lönnrot himself to create a cohesive narrative, often modeled on epics like the *Iliad*, *Ramayana*, or *Beowulf*. His revisions included reshaping mythic figures—demoting some deities and elevating others—such as recasting Väinämöinen from deity to superhuman sage. Fortunately, Lönnrot's notes survive, allowing scholars to trace his changes alongside the original source material.

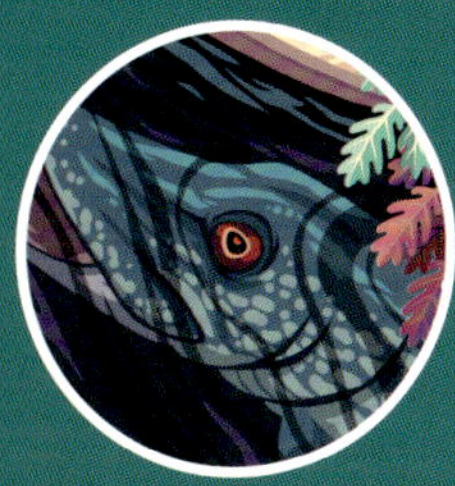

While on his many adventures, Väinämöinen slew a monstrous pike fish and used its jawbone to make the first kantele—an instrument whose music is so fine, even the gods are charmed.

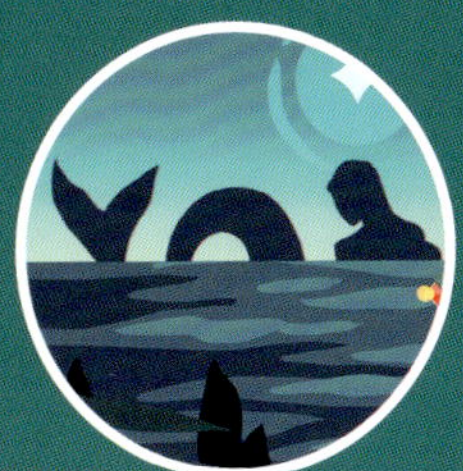

Väinämöinen wishes to wed a girl named Aino, but she refuses him, choosing instead to throw herself into the water. When he later catches a mermaid, he doesn't recognize the transformed Aino and releases her.

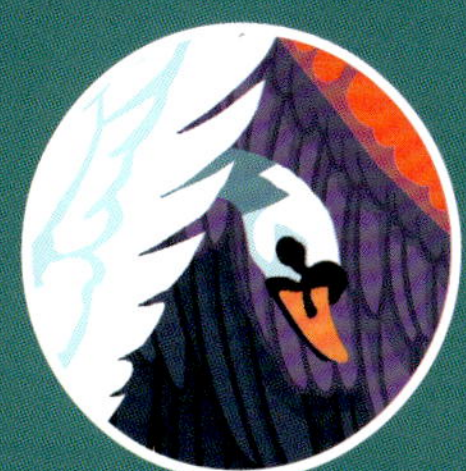

The hero Lemminkäinen is tasked with the impossible: killing the Swan of Tuonela. Before he succeeds, he is killed and dismembered, symbolizing the sacred and untouchable.

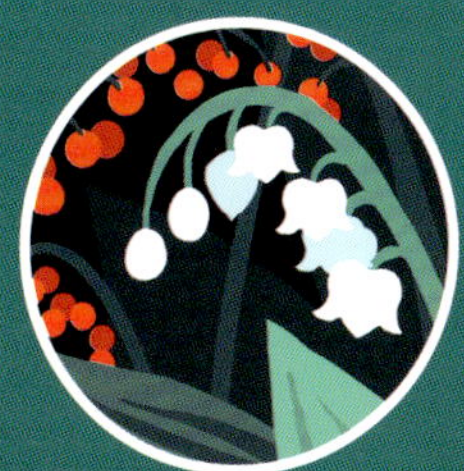

Lily-of-the-valley, with its sweet bell-like blossoms, is Finland's national flower. However, its red summer berries are poisonous.

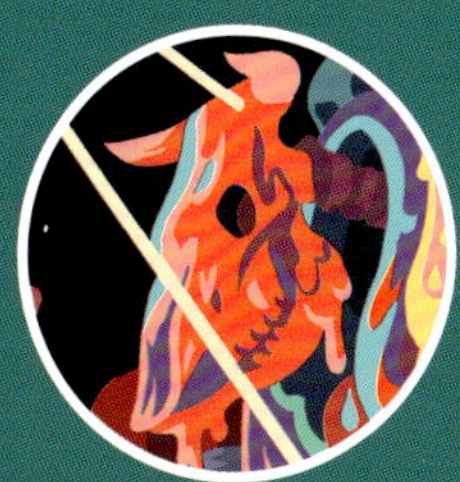

Before forging the Sampo, Ilmarinen makes numerous imbalanced creations that ultimately fail. One example is the metal heifer that refuses to stand and be milked.

THE WORLD TREE

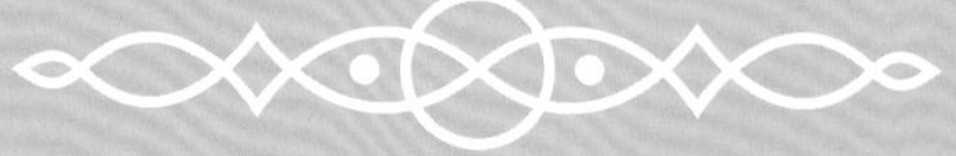

The World Tree is an ancient living pillar that holds together the structure of the universe. It is the mythic axis around which everything spins, the focal point and center of the world.

With its branches in heaven, its trunk in the mortal realms, and its roots among the underworld, the World Tree acts as a cosmic bridge that channels energy, spirit, and time. It links the divine to the mortal, life to death, spiritual to mundane. To climb the World Tree is to journey between death and rebirth, ignorance and illumination. It represents order amidst chaos, endurance through cycles, and the continuity of life. Simultaneously, it reflects the interconnectedness of all things. What happens in one realm affects all others.

In Norse myth, Yggdrasil holds the nine worlds in its vast limbs. In Chinese cosmology, Jianmu connects the Earth to the heavens and serves as a divine passage. The Aśvattha of the Hindu tradition is reversed, the roots of the tree originating in the heavens with the branches in the material world. This reminds enlightenment seekers that spiritual insight requires turning perception upside down. In Mayan mythology, Yaxche is a ceiba tree placed at the center of the world, with four more trees—in the colors red for blood, black for death, yellow for maize, and white for purity—placed at each of the world's four edges. In Finnish mythology, Taivaanpylväs is not a tree but a pillar that stands in the far north holding up the dome of the heavens that rotates on the nail of the sky.

The World Tree is a constant within a shifting universe, offering wisdom to those who seek it and a foundation when the world seems unstable. It offers orientation and serves as a reminder that all things are connected, above and below, within and beyond.

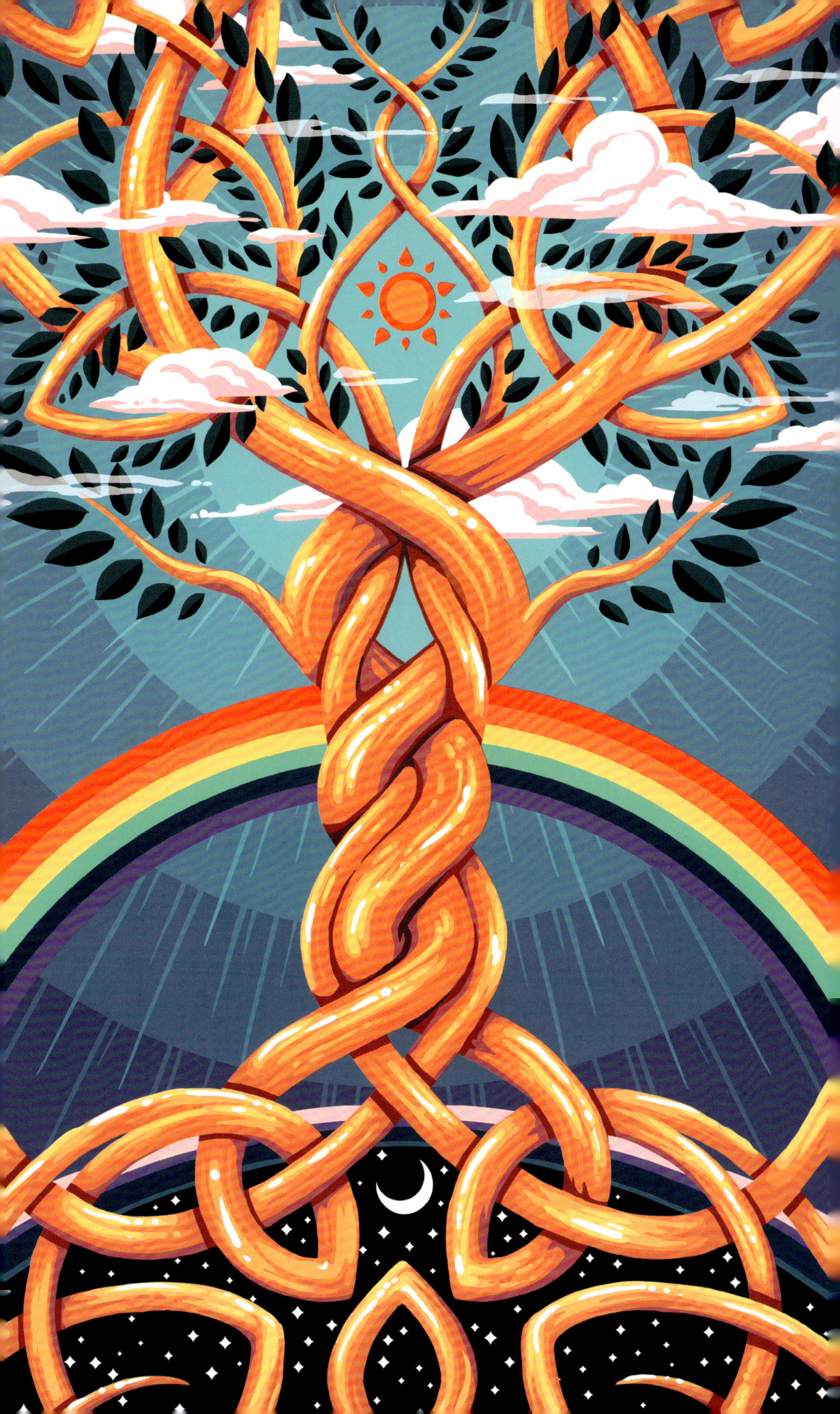

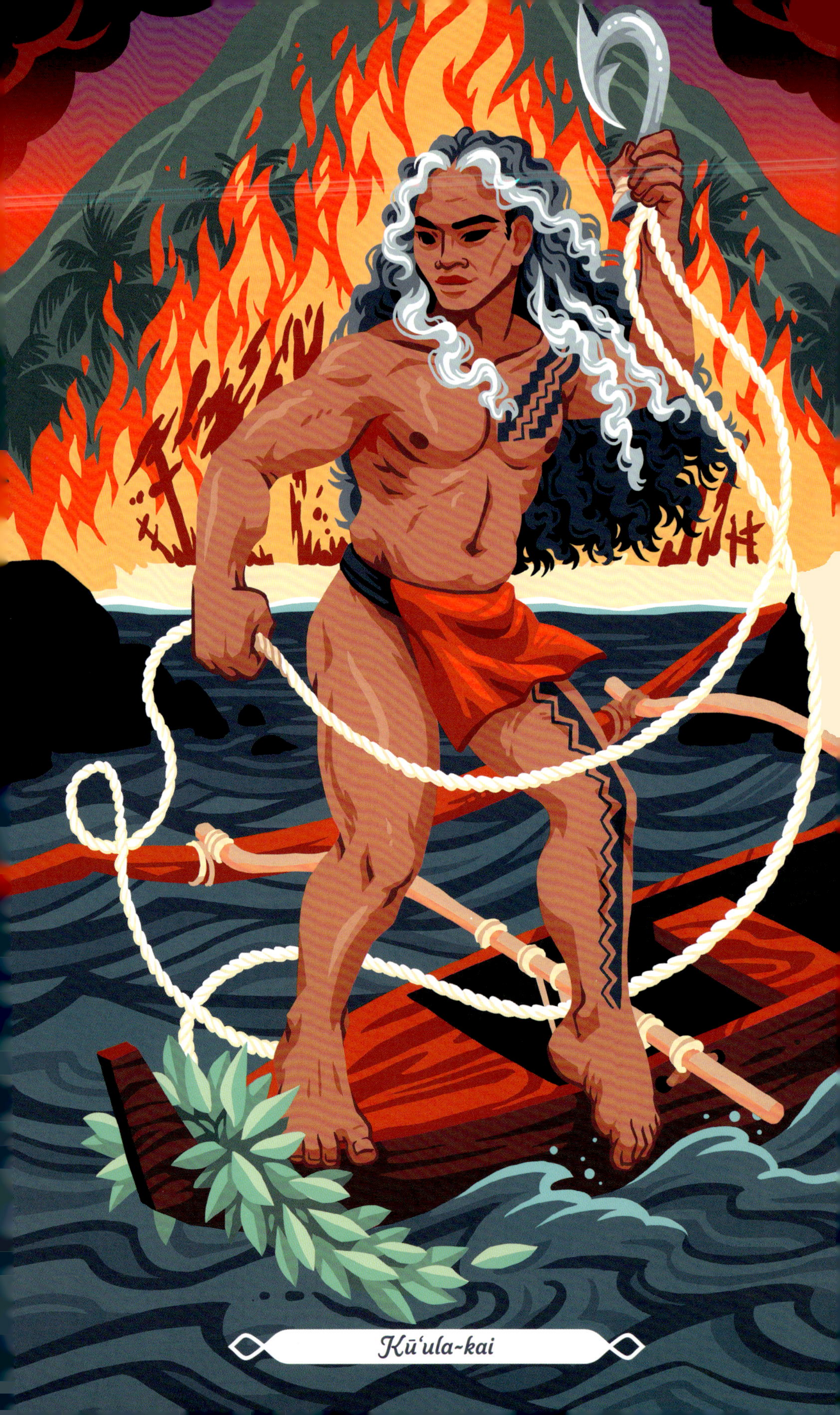
Kūʻula-kai

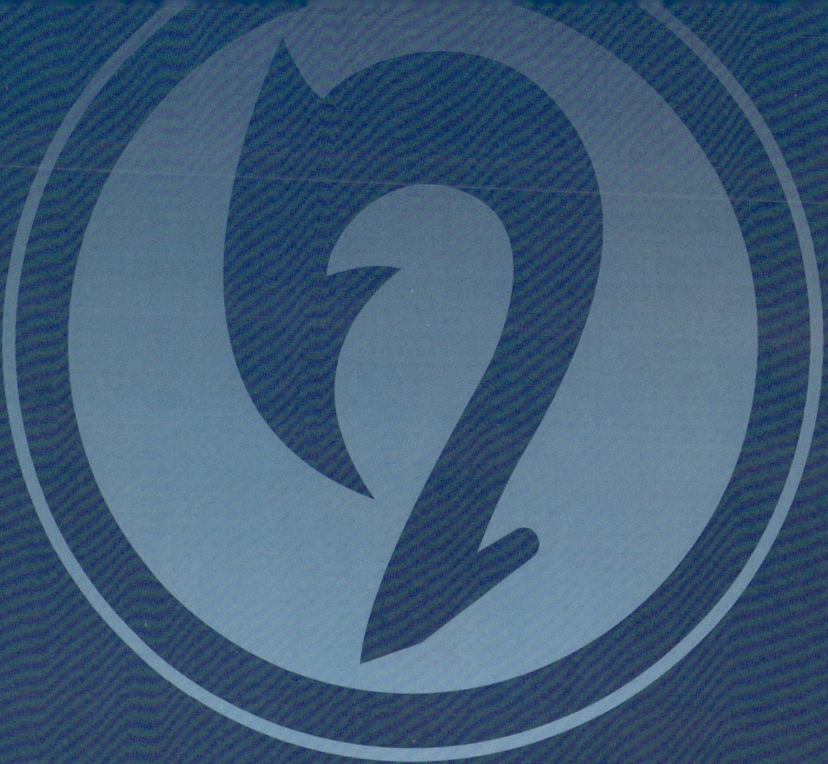

KŪ'ULA-KAI

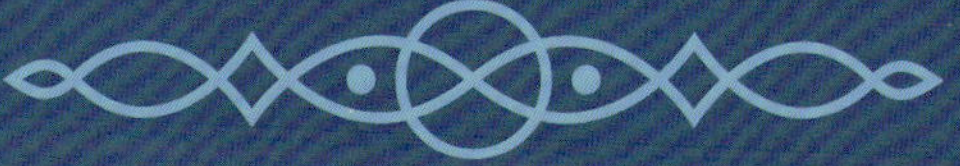

HAWAIIAN MYTHOLOGY | HAWAI'I

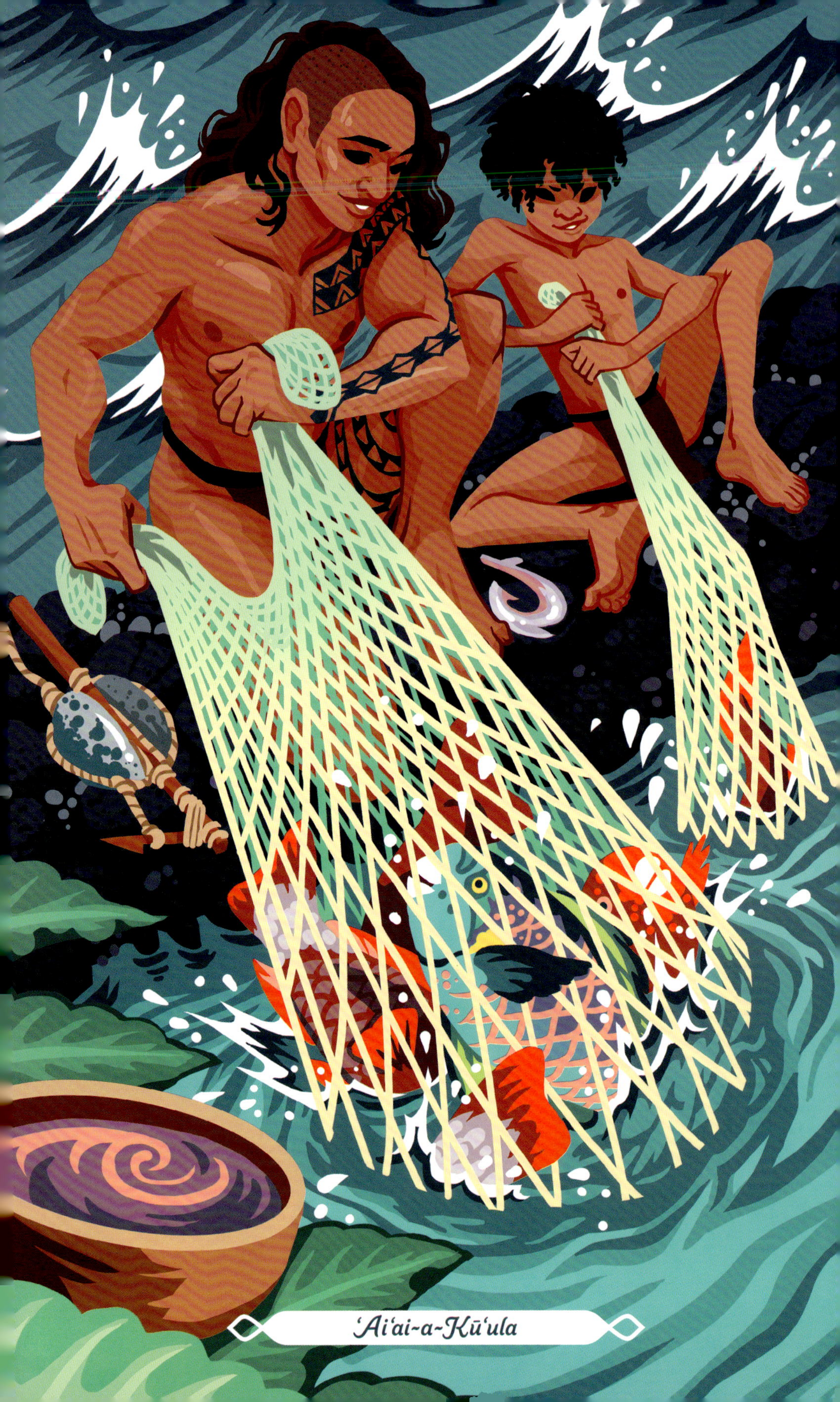
ʻAiʻai-a-Kūʻula

Many ages ago, the god Kū‘ula-kai lived as a human on the Hawaiian island of Maui with his wife, Hina-puku-i‘a. Although he was mortal, Kū‘ula possessed mana kupua, or supernatural powers, and could control the fish of the sea.

Kamohoali‘i, the *ali‘i* (chief) of the island of Maui, heard of Kū‘ula's skill and appointed him as head fisherman for the whole island. Kū‘ula agreed and set about creating the first aquaculture farming fishpond. He surrounded a shallow reef with lava rock walls twenty feet thick and ten feet high and broke it up with a narrow canal that lead to the sea. In the canal, he placed a grate made of wood and ferns that allowed small fish to enter and prevented larger mature fish from leaving. He then used his power to summon all sorts of fish to stock the pond, continuing to nurture, feed, and breed them.

In this way the island thrived, and the ali‘i's table was always overflowing with delicious and rare fish. For many years, Kū‘ula and Kamohoali‘i lived in harmony, and during this peace, Kū‘ula's wife Hina gave birth to their son, whom they named ‘Ai‘ai-a-Kū‘ula.

This tranquility was broken when one day Kūʻula came to his fishpond and found the wall shattered and half his fish eaten. Dismayed, he watched over the pond day and night until he finally spotted the culprit: the giant eel Ko'ona, returning to pilfer more fish. Normally the eel lived off the island of Molokaʻi and was worshipped there as a mighty shark-killing god. Unfortunately, Ko'ona had found the easy meal Kūʻula's fishpond provided and relocated to be closer to the feast. Kūʻula watched as the eel once again broke the walls and gluttonously gorged himself on the fish before returning to his nearby den to sleep off his meal.

Quickly, Kūʻula devised a way to catch and kill the thieving eel. He summoned the people throughout Maui to make two ropes of tree bark hundreds of feet long. He attached both ropes to a large fishhook called Mānai-a-ka-lani and gave the other end of each rope to the people on the shore. Then Kūʻula went out in a canoe to where Ko'ona rested. He dove deep to where the eel lay and hooked his mouth with Mānai-a-ka-lani. With this done, he gave the ropes several quick jerks, signaling to the people that it was time to pull.

And pull they did. It took the effort of the whole island to drag the monstrous eel onto the beach, but they finally succeeded. The island cheered Kūʻula's victory, and that night—and for many more days—they feasted on delicious eel meat and helped repair the fishpond.

While the people of Maui were happy, the people of Molokaʻi were furious and sought revenge on Kūʻula for the death of Ko'ona. A man from Molokaʻi infiltrated Kamohoaliʻi's court and slowly gained the aliʻi's trust. Once that was done, he began telling lies about Kūʻula, making Kamohoaliʻi believe the fisherman was plotting his ruin. Enraged, Kamohoaliʻi ordered Kūʻula and his whole family burned alive in their house.

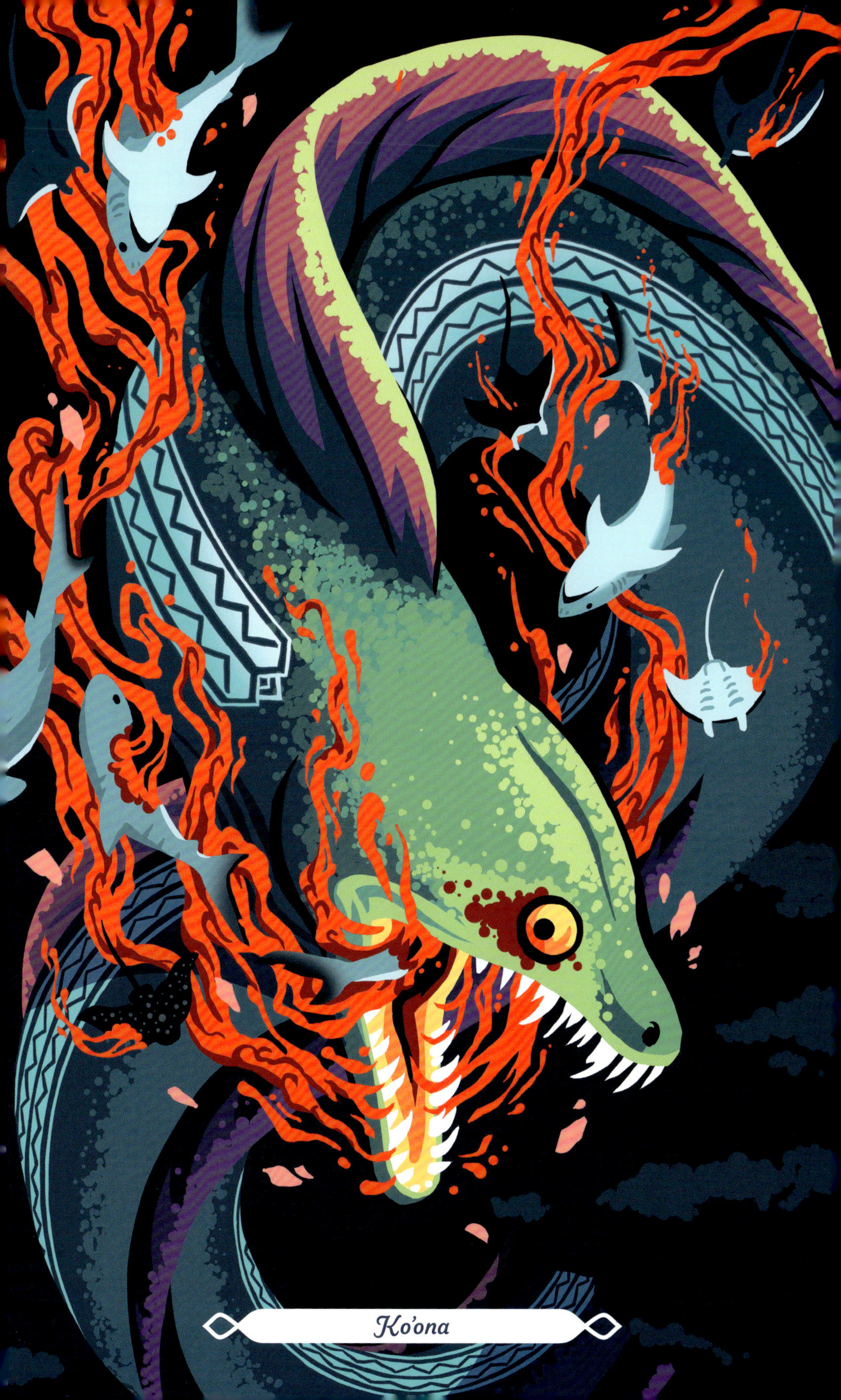
Ko'ona

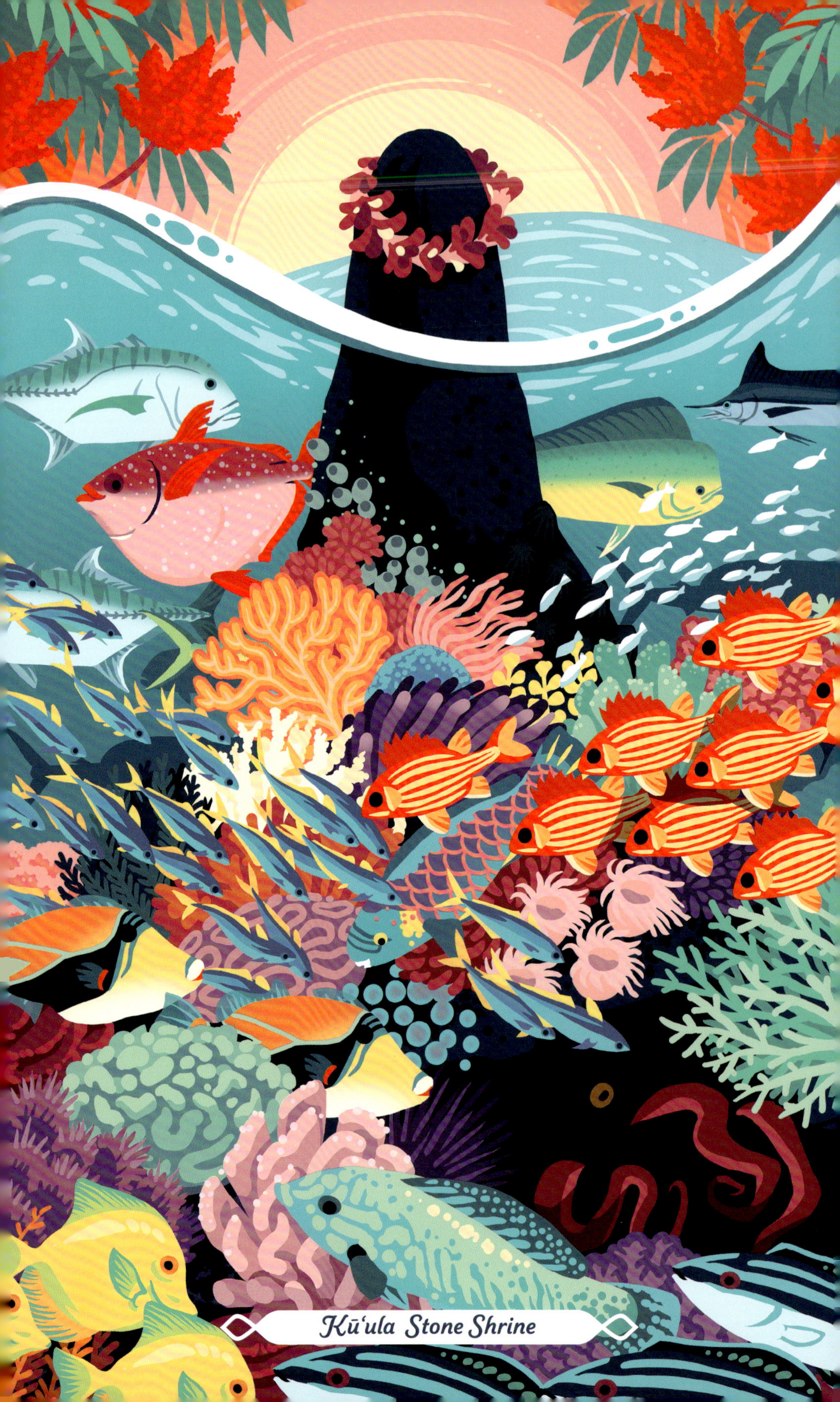
Kūʻula Stone Shrine

When Kūʻula saw Kamohoaliʻi's people placing firewood around his house, he realized what was happening. He turned to his son ʻAiʻai and gave him the giant fishhook, Mānai-a-ka-lani; the decoy stick, Pahiaku-kahuoi; the cowrie shell octopus lure, Lehoʻula; and the fish-summoning stone, Kūʻula-au-a-Kūʻulakai. Kūʻula told ʻAiʻai it would now be his task to feed the people—or starve them—then helped his son escape. Finally, Kūʻula and Hina-puku-iʻa shed their mortal bodies, disappearing into the sea and taking all the fish in the ocean and the pond with them. Kamohoaliʻi's people didn't see the escape. They set the house on fire and believed that the father, mother, and son had all died.

The orphaned ʻAiʻai wandered deep into the island, bereft, until he met a group of children playing in the woods. ʻAiʻai befriended them, and later they invited him home, where their parents cared for him for many days.

Meanwhile, disaster unfolded along the shoreline. Since Kūʻula's apparent death, no fish—large or small—were to be found. The people began to grow hungry, and even ʻAiʻai's new family feared what would become of them.

Seeing his kind caretakers in distress, ʻAiʻai decided to repay their generosity. He brought them to the fishpond and erected a stone shrine in honor of his father—later such shrines would be widely known as Kūʻula stones. He showed the family the rituals tied to the stone and told them to always offer two fish from their first catch: one for Kūʻula, one for Hina. The family agreed. They took their baskets to the water, and they were soon overflowing with fish. They offered two to the Kūʻula stone and returned home with full bellies.

Soon after, ʻAiʻai left his new friends to wander throughout the Hawaiian Islands. To those who were kind to him, he helped build fishponds and erect Kūʻula stones to summon fish.

As for Kamohoaliʻi, he choked on a fish and died.

BEGINNING AROUND 1800 B.C., aboriginal peoples from Maritime Southeast Asia began exploring the Pacific. Skilled seafarers, they used outrigger canoes and celestial navigation to traverse vast distances. They ventured into Micronesia and Melanesia, eventually settling the previously uninhabited islands of what is now Polynesia. Over centuries, they reached remote islands such as Aotearoa (New Zealand), Rapa Nui (Easter Island), and Hawai'i . Alongside physical tools, they carried oral traditions, spiritual beliefs, and social customs. This shared heritage explains the remarkable cultural overlaps seen across Polynesia, including legends of the Trickster demigod Māui, present in Māori, Hawaiian, Samoan, Tahitian, and Tongan mythologies.

After initial settlement, geographic isolation fostered distinct island cultures, with Hawaiian society being the only one to engineer advanced aquaculture fishponds for raising and farming fish. The first fishponds were built around the fourteenth century, during a period of population growth and agricultural expansion. These included small inland freshwater and brackish ponds for taro and fish, as well as massive seawater ponds bordered by lava rock walls—some wide enough to walk on. Coastal ponds typically housed more than twenty species of marine life, providing chiefs who maintained them a reliable supply of select fish.

By the early 1900s, roughly 360 fishponds existed across the islands, producing an estimated two million pounds of fish annually. Their abundance elevated their origin to the divine, with fishponds attributed to Kū'ula-kai, the Hawaiian god of fishing. Today, many lie abandoned, but others have been preserved or restored by local groups, increasing fish stocks both inside and beyond the ponds.

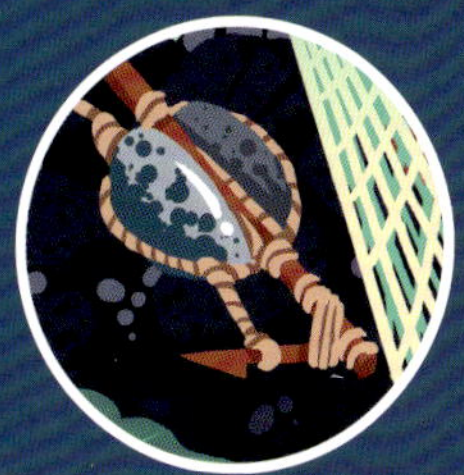

The *leho he'e* is a traditional octopus lure made of a bone hook attached to a wooden shaft, cowrie shell, and stone sinker. The lure is cast hundreds of feet deep and shaken to entice octopi.

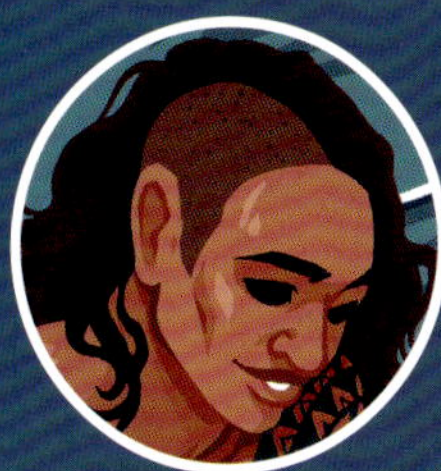

Haircuts and styles among indigenous Hawaiians could change often and signify many different life experiences. For example, the *'oki kīkepa*, or shaving one side of the head, was a ritual haircut for mourning.

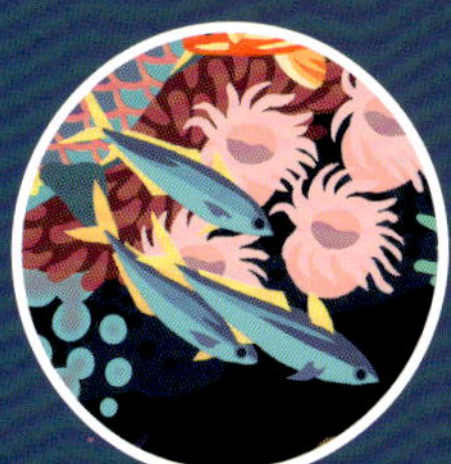

In the case of a drought, traditional Hawaiians would pull an opelu fish from the sea and strike upon a rock to call the rain god's attention and request assistance.

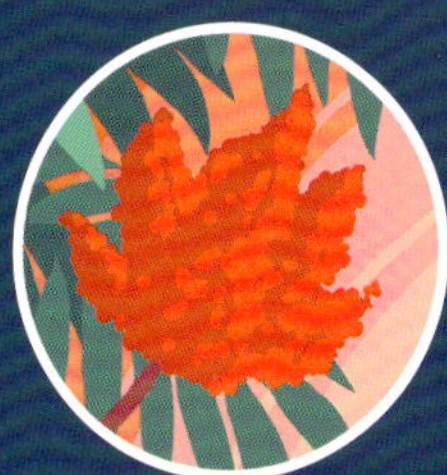

Pua ka neneleau, momona ka wana. "When the neneleau blooms, the sea urchin is fat." These clusters of tiny red flowers are inland signs that the sea is ready to be harvested.

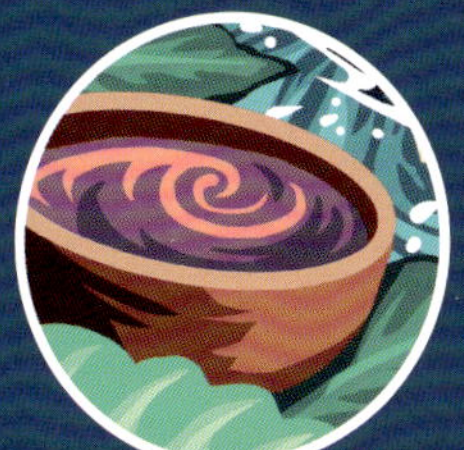

The traditional expression *he ipu ka'eo* translates to a bowl full of poi, or mashed taro root. It is used to mean a smart or knowledgeable person.

THE PRIMORDIAL CHAOS

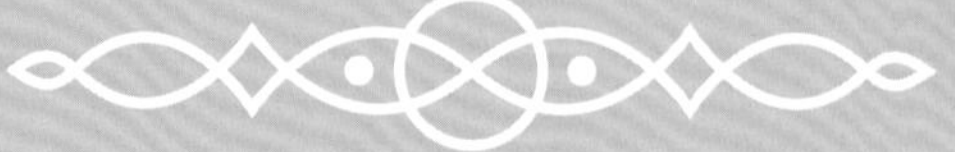

In many creation myths, the universe begins in a state of Primordial Chaos—vast, formless, dormant, neutral, and undivided. Then, through a cosmic shift or divine act, the void is ruptured, and from that split emerges the structured order of the world.

Primordial Chaos is free, unrestricted, pure potential. It is the subconscious realm of emotion, instinct, and unformed thought. Primordial Chaos is not evil, because there is no good to mirror and oppose it. Instead, Chaos is all things at once, without boundary or distinction. When this chaotic energy is finally split, everything divides: spirit from matter, sacred from profane, life from death. This separation and contrast allow order to form, with negativity pushed away and positivity elevated. Symbolically, the world awakens from nebulous dreams to conscious organized thought.

In Greek myth, Chaos is the gaping void from which Gaia (Earth), Tartarus (Underworld), and Eros (Desire) come forth, and from which Erebus (Darkness) and Nyx (Night) are born. In Egyptian belief, Nu is the endless dark water from which the first mound of earth emerges and the creator sun god Ra rises. In Chinese cosmology, the universe begins as a Cosmic Egg. When it cracks, the shell becomes the sky and earth, the yolk becomes the world and gods, and the giant Pangu separates yin and yang. In the Book of Genesis, the earth is formless and void until God speaks and begins to separate light from dark, sea from sky.

Primordial Chaos is the blank page, the moment before the idea, the breath before the performance. It's the space where nothing has yet taken shape, and anything is possible. The fertile void from which life, consciousness, and meaning emerge.

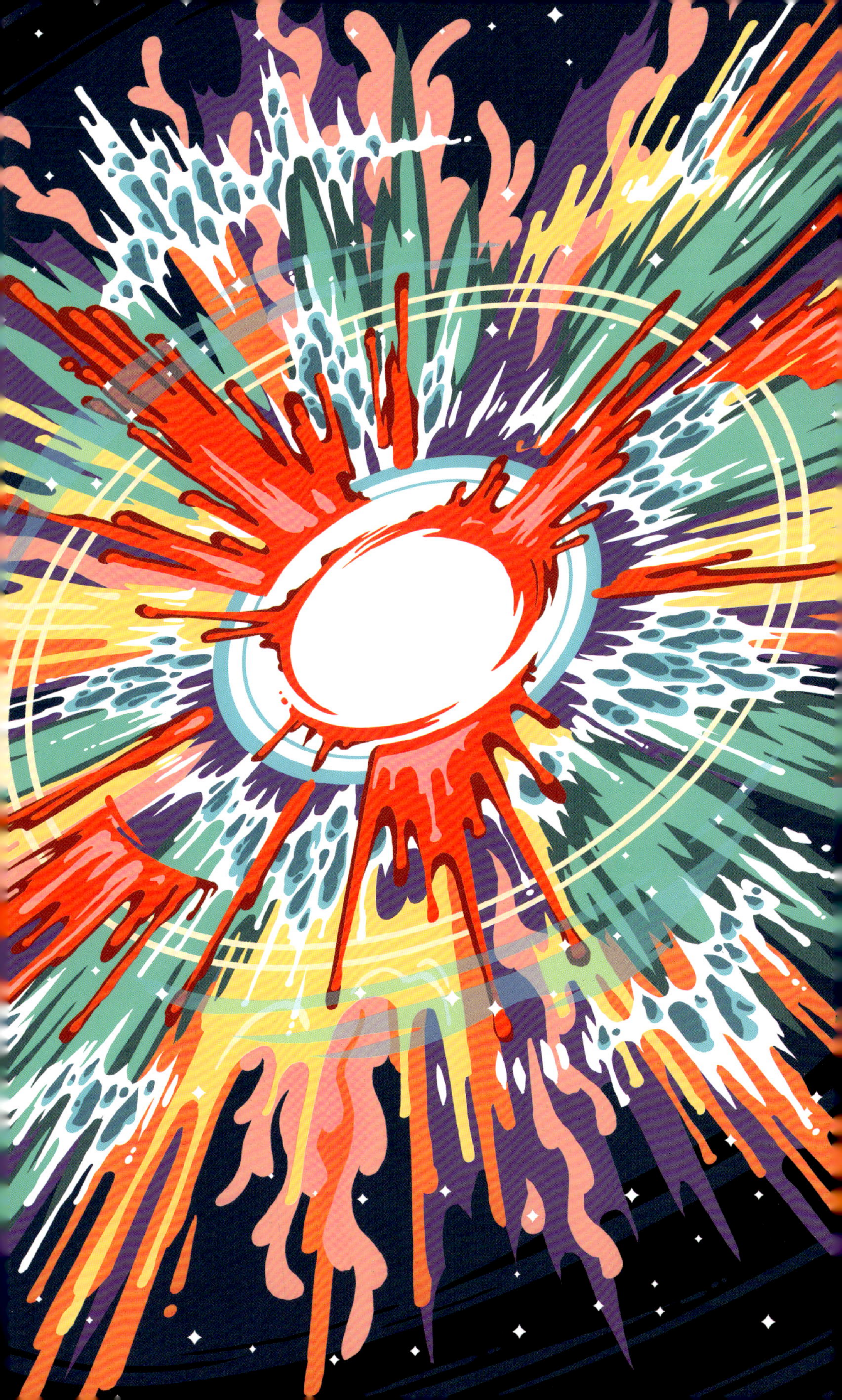

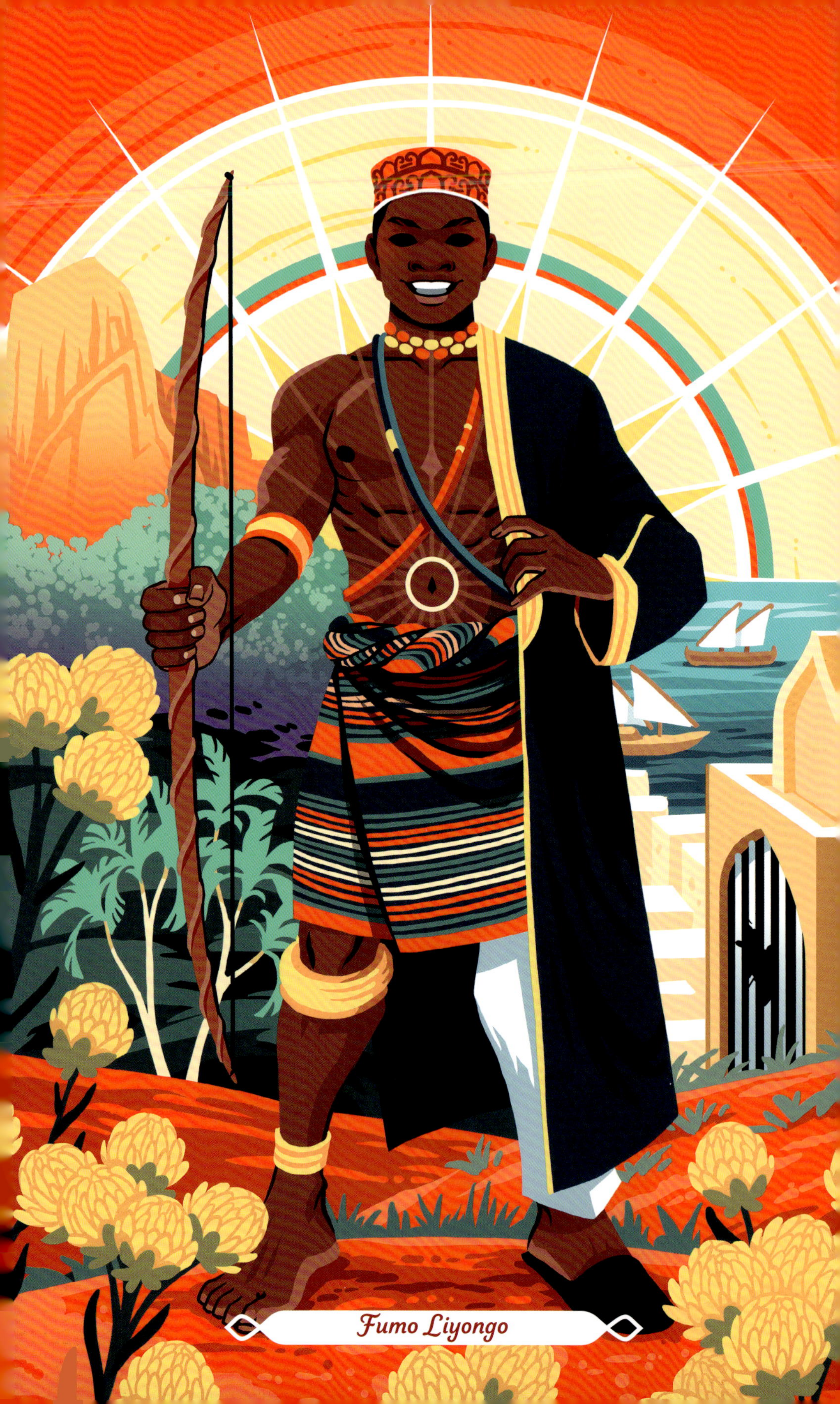
Fumo Liyongo

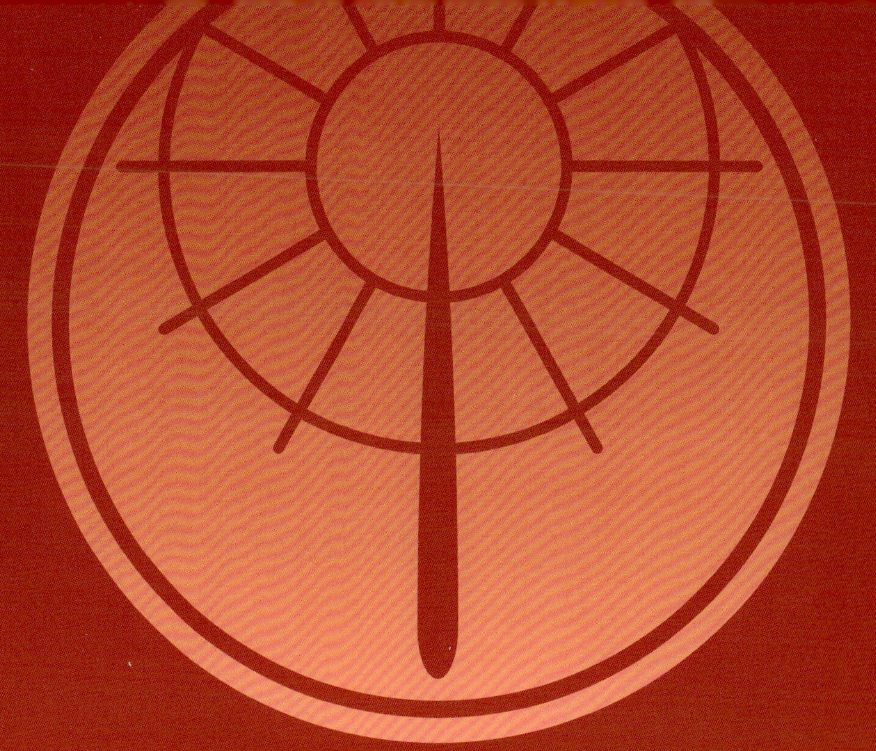

The Epic of FUMO LIYONGO

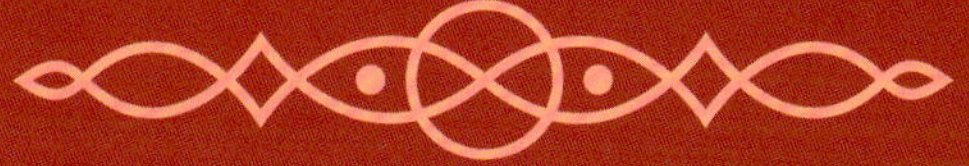

SWAHILI EPIC | SWAHILI COAST (PARTS OF MOZAMBIQUE, KENYA, AND TANZANIA)

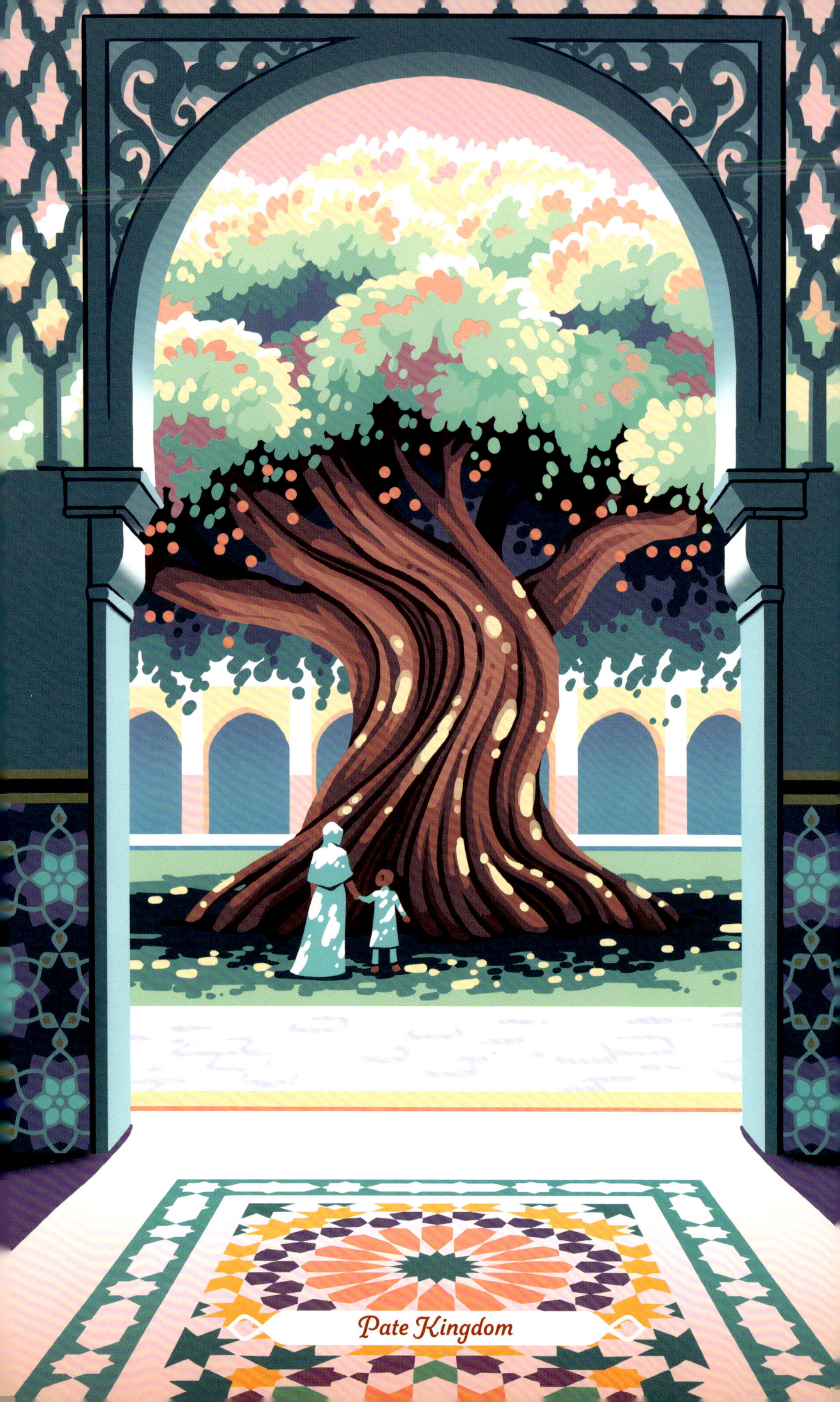
Pate Kingdom

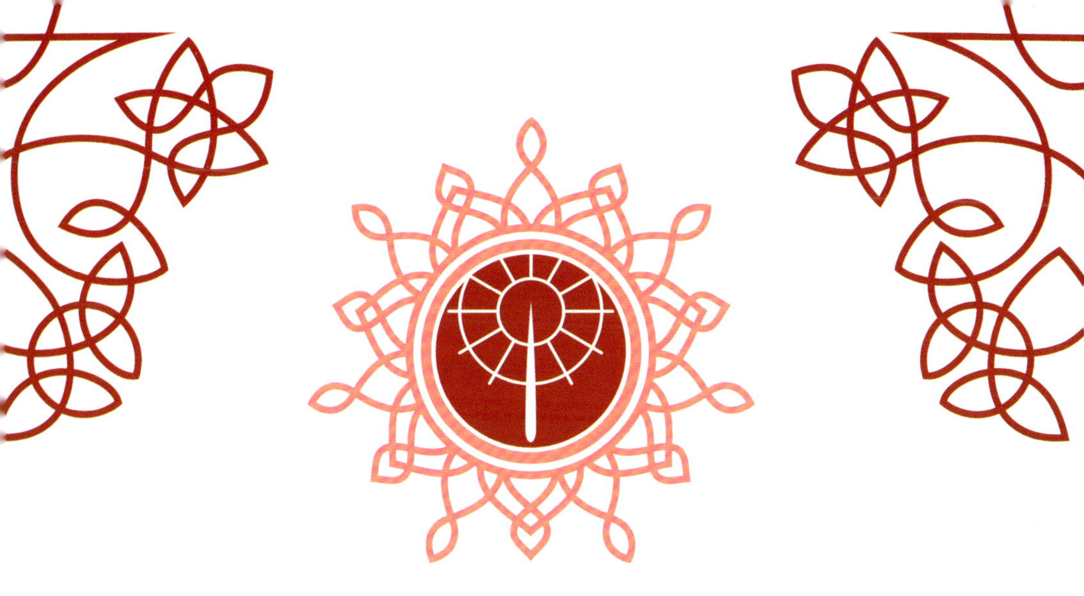

Fumo Liyongo was born to the royal family of the coastal Swahili kingdom Pate. A handsome, tall, strong, and fierce warrior, as well as a master of utendi, Swahili poetry, he was loved by the people and favored by many to take the throne.

Unfortunately, Liyongo was born just as the customs of Pate were changing. For generations, power was passed down through the matrilineal line. Because Liyongo's mother, Mbowe, was sister to the ruler Bwana Mvita, Liyongo was the rightful heir. But Pate had begun to adopt Islamic law, forming a sultanate where inheritance now followed the patrilineal line. This change meant the crown would pass not to Liyongo, but to Bwana Mvita's son, Daudi Mringwari.

Fearing that Liyongo's popularity would get in the way of his son's ascension to the throne, Bwana Mvita accused Liyongo of conspiracy and imprisoned him. But Liyongo remained unafraid. He had a secret known only to his mother: He was invincible. No sword or spear could harm him; nothing except a copper needle through his navel. In prison, Liyongo's spirit remained unbroken. He sang songs of truth and justice, his deep voice moving the city to tears. One day, his mother visited him and handed him a loaf

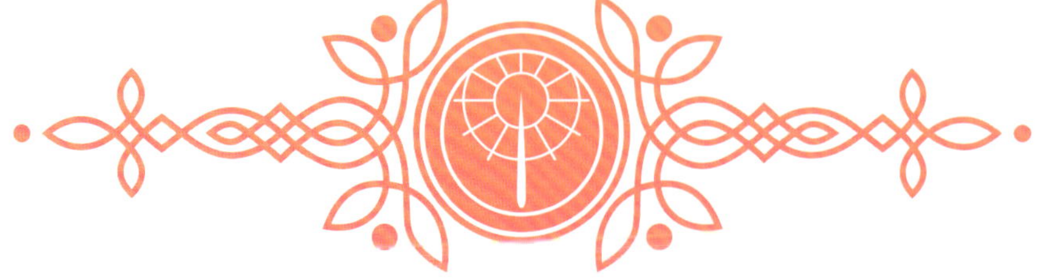

of bread—with escape tools baked inside. Liyongo used the tools to free himself and fled inland.

His escape took him to the land of the Oromo people, where tales of his strength and song had already spread. Their king invited Liyongo to his court, where he met the king's daughter—a princess who matched him in courage and wit. They fell in love, married, and had a son, Mwana Oromo (sometimes known as Mwana Galla). Although his life among the Oromo was rich and peaceful, Liyongo's heart ached for Pate. Eventually, he left the kingdom, sorrowfully parting from his wife and son.

Back on the Swahili coast, Liyongo did not return to the palaces. Instead, he disappeared into the bush, where no sultan ruled. Among the bush hunters and warriors, he learned their customs and soon became a legendary outlaw—a warrior-poet who defended the oppressed, punished the corrupt, and gave voice to the people through his songs. He became a symbol of resistance against tyranny.

As Liyongo's reputation grew, so did the fear that Daudi Mringwari, now sultan, had of him. Terrified of Liyongo's influence, Daudi Mringwari placed a bounty on his head. A group of bushmen took up the offer and approached Liyongo, pretending to be friendly hunters. They invited him to help gather fruit from a tall tree, taking turns climbing it. When they urged Liyongo to climb—planning to ambush him—he grew suspicious. Instead, he used his bow to shoot the fruit down. Awed by his sharp instincts and skill, the men fled, abandoning their deadly plan.

Frustrated that Liyongo was still living and now more famous than ever, the desperate sultan turned to Liyongo's grown son. Promising Mwana Oromo wealth and status, the sultan offered him everything—if he would kill his father. Blinded by greed, Mwana Oromo agreed.

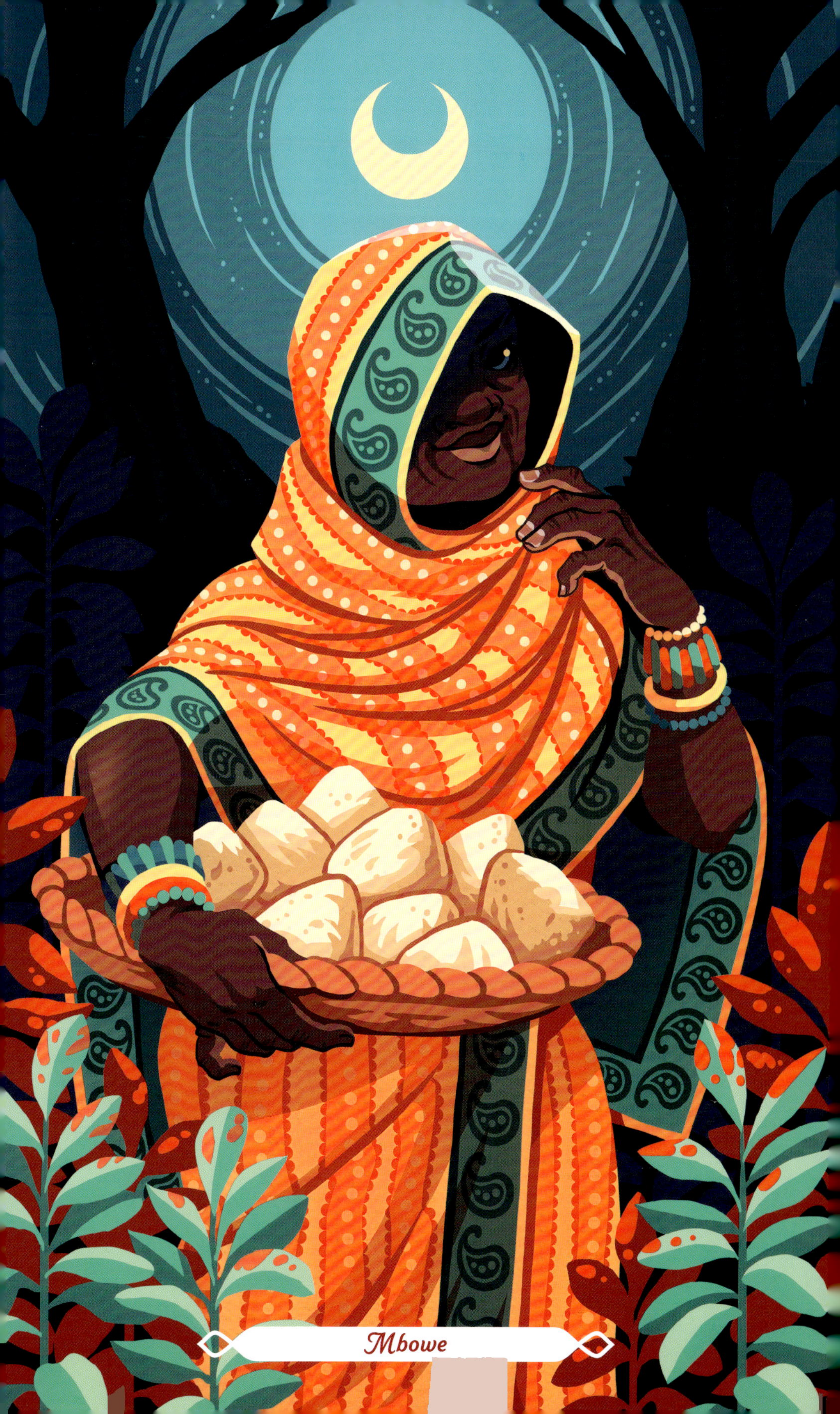
Mbowe

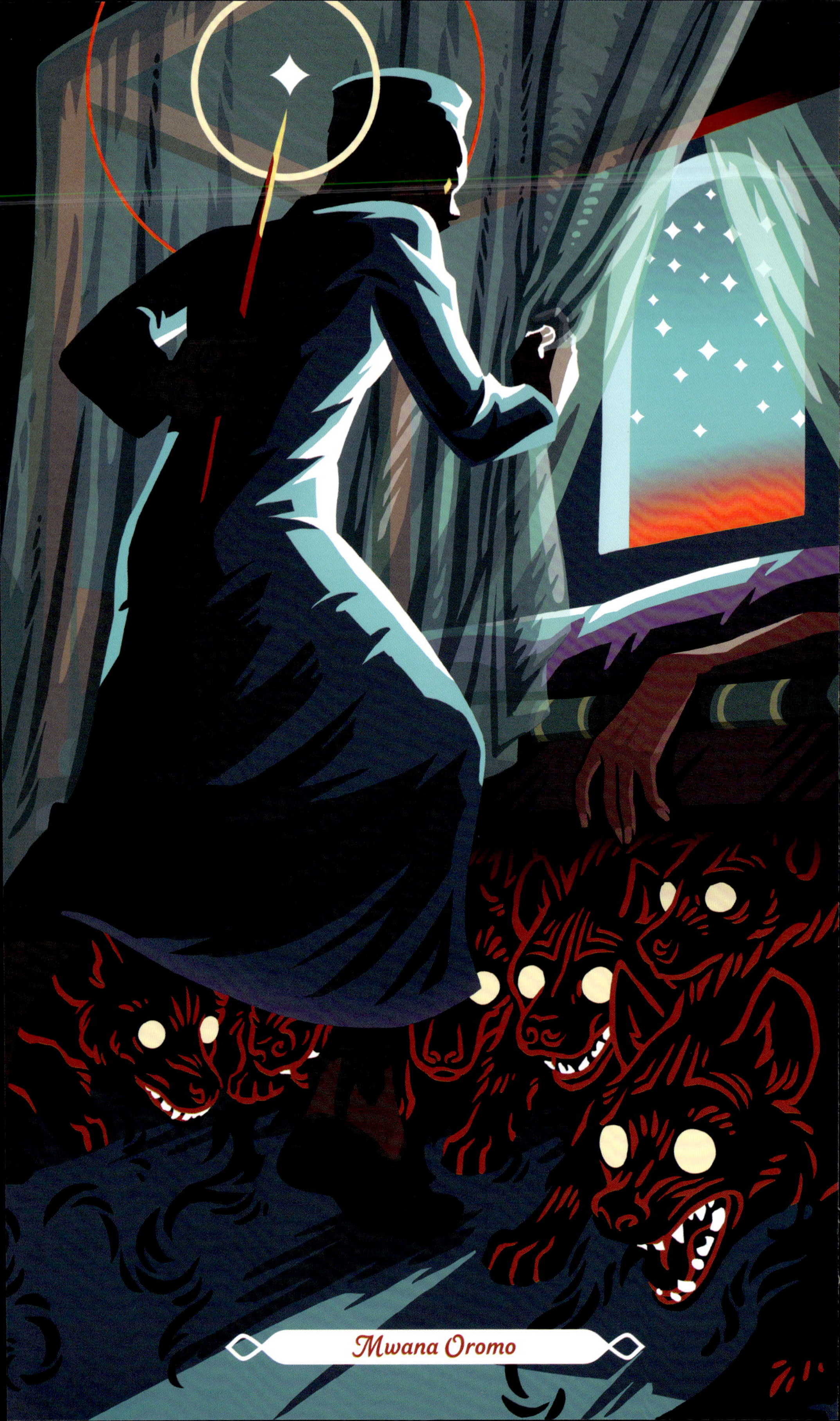
Mwana Oromo

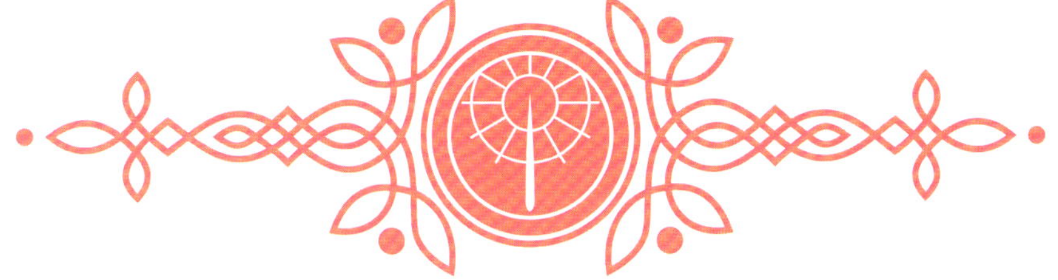

Knowing he could never defeat Liyongo in battle or wit, he sought his father's secret instead. He met with Liyongo, pretending to want to know his weakness out of trust and devotion. At first, Liyongo resisted, afraid the knowledge would put his son in danger. But Mwana Oromo persisted, and Liyongo, who loved his son deeply, finally opened up to him. That night, Mwana Oromo crept into his father's bedroom and stabbed the sleeping Liyongo in the navel with a copper needle.

Liyongo awoke instantly and knew he had been betrayed. He looked at his son and told him that he forgave him. Then he rose from bed, took up his bow and arrows, and left the house.

Although his strength was fading, his pride held firm. He walked into a clearing and faced the direction from which he knew the sultan's men would come. There, Liyongo stood tall and ready, drawing his bow. When his enemies arrived, they froze in fear, terrified by the sight of the battle-ready warrior.

Three days passed. Only when Liyongo's mother, Mbowe, stepped forward and touched him did they realize he had died standing, unflinching, with his bow in hand.

But death could not erase his legacy. Fumo Liyongo's songs lived on, passed down by Swahili poets, sung in marketplaces, and taught to children as lessons in courage, wisdom, and justice. Even now, some say he never truly died—that he waits in the forest, ready to return when his people need him most.

As for Mwana Oromo, Sultan Daudi Mringwari said he did not honor oaths made to those who would betray their own fathers. Mwana Oromo died poor and alone.

ALTHOUGH ROOTED IN LEGEND, Liyongo is believed to be based on a historical figure who lived on the East African coast between the ninth and thirteenth centuries. As both a legendary warrior and poet, Liyongo embodies the ideal Swahili hero—brave, wise, culturally rooted, and deeply spiritual, a leader whose strength was matched by intellect. His death on his feet is a symbol of dignity, resistance, and endurance. More than a tale of glory, his legend reflects the social, religious, and political transformations shaped by trade and growing connections with the Middle East and India occurring at the time.

A central theme of the Liyongo epic is conflict between tradition and change. Liyongo is born during a shift in Pate from indigenous customs to Islam and new political structures. His exile and rebellion can be read as resistance to this cultural transition, while his restless search for belonging reflects the difficulty of forging identity in a world of mixed cultural influences.

This transitional period also appears in references to neighboring peoples. In classical versions of *The Epic of Fumo Liyongo*, he visits the "Galla" kingdom, a term once broadly applied to non-Christians or non-Muslims. Today, however, the name is recognized as pejorative, replaced by the communities' self-identifications, such as Oromo, Afar, or Dinka.

The many poems attributed to Liyongo emphasize patience, humility, justice, loyalty, and resilience. Blending humor with wisdom, they continue to be performed at ceremonies, weddings, schools, and religious settings, inspiring modern poets and musicians across the world.

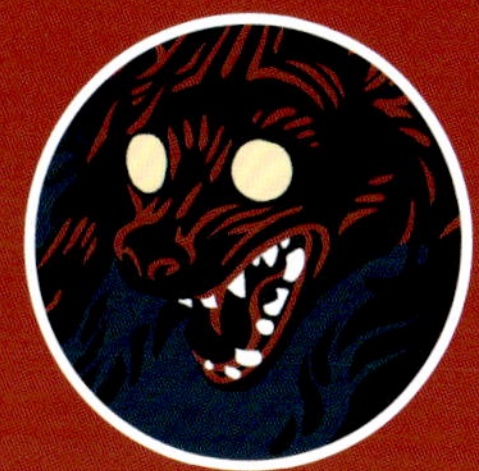

In East Africa, hyenas symbolize immorality, greed, and trickery. They are cunning, deceitful, and self-serving, opportunistically eating the carrion of others.

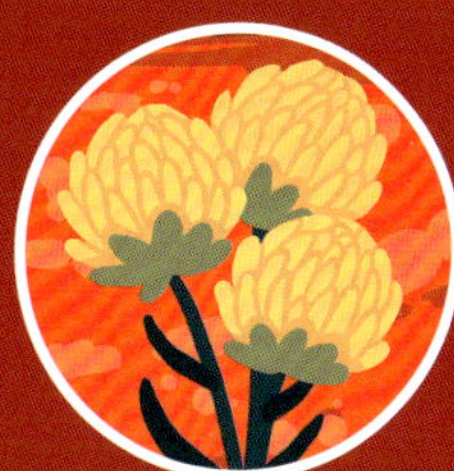

Helichrysums are also known as strawflowers or everlasting flowers. These plants are known for their vibrant blooms that retain their color even after drying and are used in traditional medicine.

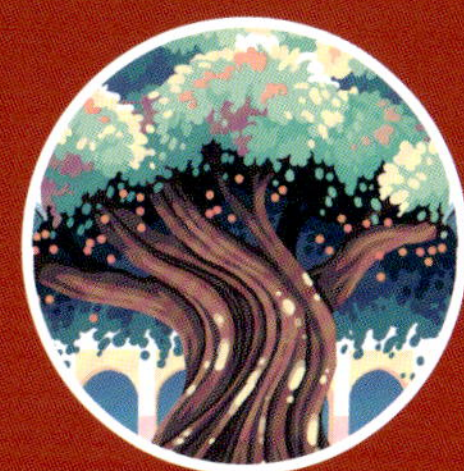

In many Swahili-speaking cultures, the fig tree is sacred. Growing old and large, it is a symbol of wisdom and resilience, its ample fruit and shade representing fertility and community.

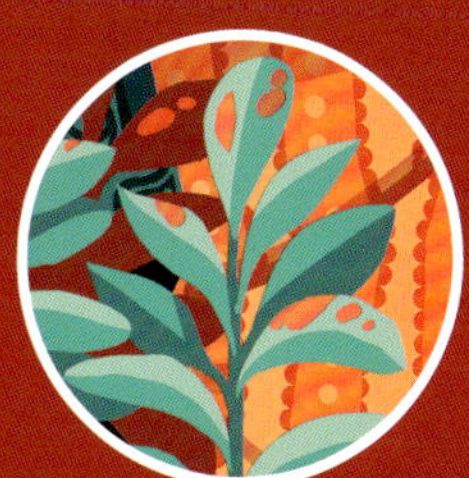

All parts of the resilient African milk bush are toxic when ingested. It is believed to have protective powers that result in the death of offenders, but its sap is also used to treat skin conditions.

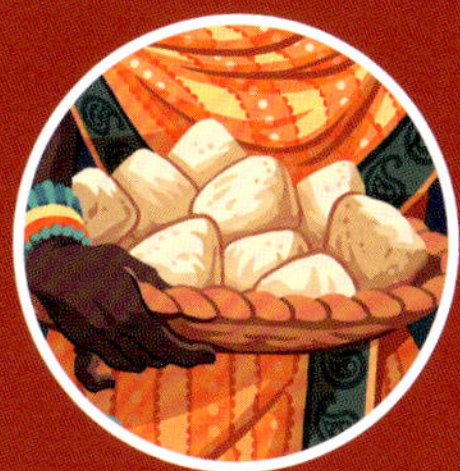

Mandazi is a sweet Swahili fried bread that is stuffed with various fillings like minced meat, mung beans, egg curry, or tools to escape a jail cell.

THE APOCALYPSE

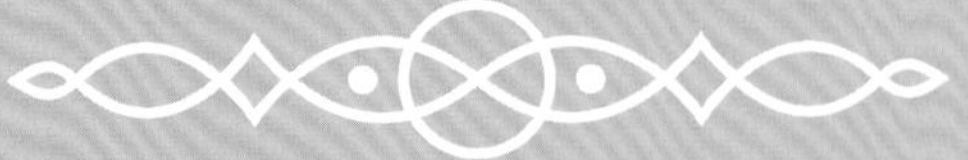

The Apocalypse myth is the story of the catastrophic destruction of the universe. It is the complete annihilation of everything, a final reckoning where the foundations of existence are shaken, undone, or consumed. It is the end of time itself.

This event is not about only devastation but also judgment. Corruption, imbalance, or spiritual decay has reached its peak, and the old ways must be torn apart. Even the gods themselves perish in the conflagration, showing nothing can escape the inevitable end. It is loss on a cosmic scale. This inescapable reckoning is the fall of complex order back into the simplicity of chaos.

In myth, the Apocalypse marks the end of an age. Yet this purge is often just the precursor. Just as a forest fire allows for new growth in the ashes, so too does a new world with new gods blossom in the void left by the destruction of the old. In Norse mythology, Ragnarök is the burning of the gods, with Odin and Thor falling in battle. From this devastation, a new green earth rises from the sea. In Hindu cosmology, the Kali Yuga ends with the arrival of Kalki, who purifies the world and restores dharma. Christianity's Book of Revelation portrays the earth being scorched by divine wrath, only for a new heaven and earth to descend. Similarly, in the Aztec tradition of cyclical creation and collapse, the current age is the Fifth Sun, which will eventually fall to make way for the Sixth, as has happened for the four ages that came before.

The Apocalypse is a metaphor for irreversible change. It is the death of a way of life and a return to the beginning.

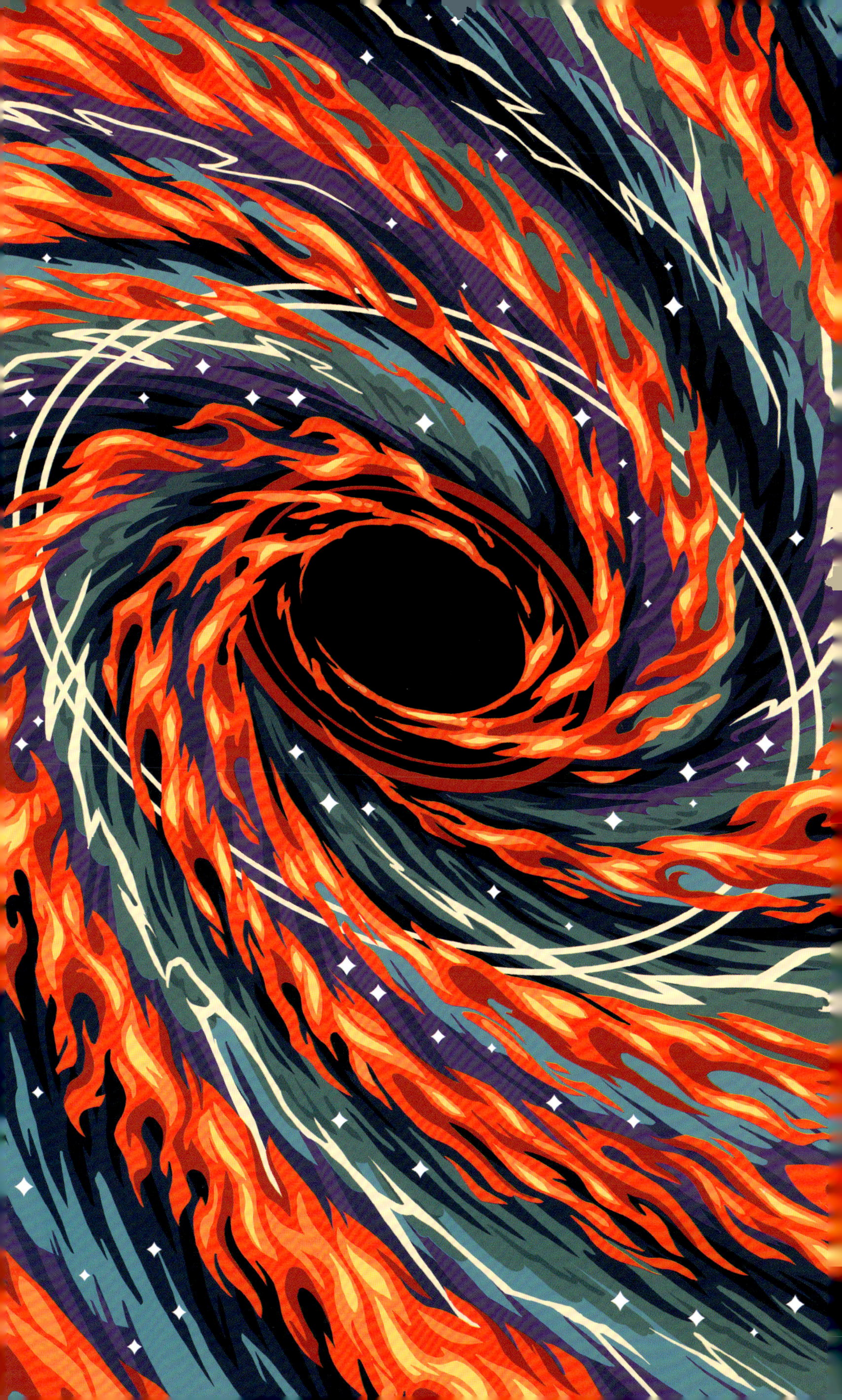

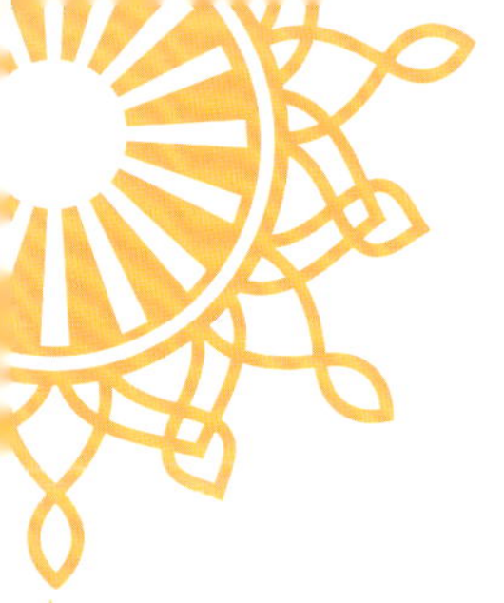

Index

M

N

O

P

R

S

T

U

V

W

X

Y

Z

Resources

Acquaviva, Graziella. "Cultural Values of Trees in the East African Context." *Kervan: International Journal of Afro-Asiatic Studies*, vol. 23, no. 1 (2019): 29–46.

Beckwith, Martha. *Hawaiian Mythology*. Honolulu, University Of Hawai'i Press, 1940, 1970.

Belcher, Stephen. *African Myths of Origin*. London, Penguin Books, 2005.

Belcher, Stephen. *Epic Traditions of Africa*. Bloomington, Indiana University Press, 1999.

Benedict, Ruth. *Tales of the Cochiti Indians*. Washington, D.C., Smithsonian Scholarly Press, 1931, 1981.

Christenson, Allen J. *Popol Vuh: The Sacred Book of the Maya: The Great Classic of Central American Spirituality*. Norman, University of Oklahoma Press, 2007.

Claassen, Cheryl, and Rosemary A. Joyce. *Women in Prehistory: North America and Mesoamerica*. Philadelphia, University of Pennsylvania Press, 1997.

Fernando, Oswaldo. *Art and Myth of the Ancient Maya*. New Haven, Yale University Press, 2017.

Frydman, Joshua. *The Japanese Myths: A Guide to Gods, Heroes and Spirits*. London, Thames & Hudson, 2022.

Horswell, Michael J. *Decolonizing the Sodomite: Queer Tropes of Sexuality in Colonial Andean Culture*. Austin, University of Texas Press, 2006.

Johnson, John William, Thomas Hale, and Stephen Belcher, eds. *Oral Epics from Africa: Vibrant Voices from a Vast Continent*. Bloomington, Indiana University Press, 1997.

Kalakaua, David. *The Legends and Myths of Hawaii*. Berkeley, West Margin Press, Mint Editions, 2021.

Lodhi, Abdulaziz Yusuf. *Liyongo's Navel: An East African Epic*. Independently published, 2019.

Longhena, Maria, and Walter Alva. *The Incas and Other Andean Civilizations*. San Diego, Thunder Bay Press, 1999.

Lönnrot, Elias. *The Kalevala*. Translated by Keith Bosley. Oxford University Press, 2008.

Macfarlan, Allan A. *American Indian Legends*. New York, George Macy Companies, 1968.

Mera, H. P. *Pueblo Indian Embroidery*. North Chelmsford, Courier Corporation, 1943, 1995.

Miller, Mary Ellen, and Simon Martin. *Courtly Art of the Ancient Maya*. San Francisco, Fine Arts Museums of San Francisco, 2004.

Pentikäinen, Juha. *Kalevala Mythology,* Revised Edition. Translated by Ritva Maarit Poom. Bloomington, Indiana University Press, 1999.

Pryke, Louise M. *Ishtar*. New York, Routledge, 2017.

Pukui, Mary Kawena. *'Ōlelo No'Eau: Hawaiian Proverbs and Poetical Sayings*. Honolulu, Bishop Museum Press, 1983.

Roediger, Virginia More. *Ceremonial Costumes of the Pueblo Indians: Their Evolution, Fabrication, and Significance in the Prayer Drama*. Berkeley, University of California Press, 1991.

Salomon, Frank, and George L Urioste. *The Huarochirí Manuscript*. Austin, University of Texas Press, 1991.

Soenoto, Faizah. "Panji Romance, Love Story in Malay Version." *Rivista Degli Studi Orientali*, vol. 78, no. 4 (2007): 195–200.

Spalding, Karen. *Huarochirí: An Andean Society under Inca and Spanish Rule*. Stanford University Press, 1984.

Wolkstein, Diane, and Samuel Noah Kramer. *Inanna: Queen of Heaven and Earth: Her Stories and Hymns from Sumer*. London, Rider, 1984.

Acknowledgments

First, I want to thank my editor Sara Neville for being the first one to ask if I wanted to tell more stories. This book and oracle deck would not have existed if she hadn't made me realize that yes, I did want to share some more favorites. Thanks to my editors Kimmy Tejasindhu and Harry Tunngal for helping me drag it across the finish line.

I also have to thank my agent, Thao Le, for always having my back and reminding me to ask for help when I need it.

Most of all, I have to thank Archer Derosa, my fearless assistant researcher. Thank you for your deep dives, your investigations, your connections, and your willingness to find documentation of obscure footwear. Even more than all that, thank you for being as excited as me about all these stories and allowing me to gush about them endlessly. This book is possible only because of you.

About the Author

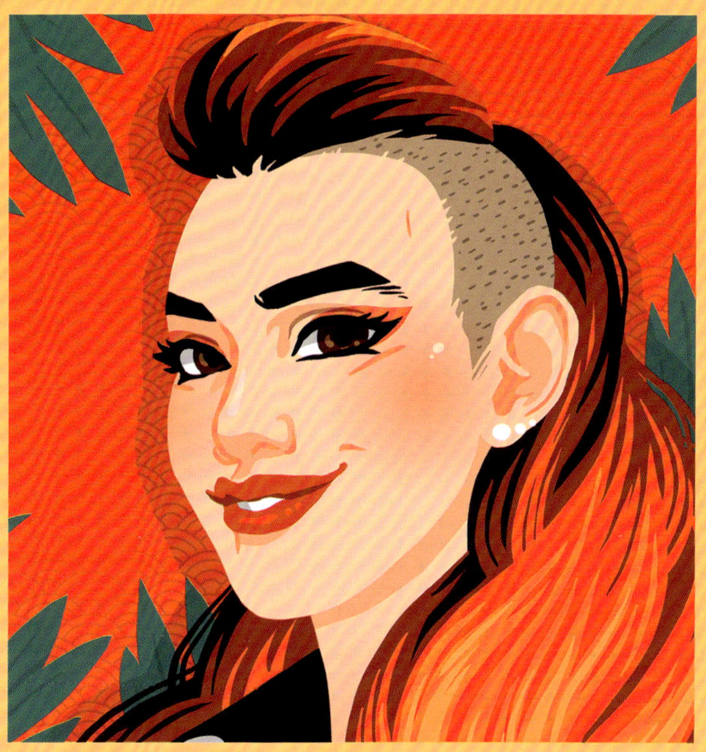

Yoshi Yoshitani is an Eisner-nominated California-based artist whose vibrant illustrations draw on inspiration from across the globe, with a particular focus on multicultural identity. Past clients include Disney, DC Comics, Valiant, Image, DreamWorks, and Netflix. Yoshi spends time researching world mythologies, listening to audiobooks, creating fashion inspiration boards, and attending comic conventions and art expos across the country.

TEN SPEED PRESS
An imprint of the Crown Publishing Group
A division of Penguin Random House LLC
1745 Broadway
New York, NY 10019
tenspeed.com
penguinrandomhouse.com

Typefaces: Commercial Type's Portrait, Evert Bloemsma's Legato, Jim Wasco and Laura Worthington's Elicit Script, and Ong Chong Wah's Chong Old Style

Library of Congress Cataloging-in-Publication Data is on file with the publisher.

Hardcover ISBN 978-0-593-57789-9
Ebook ISBN 978-0-593-57790-5

Acquiring editor: Kim Keller | Project editor: Kimmy Tejasindhu
Production editor: Abby Oladipo
Designer: Kelly Booth | Production designer: Mari Gill
Production: Dan Myers
Copy editor: Ethan Campbell | Proofreaders: Jacob Sammon and Sarah Rutledge
Publicist: Felix Cruz | Marketer: Brianne Sperber

Manufactured in China

10 9 8 7 6 5 4 3 2 1

First Edition

The authorized representative in the EU for product safety and compliance is Penguin Random House Ireland, Morrison Chambers, 32 Nassau Street, Dublin D02 YH68, Ireland,
https://eu-contact.penguin.ie.